**Secrets of a Successful
Mail Order Guru:
Chase Revel**

Secrets of a Successful Mail Order Guru: Chase Revel

Ron Tepper

Ron Tepper & Associates
Torrance, California

John Wiley & Sons
New York/Chichester/Brisbane/Toronto/Singapore

Library of Congress Cataloging in Publication Date:

Tepper, Ron, 1937-
  Secrets of a successful mail order guru.

  Bibliography: p.
  1. Mail-order business. 2. Revel, Chase. I. Title.
HF5466.T36 1987   658.8'72   87-21658
ISBN 0-471-84857-3

Printed in the United States of America

10 9 8 7 6 5 4 3 2 1

Contents

3.   Entrepreneur's Keys to Success   29

4.   Consumer Needs and Repeat Sales   55

8. How to Find Opportunities 143

9. Getting Your Foot in the Door 167

1

Introduction

Success. To most it means fame or prosperity. Attaining it can be slow, arduous, and lonely, a long journey up a steep mountain. But coming down can be instantaneous.

Ask Chase Revel.

In 20 years, he built 17 successful small businesses. He did everything from construction to publishing and real estate management. He was even a gossip columnist.

His prize accomplishment was the creation of *Entrepreneur*, a magazine and mail order company that specialized in selling business information to current and potential small business entrepreneurs. The information was provided via unique, practical "how to" manuals that detailed every phase of a business's operation. With one of Revel's manuals, a prospective small business owner was able to do everything from site location to marketing by simply following the directions.

In less than a decade, *Entrepreneur*, under Revel's guidance, produced more than 200 start-up manuals on various businesses. More than one-third of the manuals were on unique, new businesses that few had even heard about. There was never any theory involved, only practical information.

In addition to finding businesses to write about, Revel predicted new small business trends. He was the first to forecast the antique and bicycle crazes, as well as the emergence of computer and health food stores.

His uncanny, accurate forecasting made *Entrepreneur* known

1

throughout the country. It also turned Revel into the guru of the small business field. His company grossed millions of dollars, and his small business expos broke attendance records at arenas throughout the country, including Madison Square Garden and the Los Angeles Convention Center.

Virtually every major newspaper in the country wrote feature stories about him and his company, Chase Revel, Inc. He appeared on hundreds of radio and television shows, and the mayors of 17 cities proclaimed special days in his honor.

He was a celebrity and a millionaire. His posh, hillside home, with its 180 degree living room window, overlooked the exclusive shores of Marina Del Rey. Two hundred miles to the north was his hideaway, a 3,000 acre ranch in the rich San Joaquin Valley of California.

Chase Revel had it made.

For the soft-spoken Tennessean, success in business had nothing to do with theory. There was no college in his background, only trial and error. His unique marketing techniques were based on his own practical experience and an uncanny ability to relate to people and understand what they will buy, why they will buy it, and when they will buy it. His marketing and accounting skills were innate.

It was, however, in direct-mail that he excelled. He was an innovator and a gambler. He tried advertisements and direct-mail approaches that few would even contemplate, let alone try. Not every one of them worked, but those that did turned Revel's company into a $15 million enterprise in less than six years. His masterful mailing pieces ultimately turned *Entrepreneur* into a multimillion-dollar publicly held over-the-counter (OTC) enterprise.

Amazingly, he began the venture with one $44 ad.

He became the direct-mail master at selling paper—that is, manuals, books, tapes, and magazines.

In 1982, his company ran into difficulty and he found himself on the brink of losing everything. In one afternoon he came up with another mail order idea that not only brought *Entrepreneur* back from the brink of financial ruin, but enabled the company to bank nearly $1 million in less than nine months.

In 1983 Revel used his talents to start a new mail order enterprise, a simulated jewelry company. Instead of starting out with small three and four line inquiry ads, he went across the country with daring full-page ads in which he sold an old product with a new twist.

He became the first direct-mail entrepreneur to buy full-page mail order ads in *USA Today*. He proved that mail order specialists did

not need new concepts or revolutionary products in order to make millions.

He also proved that, despite the increased competition in the field, there was always room for another creative mail order marketer who had a unique idea and his pulse on the market.

He became one of the few mail order specialists in the country to make millions not only by selling paper products (through *Entrepreneur*) but merchandise as well. His simulated jewelry company astounded the mail order field when it grossed more than $5 million in less than 14 months.

Few can match the amazing direct-mail success that Revel has had. Yet his techniques remain remarkably simple and easy to emulate.

His rules apply to every form of direct mail, and if followed can virtually guarantee that the mail order entrepreneur will be able to bypass the pitfalls that have plagued direct-mail specialists throughout the country.

Thanks to Revel's candor, this book outlines his road up, his problems, his direct-mail rules, and his techniques for mail order success.

His is an unusual story, one that shows what it takes to become a success in mail order as well as in business.

Most important, he details for the first time the techniques he created and the rules marketers must follow if they are going to succeed in the most promising—but most difficult—business profession of them all . . . mail order.

2

Two Steps to Profit

"Insider's Report. How much profit does Joe's business make (exactly)? Any small business? Case history, details including how to start one."

I created Chase Revel, Inc. with that simple, straightforward three-line $44 ad in the *Wall Street Journal*. In less than 10 years, it grew into a $15 million a year mail order publishing enterprise with an internationally successful magazine (*Entrepreneur*), and I became a millionaire.

During that decade I produced dozens of direct-mail catalogs, package inserts, one-step space ads, two-step inquiry ads, and every type of marketing piece imaginable.

My first effort, however, was that simple $44 ad. Within weeks after I had placed it, everyone was sending me money to learn the ins and outs of small business and to find out the latest small business trends and fads.

Was I surprised? You bet I was. It was the first serious mail order venture I had ever tried. It taught me that the most important thing in mail order was not experience, the product, the offer, writing ability, the advertising vehicle, or the money you spend. The key to mail order success has nothing to do with computers, data base, analyzing markets, or anything even remotely related to science.

IMPORTANCE OF SENSITIVITY

In mail order there is one critical key, one element that is more determinative of success or failure than anything else. It is sensitivity.

Sensitivity is the mail order marketers' ability to understand their customers, to relate to their market, to empathize and not only comprehend what people buy, but *why*.

What motivates people? How do they feel about products?

Webster defines sensitivity as the "capability of perceiving with a sense or senses" or (someone) who is "susceptible to the feelings of others." That says it perfectly.

Out of the 230 million people in this country, many are sensitive, and many are not. Unfortunately, everyone thinks they are sensitive. There are easy techniques to test one's sensitivity. For example, go through the mail order ads in a magazine. Pick the ones you believe will work. Did you pick the right ones? You can answer that question by looking for the ad in the next issue of the magazine. If it is repeated, chances are it worked, and you were right.

For those who are sensitive, mail order can be a phenomenal business. For those who are not, mail order can be disastrous.

Mail order is unlike any other enterprise in the world. All around us we see conglomerates gobbling up smaller companies, and foreign companies copying our products and selling them back to us. In mail order if you create the right offer for the right audience, you can become a success regardless of bigger companies or foreign competition.

Anyone can, of course, duplicate a mail order product. But they cannot program human nature. Mail order ads are successful because the marketer has correctly identified the reader's need and answered it with his or her ad. It is not the product that sells, but the approach. The correct approach requires an understanding of human nature, and if you have that ability, no one can copy it.

That is what makes mail order exciting—and the opportunity it is today.

SPACE ADS VERSUS TWO-STEPS

For the mail order marketer, there are several ways to reach and attract an audience. Selling via space, that is, advertising in newspapers, magazines, or on radio or television, is one.

Space ads can be approached in two ways: one-step or two-step ads. In a one-step ad you present your entire sales message and "close" in the same ad. There may be a coupon, address, or telephone number at the bottom of the ad so customers can respond and place an order.

One-step ads require more ad space and capital.

A one-step takes more space because you have to pack your ad with information and answers designed to overcome the buyer's objections. It is your one shot at the prospect and you must answer all his objections with that ad.

I started *Entrepreneur* as a newsletter (*Insider's Report*). It was a newsletter geared to the business opportunity seeker. I was going to tell them about the hot new businesses, and how to start one. If I had placed a one-step ad that said "get all the inside information about the current hot new businesses from Chase Revel . . . send $16.75 to . . ." it would never have worked. To that audience I was an unknown.

Readers, regardless of their desire to find out about business, are not going to give $16.75 to anyone they know nothing about.

To quell their doubts, you need a great deal of space and that costs money. You must take half- and full-page ads in order to make a one-step approach successful. It is the ultimate mail order gamble, and later I took it many times.

Not everyone has the capital for expensive, one-step ads. Many mail order marketers go with the two-step ad as I did. For those venturing into the business, two-steps are a must. For me, the ad that started it all was a two-step.

Two-steps are designed to generate inquiries. They are usually small space ads, similar to the first one I placed in the *Wall Street Journal*.

The initial step is placing the small ad; step two is answering the inquiries with a well-conceived, convincing letter (or mailing piece) that is designed to close the inquiree or prospect.

Up-front expenditures are minimal, as exhibited by my $44 investment. The sole purpose is to generate a qualified name as a lead. For those who wrote to me about "Joe's business" I followed with a sales letter that tried to convince them to send me $16.75 for a year's subscription to my first newsletter, a product I called *Insider's Report*.

MERCHANDISE VERSUS PAPER PRODUCTS

In mail order there are two types of products that can be sold: paper or merchandise. Paper (books, manuals, reports, newsletters) is often the initial choice of many marketers entering the mail order field. It was mine, too. Later, I found the potential and advantages of selling merchandise through the mail.

My initial two-step consisted of a three-page sales letter by "J.C. Revel." In looking back, there is little I would change in it today. (You'll find it in Chapter 10 with an analysis.)

Before anyone gets the second part of a two-step, they have to respond to step one, the inquiry ad. What makes an inquiry ad work? Curiosity is one element that draws in response. It is one of the greatest motivators that consumers have.

Take a look at some of the top selling newsstand magazines. They all have coverlines that pique consumers' interest, make them stop and think. Next time you are in the supermarket, pick up a copy of *People*, a publication that is good to study. The cover is loaded with headlines that pique consumers' curiosity.

Newspapers work on consumers' curiosity as well. Pick up a copy of *USA Today*. Notice the multitude of headlines and the different audiences to whom they may appeal.

If curiosity can be worked into an inquiry ad you may find your mailbox loaded with letters. Everyone was curious about "Joe's business" and how much he made.

Once the ad generates inquiries, it is up to the follow-up sales letter to convert the leads into sales, and that is where sensitivity becomes even more important. The mail order marketers have to "feel" what will move people. They have to understand consumers' needs and the words that will answer those needs.

My follow-up letter generated $2,000 in newsletter subscription revenues. Suddenly I was in the publishing business. I had not even written the initial newsletter. Before I did, I wanted to see if the response warranted the effort.

DRAWBACKS OF PAPER

One of the advantages of marketing paper is you do not have to go to press unless there is a demand. Contrast this with merchandise or durable goods sold through the mail. You have to invest in the product before you place the ad. There is a large capital outlay for a product that you do not have when selling paper.

But paper is not without its drawbacks. It lacks the credibility of a durable good. For example, RCA and Sony products are sold through the mail. No one has to explain the quality of the goods, because consumers are convinced of it. They are familiar with both firms and the merchandise they offer.

Orders for paper products are harder to obtain. It takes more space

and sell. Advertising costs are higher and you need a greater markup. My 36-page *Insider's Report* newsletter, which eventually became *Entrepreneur* had a markup of five times cost. Later I successfully sold merchandise (durable goods) with three times markup.

But I am getting ahead of myself. First, why would anyone stick money in an envelope, for *Insider's Report* or any other product? Customers do not buy unless all their questions have been answered.

When I sold *Insider's Report* I had to not only tell the customers who Chase Revel was, but convince them that he knew about business, and was worth the $16.75 investment. "Who is Chase Revel?" "How does he know about business?" "What makes him an authority?" "How much money can I make following his advice?"

Those are typical queries that mail order marketers selling advice have to answer. My Revel follow-up had to answer them. To answer questions, mail order marketers have to step back from their product or offer and look at it objectively. If you were the prospect, what questions would you ask before putting money in an envelope?

If you can be objective and answer that question truthfully and accurately, there is a good chance you understand and can answer your prospect's questions.

Once again, sensitivity *is* critical.

Even if you have unparalleled sensitivity, a one-step campaign may not be the way to go, especially if it is your first crack at mail order. A one-step, full-page ad in a major metropolitan newspaper can run $10,000 or more. If you are selling $10 widgets you need 1,000 orders to break even on the cost of the ad, not to mention the cost of the product. A half- or full-page ad in the *Wall Street Journal* on a national basis is even more costly.

THE ECONOMY OF A TWO-STEP AD

In the long run mail order marketers may spend the same amount on a two-step; however, they can enter the business with a lower cost since the inquiry ad is smaller and it does not have to be "perfect" and sell the reader in one-step.

All the inquiry ad has to do is generate prospects. It may generate those even if the sales approach is not quite right. The mail order marketer then has the chance to sell them with his follow-up mailing piece, which can be loaded with every conceivable argument and fact about his product. He can pack a great deal of credibility into a follow-up piece, more so than he can in a one-step ad.

With a two-step, marketers can reach, and possibly sell, the same widget at a fraction of the cost. A two-column, one-inch ad designed to get people to send for more information may run $100 or less in a publication that charges $10,000 for a half- or full-page ad.

The key is the follow-up message, that is, the material that is sent to the prospect. It must be thorough and concise. It must answer every question and objection the buyer might have.

I have always thought of it this way: Imagine you are putting together a one-step. Compile all the possible questions you would have to answer; think of all the needs that the ad has to appeal to in order to succeed. Whatever you come up with belongs in the follow-up material that is sent to a prospect in a two-step approach.

Response to an inquiry ad is not automatic. The prospect has to be teased and tantalized. The headline on my $44 ad did exactly that.

"How much does Joe's business make?"

Intriguing question—most people in the business world would like to know the answer, especially if they are thinking about going into business. A question is always a good opener.

Even with a well thought-out headline, you cannot forecast results until you see them. The consumer is the ultimate judge, and if there were a way to predict success or failure beforehand, mail order would not be a challenge and would not offer the rewards that it does.

One way to enhance the chances of a good return is never to take the plunge unless you *believe* in the product. That is basic to the mail order business.

Never sell something you do not believe people will buy. If you do, the copy will fail to convince and the offer will fall flat. Mail order requires objectivity, logic, and common sense, but the marketer must also be passionate about the product.

I believed in *Insider's Report*. I started numerous business enterprises previously, and I knew the ins and outs of each. I knew what makes a business go—or fail. I had acted as a consultant to a number of people in business, and I was confident I could relate those ideas to anyone in a newsletter.

IMPORTANCE OF RAPID RESPONSE

A major pitfall and cause of failure in mail order is slow response time. Consumer protection agencies allow mail order firms four to

six weeks to fulfill an order, but the firm that takes that long turns off customers.

We live in an age of instant gratification. When someone orders a product they want it *now*, not in six or seven weeks. When they send for information they want it *now*. Your chance for reorders or additional sales (of other products) increases dramatically as fulfillment time decreases.

In 1983, when I started my simulated jewelry company and sold through the mail, one of the key reasons for my success was that I guaranteed fulfillment within four days after receiving the order. Simulated jewelry companies were not new, but a four-day fulfillment time certainly was.

Rapid response is critical. Delay, and customers believe that your response time is an indication of what future service will be like. If it takes four weeks to get them information on a newsletter, how long will it take to get the newsletter? Will they ever get it?

DON'T FORGET THE PROSPECT'S NEEDS

The J.C. Revel letter (see Chapter 10) hammered at the prospect's needs. Every subscriber would be the *first* to learn about new and highly profitable businesses, every subscriber would be the first to learn how to take advantage of them, where to set up a new business, the profit potential, and how to avoid the pitfalls.

It addressed the prospect's needs—to make money, increase status, and learn how to do both with little effort.

It also sold prospects on my ability to help them attain those goals. I was a successful businessman who had owned a number of thriving enterprises, and had made millions in several of them. I was retired and anxious to help other budding entrepreneurs.

My letter contained a slightly dramatized version of how I had become a success in previous businesses. I stressed that anyone who knew and used the same principles I did could duplicate my success. The newsletter would provide that information.

SELL THE SIZZLE, NOT THE STEAK

The mailing piece did not detail the principles. The principles are the "steak," the meat of the newsletter; the solid information the buyer wants. If you supply the information to the buyer in a direct response

sales letter, there is no need for him or her to send money. The marketer must talk to the prospect about the principles, and how they helped, but never describe or detail them.

The direct-mail letter has to tease the reader; it must contain "sizzle," not "steak." For example, if you are selling "10 ways to financial freedom," you would not name the 10 ways, only the results and benefits derived from using them.

The J.C. Revel letter had everything that a good direct-mail piece should contain, with one exception—testimonials. Testimonials enhance the credibility of a mailing piece and improve response. If prospects know that others have bought and succeeded before them, it is a selling point.

Obviously, at the time, I did not have any success stories; there were not any people around who had subscribed to my newsletter and become a success. That would come later. In lieu of the success stories, I offered a money-back guarantee. Even without success stories, the checks began to arrive. I moved a duplicating machine into my garage, and began cranking out my first issue of *Insider's Report*.

The information in *Insider's Report* could not be found in a bookstore, college library, or government printing office. That's important when selling paper by mail. You need a unique, noncompetitive product; something that cannot be purchased at the corner drugstore.

Merchandise sold through the mail is different. You can sell RCA television sets, Sony VCRs, or other items found at retail stores. Because they are available at retail stores, prospects are familiar with the item, and know its value and brand name. The presence of merchandise in retail outlets enhances the item's credibility.

Why buy merchandise through the mail when it can be purchased at a department store? Convenience. It saves time. Consumers do not have to wait in line or spend time shopping.

Mail order paper products are not items that can be found at retail outlets. If they were, no one would buy them through the mail. They would stop at a retail outlet and thumb through the material (first) to make sure what they were buying was worth the investment. And they would buy it right there.

MERCHANDISE VERSUS PAPER-MARKETING COSTS

Sell merchandise through the mail, and your ad cost should run about 20 to 25%. The product cost is 30 to 35%. To make a profit, the mail order marketer should be marking the cost up somewhere

around two and one-half times. Two and one-half times is sufficient, especially if the item is known to consumers.

With paper, costs differ dramatically. Marketing costs are much higher, although product cost can be lower. Still, the mail order marketer must mark up paper cost around five times in order to make a profit.

I had more than a five times mark up in *Insider's Report* when I started to sell it, and prospects bought it. For a short time, I thought there was nothing that would stop or slow my newsletter's growth. I was wrong.

Despite the heavy response to my initial ad, it had a weakness which I did not discover until it was almost too late. At first the ad pulled dramatically. Suddenly, it began to die. I watched inquiries dwindle and the dollars with them. Something had to be done. I had no desire of running a newsletter for a couple of thousand subscribers at $16.75 forever. There was not enough profit in it.

I scrutinized the ad and body copy. For an inquiry ad, I could not do much with the body, but I could change the head. I did. This time it read:

Who's Making a Bundle?"

A subtle but important difference. With the new head, I created a two-step that pulled for four years before response diminished.

Why? In mail order, a head represents 60 to 70% of the ad's appeal.

SPECIFIC VERSUS GENERAL HEADLINES

"How Much Money Does Joe's Business Make?" and "Who's Making a Bundle?" may not sound too different, but they are worlds apart. The two heads demonstrate specific and general headlines.

"How Much . . .," the first headline, was specific. The word "business" qualified readers and led them to believe the ad (and follow-up information) would tell them about *businesses* they might open. It eliminated those who might not have been interested in opening a business, but were interested in making money. Yet those who had no intention of opening a business could still be potential customers. I accidentally neglected the audience of investors who purchase stocks, bonds, real estate, and so on. They might never

open their own business, but they certainly could be curious about "who's making a bundle."

"Who's Making a Bundle?" could have referred to people who were making money through real estate, stocks, or a half dozen other investment opportunities. It was more general and appealed to a wider audience.

General headlines bring in greater numbers of respondents, and may lead to more sales even though the percentage of conversions may diminish.

My inquiries more than doubled. The *Journal* came back to life for me. The percentage of inquiries from "Who's Making a Bundle?" who purchased once they received my follow-up letter dropped, and for a logical reason. The audience was broader, but not all were qualified buyers. Still, there were advantages in that broader market.

For example, suppose my two-step with the first headline generated 100 inquiries each time it ran. Suppose again that 25% of those who responded ultimately bought the newsletter. That gave me 25 orders.

Now, take the new head. I ran it in the same publication, but the response per insertion jumped to 300. This time, however, only 20% bought the newsletter when they received the packet. That meant 60 orders, or more than double the subscriptions I generated from the first ad.

This held true in every publication in which I inserted the ad: Inquiries increased, the closing percentage dropped, but the total number of orders went up.

The new head appealed to anyone interested in making money. Many were simply curious. They had no intention of ever opening a business, but they wanted to know who was making a bundle and how they did it.

NOT EVERYONE USES THE PRODUCTS

Buyers may intend to use the product, but for one reason or another they never do. That lesson was brought home to me when I expanded my product line and began producing "start-up manuals" on individual businesses.

The manuals were practical, "how to" guides on business. For example, if you wanted to open a hamburger stand, I would sell you a manual containing information on everything from site location to marketing to recipes.

People would purchase three, four, or even a dozen at one time. Why would somebody buy so many? Why not buy one, read it, and if it is not to their liking, purchase a different manual? Logically, that would be the way you would imagine a consumer would act. Consumers, however, are not logical. Neither are opportunity seekers. Many were unsure about the kind of business they wanted to enter so they bought information on any—and every—business that interested them.

Many never intended to go into business. They were merely curious and wanted to find out about available opportunities. Once they read the manual, and saw it required more effort and work than they were prepared to put out, they dropped the idea.

In later studies, I found less than 10% of those who bought the manuals actually used them. The same was true for the information contained in *Entrepreneur*.

Nonuse is an interesting phenomenon that is particular to mail order paper products. It not only happens with business advice products, but courses that are sold through the mail, as well. The customer may have every intention of using the paper, but when it arrives he or she either is too busy, has lost interest, or finds that the rewards are not worth the effort.

This seldom happens with merchandise. If a camera, television, VCR, compact disc, jewelry, or other similar item is purchased through the mail, it is used.

Why do people buy if they have no intention of using the product? Because the mail order marketer has successfully appealed to their needs. Those needs can range from curiosity to greed. Appealing to those needs was not the only reason for my success.

I punched holes in business fallacies as well. A Bank of America report, for instance, might report that a hardware store nets 3.2%, a figure supplied by the hardware store owner.

It was misleading. All bottom line figures of privately held businesses are. Sole practitioners try to make their profit as little as possible for tax purposes. They take small salaries, but have their company pay for all their fringe benefits, including entertainment, insurance, automobile, and much more. It is all an attempt to diminish their tax liability.

That is not the case, of course, with the large publicly held companies which want to make the bottom line appear as healthy as possible because of shareholders and the impact earnings have on the price of the company's stock.

The small business owner purposely (and understandably) de-

pletes the bottom line. Buried within the business, however, is sub-stantial profit. I knew it because I had been in business. Many enterprises showed a 30 to 40% profit, sometimes higher.

Years later when *Entrepreneur* became nationally known, I was criticized by some in the media for being too upbeat about small business in my manuals and reports. They claimed the earnings fig-ures for some of the businesses in our manuals were exaggerated.

MAIL ORDER PROFITS

They were not. All it takes is common sense and an in-depth ex-amination of a company's books to determine what the business really makes. It is not uncommon for a mail order firm to show a gross profit of 50%.

Mail order does not require fancy offices or high overhead, nor does it require dozens of executives and other management employ-ees. I ran Insider's Report out of my garage when I was grossing more than $100,000. There are few businesses that can be operated that way.

Unfortunately, when it comes to profits, bankers cannot get away from that reported bottom line. Just as it is easy for the small business to bury earnings, it is equally easy for the large corporation to hide problems. To determine a good investment, it takes more than a cursory glance at a profit and loss statement. That is one of the rea-sons many banks are having financial difficulties today.

EVOLUTIONARY, NOT REVOLUTIONARY PRODUCTS

Insider's Report was first in the market but it was not a radically new product. Radical, revolutionary products sound exciting, but they are tough to sell. If you try to market something to consumers that is too new they have a difficult time understanding it, and you stand an excellent chance of failing, although the product may be exceptional.

Years ago, I worked for an electronics firm in Chicago. The com-pany came up with a phenomenal cash register, one that not only rang up sales, but tracked a half dozen other things at the same time. We were able to get one department store to install it.

It was a failure because employees would not accept a cash register that was run by a computer. At the time, computers were new and

strange. As a result, we had to remove the cash register and the product failed.

Today, computerized cash registers are standard in almost every department store, because consumers and clerks have come to know and accept computers. High tech is in and the computerized cash register is part of it—an evolutionary product.

An excellent illustration of consumer fascination with and acceptance of high tech is *Sharper Image*, a slick, four-color monthly catalog mailed to more than one million businesspeople. *Sharper Image* and other similar books are loaded with evolutionary products, and they sell because consumers have learned to accept computers and the many electronic innovations that have developed along with them.

If *Sharper Image* and other catalogs had been trying to market the same products in the 1950s, there is an excellent chance they would have failed. The breakthrough in high tech products opened the door for a myriad of mail order merchandise items that revolved around the computer. High tech, however, is certainly not the last industry that will lend itself to mail order. Astute marketers who keep their eyes on trends have every opportunity to create another successful *Sharper Image*.

The creation of *Sharper Image* was not an accident, nor was it luck. The creation of *Entrepreneur* was not a matter of luck, either. I came up with the right concept (a business opportunity magazine) at the right time (when entrepreneurial interests were on the rise). Oftentimes those outside the industry look at successful mail order breakthroughs and they credit the company's rise to luck or fate. Luck, hell. Certainly you need it, but I have never seen a mail order product succeed because someone was lucky.

LOOK FOR GAPS IN THE MARKET

The mail order marketers who make it are those who understand where the gaps and opportunities are in the marketplace. They are not concerned with exciting products, only an exciting niche in the market.

There is no shortage of products. There is a shortage of good mail order marketers who are willing to take the time to study the consumer (or whomever you want to sell a product to) before they come out with a product.

I never sold a product without being convinced there was a potential market. I sold subscriptions to *Insider's Report* because I had

spent time in the consulting field and could see how hungry middle management executives and budding entrepreneurs were for information.

As a teenager, I used to read ads in magazines and study the ones that were repeated. If you find an ad that is repeated on a regular basis there is a good chance it is doing the job—the product is selling. No one repeatedly spends money for an advertisement unless the ad is profitable.

I used to look at those ads and try to understand why the product sold, what made people buy it. It helped develop my sensitivity to the marketplace, my understanding of what motivates buyers. I still do the same thing.

I would rewrite ads. I tried to substitute better, more potent words. I do the same thing today. If you want to be good at anything, you have to work at it, hone your skills. The best football players practice the longest and hardest. The same is true of every athlete, and virtually anyone who has been a success in mail order.

REAL VERSUS RATIONALIZED BUYING REASONS

People buy for emotional reasons (e.g., to gain status, to earn more money, to be healthier, etc.) Later they rationalize these emotional reasons with logic.

Good mail order ads play on the emotions. For example, take solar energy. Thousands of consumers have converted hot water heaters to solar energy. However, if they logically examined the cost and savings of this switch, they would not have purchased this type of product.

But switching to solar energy can be rationalized in buyers' minds because they believe they are helping to improve the environment and lower energy usage. Good, logical reasons. But their real motivations for buying are their emotional reasons. A solar purchase makes buyers feel good. It gives their ego a boost. They can discuss how they are doing their part for their country and humanity.

Ridiculous? Not at all. It is the true reason for the purchase. Those who are sensitive to buyers understand the differences between emotions and logic. They know how to stimulate buyers' emotional response, and they leave them with a logical reason to defend their purchases.

People buy for fun, too. That is why the Pet Rock sold. It was a

humorous conversation piece. People love to give humorous gifts, and humor is a strong motivator.

Not all consumers are the same. They differ from market to market, and it is important for marketers to understand the differences. A 35-year-old male Philadelphian may not respond the same way as a 35-year-old male in Los Angeles. (Actually, the Philadelphia consumer differs radically from his counterpart in Los Angeles.)

The way for marketers to come close to pinpointing those differences (and the response that goes with it) is through the most important research tool available—*Editor & Publisher's Annual Market Survey*. If you intend to sell nationally (or even in one market) this book is a must.

Editor & Publisher contains information on every market, describes prime industries, where people are employed, and dozens of other useful facts that helped me analyze buyers in cities I had never even been to.

It is a bible to the mail order marketer. It dissects markets, tells you who lives there, what they do, and how much they make. For example, the two key industries in Bakersfield, California, are agriculture and oil. That information tells the marketer Bakersfield is a blue collar market, as opposed to a community of white collar service businesses. That gives the marketer a clue as to the category of products that might sell via mail order.

Compare Bakersfield to Houston, Texas. Texas, of course, is one of the country's prime oil producers. Therefore, some may reason that Houston has a heavy blue collar population as well. *Editor & Publisher* indicates there are 1.1 million wage earners in Houston, with 187,000 employed in manufacturing—possibly oil or oil-related businesses. But there are nearly 950,000 in nonmanufacturing (or white collar) occupations.

Obviously, mail order marketers who relied on Houston's geographic location instead of its actual industries could be in trouble if they marketed a product geared to the blue collar worker. I have said before that marketing firms put too heavy an emphasis on data base when dealing in the mail order field, but that does not mean statistics should be totally ignored.

There are important ramifications for mail order marketers when analyzing Bakersfield and Houston. As a rule, blue collar workers are more trusting and less likely to question the motives of an ad or mailing piece. White collar workers are more dubious. They want more proof and credibility before making a purchase. In analyzing white collar workers it is easy to see why they have doubts. Most

white collar workers live in cities that are crowded and impersonal. They spend one or two hours a day on the freeway or expressway, honking horns and exchanging unpleasantries with other drivers. Crowded conditions foster a lack of courtesy.

On the other hand, many blue collar workers dwell in areas that are more rural. There is more space, less crowding, and far less irritation and suspicion of their neighbor.

Editor & Publisher will not, of course, relate the psychological attitudes of the buyers to the mail order opportunist. If it did, there would be no risk involved in the business. But common sense and sensitivity can give anyone in the field an excellent insight into the potential customer once they know the demographics of their community.

Editor & Publisher goes far beyond occupations. It breaks down the number of households; types of transportation; number of automobiles; and even the shopping centers, chain drug stores, and supermarkets.

By going through *Editor & Publisher*, I was able to pick test markets for products. If a test goes well in one blue collar market, it should do well in another.

I was not a sophisticated, experienced mail order specialist when I launched *Insider's Report*, but I learned by carefully monitoring ad results, comparing markets in *Editor & Publisher*, and trying to analyze why some areas differed from others.

KEYS TO GOOD COPYWRITING

Creating a successful mail order campaign involves more than selecting the right market. Copywriting is, of course, a critical ingredient. What makes a good copywriter? The ability to relate; to understand people, their motives, and attitudes.

Read the daily newspaper and attitudes jump out at you. Drive the freeway or expressway and you cannot miss them. Never go by what you believe people will buy; go by what you know they will buy. I determine that by observation and by monitoring every ad.

I also assign a code to each ad. That is, I give each ad (and mailing piece) a specific number or code that is returned to me with the order. The code is usually located on the back or bottom of the order form. If a consumer's response is through a call, he or she usually has to ask for a specific operator "number." That number is actually the

code. It indicates to the marketer what publication or radio or TV station was responsible for the call or order.

Coding is critical in mail order. I found myself placing 10, 20, sometimes 50 ads a week. Responses came from every city in the country. Without accurate coding, I would never have been able to determine which media pulled best, which were cost-effective.

Tracking ads is more than a matter of coding, counting the responses, and determining their cost and profit. There is a subtle ingredient that has become of paramount importance when it comes to mail order—the "back-end" or postpurchase sales you get from a customer.

For example, in some instances my "Who's Making a Bundle?" inquiry ad cost me $100 to place. In return I might receive 50 inquiries, and from those my follow-up mailing piece would convert 20%, or 10, for a gross sale of $165.

Now, subtract the $100 ad cost, which leaves $65. Then subtract the cost of the mailing piece and postage. If it cost me 10 cents for the printing of the mailing piece, that's $5. Postage ran another $11 (50 × .22, although postage in 1973–1974 was cheaper).

My $65 profit shrinks to $49, but there is more to deduct. I have to print, write, and research 10 monthly newsletters. Printing for a 36 to 40 page report could run another $1–$2 per issue, or $24 per year.

Profits are down to $25 for the year's subscription. Is it worth it? Yes, and for a reason that is not immediately apparent.

Initially, there is the quantity aspect. If I have 1,000 subscribers I will earn about $25,000 a year. When I ran "How Much Money Does Joe's Business Make?" my subscriber base was in the 1,000 range. When I changed the head, subscriptions jumped and I soon found myself with 10,000 subscribers, or a gross of $250,000 a year.

Of course, $250,000 is an excellent gross profit but it was not the reason I continued the newsletter and eventually turned it into a magazine.

THE BACK-END POTENTIAL

I discovered the back-end, or what is called postpurchase sales potential. Postpurchase selling can generate more dollars for marketers than the initial sale.

The underlying principle of the back-end is that once a prospect becomes a customer he or she can be sold again and again—and

again. Someone who spends $10 for a product may spend 10 or 20 times that amount with the same company in the future if he or she is handled properly. For example, each issue of *Insider's Report* had one or two reports on a current, hot, profitable business. The initial subscribers received those reports but those who began their subscription with subsequent issues missed them. Oftentimes, they wrote asking to buy a copy of the missed report.

I charged $3.50 for a reprint, but as the subscriber list grew, I found myself filling more and more reprint orders. I began to advertise them as a separate item that could be purchased, and soon found that orders for back reports escalated rapidly.

I started packaging the reports. Buy five for $15 instead of $17.50, I offered. I began to segment them. Retail reports were put in one binder, service businesses in another, manufacturing in a third, and I marketed each.

I discovered many charter subscribers could be resold reports they had forgotten about and even discarded. I also found that prospects who did not want to subscribe to the newsletter were often willing to purchase a report. Once they became a report buyer, I retained their name and it was not unusual to have them purchase 5 or 10 additional reports during a 12- to 18-month cycle.

By 1980, 50% of my gross sales were from reports, which I had renamed "start-up manuals." Equally as important, the report sales showed me the value of obtaining a "qualified name" and the ultimate back-end purchasing value of that name.

In mail order, when someone responds to an offer (or inquiry) they have qualified themselves as buyers or prospects. I might only earn $25 gross profit from an inquiry ad that generated 100 responses. However, there was at least 10 times that amount in the back-end or postpurchase sales potential of those names.

Because of the sales that can follow the initial purchase, some mail order companies are content to either break even or lose money in order to obtain a qualified name.

A qualified prospect's name is not only of value to mail order companies, but to others as well. By 1980 the list of buyers I had compiled for *Entrepreneur* was generating $350,000 a year through list rentals.

The buyers for the simulated diamond business I created in 1983 are equally as valuable. Initially they made an investment of about $25 (to buy a one-carat simulated diamond), but once they bought they found their order came not only with the stone but with a catalog outlining the different settings they could have if they returned their

diamond. As a result, each $25 order turns into an average sale of $177. By fulfilling orders rapidly, a simulated diamond customer will spend anywhere from $500 to $700 with us during the first 12 months.

That is an example of the value of postpurchase selling. It is also one of the exciting things about the mail order industry. With heavy repeat sales, it is one of the few businesses where you can use your skills and a small investment, and suddenly find yourself on the brink of riches. There is no other business like it in the world. For the investment, there is no business with a greater potential reward.

PREDICTING MAIL ORDER SUCCESS

However, not every mail order venture is a guaranteed hit. In fact, for every five I try, four fail. Unfortunately, it is impossible to predict which one will be the hit because human nature—the element that dictates whether your product will go or die—is constantly changing.

Most mail order ideas that fail do so because the right words were not put together in an ad or mailing piece. The failure usually has nothing to do with the appeal of the product.

Products seldom fail (unless they are so outrageous no one will buy). More often it is the mailing piece, the words, the way they were structured, the manner in which they addressed the potential customer's needs. Oftentimes, a marketer will have the right offer and words, but he or she goes to the wrong market; hence the importance of *Editor & Publisher*.

My simulated jewelry company (Van Pler & Tissany) was not an original idea. In fact, hordes of mail order specialists had tried to sell high-line costume jewelry through the mail before I came along. Many had the right offer, but they went for the wrong market. I simply changed direction, and with one $700 ad I started a business that grossed $5 million in 14 months.

The new direction I selected for Van Pler & Tissany is an example of what I mean when I refer to sensitivity to the marketplace. Sensitivity cannot be taught. Either you are sensitive or you are not. Either you understand the basic motivations of people or you do not.

CHARACTERISTICS OF MAIL ORDER MARKETERS

What kind of people are sensitive? That is, what characteristics make a good mail order specialist?

Salespeople are sensitive. That does not mean you have to be a top salesperson in order to be a success in mail order. I have known numerous successful mail order marketers who were introverted and withdrawn and hated sales, but they did well because they were sensitive to people's needs.

For as long as I can remember, I have loved sales and been good at it. I am also interested in people, and what makes them do things. As a teenager, I sold ointment door-to-door in Tennessee, and I did well.

I grew up on a farm and it taught me about life. It toughened me. For example, you cannot stay in bed on cold mornings because someone has to milk the cows and feed the chickens. You cannot stay indoors and watch television during the winter because there is no television.

Children who grow up on a farm learn to relate to people at an early age. When you relate to people, you can sell them. That's why I was a good salesperson. It was also one of the reasons I liked mail order. A good mail order campaign is like a good sales program. The difference being that instead of selling to one person at a time you can sell to millions.

Good salespeople understand what makes people purchase goods. If you can master that your chance for mail order success increases dramatically.

Good salespeople and mail order marketers never stop learning. They learn by observing. Did you ever spend an afternoon in a shopping mall watching people? Did you ever observe how they approach goods and salespeople? Did you ever notice what type of windows attract them? By watching, the mail order specialist can become more proficient. Observation and research are required training in this business.

Success in the business depends on a knowledge of the attitudes that people have. Attitudes are no more than feelings. They reflect a buyer's needs and thoughts. Attitudes are vastly different today than they were when I was growing up in the 1950s.

TRENDSETTERS OF ATTITUDES

All attitudes are created by the 18- to 30-year-olds. That's the age bracket when most of us are vocal and outspoken. We are searching for identity and purpose. At that age, we go for new products, create new trends, and introduce new ideas. Eventually those attitudes af-

fect the attitudes of the over-30 crowd, an audience that emulates the 18 to 30-year-olds.

Just about the time the 18- to 30-year-olds tire of an attitude, it is picked up by the over-30 crowd. That subtle change is important for mail order marketers to understand. Later in this book, we will take a closer look at some of today's—and tomorrow's—attitudes and how they help determine what can be sold through mail order, and to whom.

Even if you are sensitive, and understand attitudes and how they change, success does not come easy with mail order. At times I not only worked long hours, but I gambled every dime I had, and took chances that few would.

When my company grew, I hired, fought, and fired executives and employees. There are few entrepreneurs who can have a million dollars in the bank without taking chances. It is part of the game.

Turning points? There were many. In 1977, four years after I launched *Insider's Report*, I came up with an idea to combine a business opportunity show with seminars. The seminars would all be built around a "start your own business" theme.

To stage the show and promote it, I needed $60,000. My company was fairly successful but I still had to juggle bills (and creditors) in order to raise the money. I gambled. I hocked it all. If we did not draw, my company would probably belong to creditors.

Some feel that risking their bank account is a gamble. To me, it isn't even close. True gambling is putting all you have on the line. I did.

I was convinced, however, that the show would be a success. I even had the Los Angeles Convention Center put in 20-foot aisles to accommodate the crowd I anticipated. When I said 20-foot aisles and predicted 50,000 people, the Convention Center management stared at me as if I had lost my marbles. Most shows have 10-foot aisles, some even as narrow as 8 feet. Reluctantly, they went along with the request.

Despite the preparation, we were not ready for the massive crowds that hit the day the show opened. We had a near riot and made thousands of people angry because of our poor preparation. One disgruntled attendee took a swing at me, and dozens of others felt like doing the same. Yet, the show made it and I hit it big. In three days I made $500,000. Nice return for a $60,000 investment.

That show was the prototype for 40 others, each held in a major city. Before I finished, we had grossed millions. Much of the money

came from a six-page mail order supplement I had designed that promoted the show.

The supplement, which I had inserted in the Sunday newspaper before each show took place, was done in an editorial format. There was a coupon that could be used for ordering seminar tapes or copies of our start-up manuals if they could not make it to the actual show.

The supplement was an incredible marketing tool. It not only drew thousands to the show, but I made back 150% of its cost in mail order orders in Los Angeles. In other cities the return was not as high, but in nearly every city we received a minimum return of at least 33% of the supplement's cost.

Usually, that return is not sufficient for a mail order company marketing paper products. But with the shows the mail order piece (the six-page supplement) served a dual purpose. It generated orders *and* drew people to a consumer show where each customer might spend anywhere from $25 to $100 once inside the door.

EDITORIAL/ADVERTISING TIE-INS

The supplement was also the first advertising vehicle of its type to be structured entirely in an *editorial* format. It was dramatic evidence of the credibility that editorial material has in comparison to advertising. To most, although the supplement was labeled "advertising supplement," it appeared to be a special section put together by the newspaper to salute the show.

The results showed how important good, positive publicity and editorial coverage can be to a company, especially a firm in the mail order business.

The show was not my only gamble. I gambled through the mail as well. Nearly all my products were sold through the U.S. post office. In mail order you need a thick hide in addition to being sensitive to the public's needs.

The post office watches you closely, and consumers are suspicious, and will call and complain if their order does not arrive almost instantaneously. The more money you make the more watchful eyes you encounter. The countless pieces of junk mail that invade each mailbox daily have not enhanced the industry's image, either.

Yet it is one of the most rapidly growing industries in the United States. Time and convenience, two of the most critical considerations that consumers have today, have helped turn mail order into one of the fastest growing businesses in this country.

Despite the difficulties and the risks of the business, there are rewards. If you run an efficient mail order operation the profits are enormous. It is also a cash business and does not have the receivable headaches of many other enterprises.

Our company was productive. We charted and monitored every ad and mailing piece. We did not sell junk, either. Our manuals were vast resources of information. They had detailed business information that could not be obtained elsewhere.

I mailed more than a million catalogs a month. Many times I had to commit tens of thousands of dollars months in advance in order to get a catalog printed. Yet, I never knew if the catalog would draw replies until I actually paid the printer and postman and waited for a response.

Along the way we created unique mailing pieces, ad approaches that the entire industry copied, package inserts, and every type of mail order response mechanism available. They are all detailed in later chapters.

In the end, *Entrepreneur* succeeded and grew into a $15 million a year enterprise.

What other industry could show that kind of return for a $44 investment?

when advertising event

give coupons for % off

from products for those
who don't go

3

Entrepreneur's Keys to Success

Attitudes influence manufacturers, manufacturers create new products based on these attitudes, consumers select products that relate to attitudes, and suddenly trends are established.

It isn't as complicated as it sounds. Behind it is the theory that the consumer is the ultimate master, the selector of which products and services will become a success.

For example, consumers developed an interest in exercise, manufacturers recognized that new attitude and came out with a variety of products that fit the exercise craze. We saw everything from high tech jogging shoes to aerobic bicycles. Some products caught on, others did not.

Trends can be long term or short term. If it is short term, consider it a fad. Guess right as to whether you are looking at a fad or trend, and you can make money. I made a bundle because I showed people that I was able to pick and forecast trends with uncanny accuracy through the pages of *Insider's Report* and later *Entrepreneur*.

HOW TO UNCOVER NEW TRENDS

Insider's Report became the country's leading forecaster in the small business area. We not only predicted new business crazes, but we

gave mail order marketers thousands of ideas about new (and recycled) products that could be marketed.

The techniques we used to uncover new trends were no mystery. In order to keep on top of trends, you have to read constantly, and then analyze what you have read. The clues to new attitudes and trends are printed in the daily newspaper and televised almost nightly.

No one beat us when it came to reporting new trends or fads. I subscribed to dozens of newspapers, magazines, and periodicals. I assigned researchers to scour the pages and clip any item that might give us a clue to new businesses or attitudes.

As a result, *Insider's Report* grew rapidly. We not only had business opportunity seekers subscribing, but manufacturers who were looking for opportunities to expand their product lines were buying our reports as well.

By the third issue, I turned *Insider's Report* into a magazine. My motive was strictly profit, and the savings I would realize in postage. In direct mail, postage can siphon your profit and break a company before it even gets off the ground.

BULK MAIL VERSUS FIRST CLASS

When I started *Insider's Report*, magazines enjoyed a special post office rate, while newsletters either went first class or bulk. With the size of the newsletter (36 pages) it was not cost-effective to mail first class.

Many mail order specialists dislike sending anything bulk mail but you have to go with the most economical way. A 36-page catalog costs approximately 83 cents to mail first class. Contrast this with a 12-cent expenditure for bulk mail. Consumers are accustomed to catalog bulk mailings. They accept it.

As far as envelopes containing direct mail, there has always been a controversy over first class versus bulk. Naturally, it is hard to beat the impact of a personalized letter with a single 22 cent stamp affixed to it. But there are ways to get around the bulk drawbacks, and make a bulk envelope equally as effective as a first-class mailer.

Through the years, I have seen numerous first-class mail order packages ignored because they were poorly packaged. At the same time, I have seen bulk mail envelopes succeed because they were well-packaged.

The key is the envelope's appearance, what it says, and how the

prospect perceives it. I'll discuss that in greater depth in a later chapter.

In every business that succeeds you find at least one innovation or idea that marks the beginning of rapid growth. With *Insider's Report*, I had several. Nearly every one of them occurred in 1977, a full four years after I started the publication.

Our first year was, of course, one of rapid growth in which *Insider's Report* went from a newsletter to magazine. But 1977 was 12 of the most thrilling months I have ever lived through. Almost every idea and mail order innovation that I developed increased business.

First, I decided to give the magazine a more exclusive appeal. I formed an association and called it the International Entrepreneur's Association (IEA). I was always under the misconception that an organization needed to be nonprofit in order to call itself an association. I was wrong. Any business could use the name.

I selected the word association for several reasons aside from it sounding more exclusive. The most important was the term's inherent marketing value. Association means a nonprofit organization to most, and nonprofit groups have more credibility in the eyes of consumers than businesses that operate for a profit. Associations, of course, can be quite profitable.

With the association, people could no longer subscribe to the magazine, they had to belong to IEA, and spend $35 a year for membership. As one of the benefits of membership, they received the monthly magazine.

I put a separate cover price on the magazine, $7.50, and called it the "most expensive magazine in the world." It gave the publication a high perceived value in the member's eyes. It did several other things, too.

It brought us to the attention of the advertising agencies on Madison Avenue. I wanted them to notice the publication and place ads in it. What better way than to put a high price tag on the cover and call it the most expensive magazine in the world.

SPARKING CURIOSITY

The line also sparked curiosity. I put it on the outside of most of our mailing pieces, and our returns jumped dramatically. Using that copy line on the outside of direct-mail pieces turned out to be a sure way to get prospects to open our solicitations.

The copy did more than help us with direct mail. I wrote an ad

interesting idea to try

with the most expensive magazine in the world as the headline. I budgeted $25,000 and placed a full-page in 6 or 7 prestigious business publications. My hope was, once again, to attract the attention of the advertisers on Madison Avenue.

At the bottom of the ad there was a coupon which readers could send in for a $3 sample copy. I expected that at best I would break even on the ad. Making money, however, was not my concern. I was doing it for image. I was astounded when the returns came in. Instead of losing money or breaking even, each ad returned anywhere from 300% to 400%.

With each copy I sent a direct-mail subscription piece and we converted a high percentage of those who sent in their $3. After analyzing the ad, I could see why it drew. (We've all heard of hindsight, of course.)

It was the curiosity element. Everyone wanted to see what the most expensive magazine in the world looked like. It's the same curiosity that sparks people who are visiting Los Angeles to drive through Beverly Hills to see Rodeo Drive or the homes of the stars.

In 1977 I decided on a name change as well. *Insider's Report* went well with the newsletter, but in hopes of attracting more executives to subscribe, I revamped the entire product and renamed it *Entrepreneur*.

More than a decade ago the word entrepreneur certainly was not commonplace. I did not change the name for any frivolous reason. We spent an entire day brainstorming, trying to come up with a suitable title. The moment I heard entrepreneur I loved it.

It was a French name, and certainly not well-known in this country. Rarely was it ever seen in print, and about the only time it did appear was when a foreign show promoter was referred to in the newspapers.

I chose the name because of the *curiosity* factor. I was confident the name would stop people at the newsstand. Even if they could not pronounce it, I felt it would still stop them. I was also confident they would pick it up and look at the title more than once. Underneath the title I put the line "the business opportunity magazine." That explained what the potential buyer needed to know.

It was a gamble. As a rule, you want to give a product or company a name that describes the business. Adopting one that no one understands is, at best, foolhardy. Within six months after we started using it the media discovered the name and made it a part of our vocabulary. My reasons for selecting *Entrepreneur* had nothing to do with possible media acceptance.

I viewed *Entrepreneur's* audience as twofold: those who were mail order oriented and received the publication in their homes, and the newsstand buyer. I was careful to distinguish between the two. The audience that browses through publications on the newsstand has already proven they are readers. It takes little effort for them to pick up a magazine—especially one that has an unusual name—and scan the pages.

On the other hand, the direct-mail recipient is not necessarily a reader. I never overused the word (entrepreneur) in our mailing pieces. I preferred "the most expensive magazine in the world" or the "business opportunity magazine." Our mail order prospects had not proven (to me) they were ready to read. I stood a chance of losing them before they even opened my mailing piece if I hit them with the term before I carefully explained the product.

CHOOSING NAMES AND COPY

Copywriters are always inventing clever phrases, but in the mail order business the marketer has to be careful never to use language that is so "in" it will leave the prospect out. Unfortunately many mail order firms fall into this trap.

I had utilized new terms previously with much success because I had never "overestimated" the linguistic ability of our potential customers.

Curiosity is potent, but you have to evaluate carefully every segment of your audience. I was certain my newsstand readers would accept the new title more readily than those who received solicitations at home.

I changed packaging as well. I went from newsprint to glossy stock with black-and-white and color photos. The cover was a heavier stock, usually a four-color production.

Upgrading the appearance was a positive step, but changing the name of a successful product was a risk. You do not see McDonald's changing its name to the Burger Barn or Ringling Brothers to Smith Brothers. It takes a long time to establish a name, and changing it is nearly always a mistake. However, I felt a switch would have a positive impact on our image and enable us to reach a larger market. I was right.

IDEAS THAT SELL—AND WHEN

Another plus for the magazine was the number of new trends and businesses we were spotting and writing about. Although a recession year, 1977 was a remarkable year for innovation. I haven't seen one to equal it since. I would guess if we go through another severe recession we may see an equal number of good ideas. During hard times there is usually an abundance of new ideas. People are less content; they are searching, creating, and taking risks. For now, however, 1977 stands as one of the most creative years in small business history.

I am not, incidentally, talking about the creation of new products. I am referring to the development of new business concepts. For example, there were computer stores. At the time *Entrepreneur* wrote about them, there were only two in California.

I predicted every city in the United States would soon have one. When I made the forecast, most readers did not even know what a computer store was or how it operated. I could see the potential.

Initially the stores were meant for computer afficionados, the pros, the people who were engineers or data-processing fanatics. That segment of the market was not large enough to make an impact, but they were the catalyst that served to introduce consumers to computers.

In our April 1977 issue, I predicted the emergence of the business. I also forecast that this was no fad, that it would be a long-term, solid business with steady growth.

I did not need to be a genius to say that. All I had to do was analyze the industry. There were 23 computer stores in existence. They catered to the engineering-types, and sold them hobby kits which consisted of components that had to be put together. Most of the time you needed an engineering background in order to read the instructions and put the kit together.

You had to know computers, and how they functioned before you would feel at home in one of the stores. I likened it to the early days of high fidelity, when the sound afficionados bought components from specialized stores and put them together at home.

The computer industry was going through the same growing pains. I could envision that it would not be long before the hobby kits were replaced by computers that were already assembled, much as the high fidelity components were eventually replaced by fully-assembled stereos.

If computers were going to become the rage, someone had to sell them. There were no stores marketing or servicing them. Therefore it made sense for a specialized computer store to emerge.

WHERE OPPORTUNITIES COME FROM

New technology always creates new opportunities. It may destroy old industries, but in the birth of the new technology is the seed for new business. Mail order entrepreneurs should always examine breakthroughs closely because invariably there is a chance to make money.

The computer store pick was a coup, but my favorite remains the lo-cal bakery, which I first saw in 1977. I forecast its emergence about the same time. I had spotted one on my way to work one day. I visited it, studied the operation, made a few calls, and could not believe the opportunity.

The bakeries originated as placed where diabetics could buy sweets and bakery products that were in low in sugar. The breads and cakes were all made with cheap, day-old (or more) stale bread, which contained less sugar.

The owners were amazed when they opened. Instead of diabetics, they attracted health addicts, people trying to lose weight, and those trying to cut down on their sugar intake. The diabetic bakery had a huge market, one that was much broader than the originators even imagined.

I remember the concept for another reason. When I wrote about it, the owners tried to obtain an injunction and prohibit us from selling the report. They had two dozen bakeries in Southern California and were not interested in competition.

They never did get the injunction, and the lo-cal bakery remains one of the finest, high profit business opportunities I have ever seen. Amazingly, while the country has become saturated with computer stores, lo-cal bakeries remain an oddity. They have not expanded much beyond California, despite the hunger that American consumers have for lo-cal products. It remains a prime opportunity.

In 1977, *Entrepreneur* became the first magazine to cover such fad businesses as roller skating and skateboard parks. Skateboard parks became a sensation, and eventually every national magazine wrote about them. *Entrepreneur*, however, was the first and that gave us tremendous credibility among consumers—and the media.

The media began to look to us a source of new business infor-

mation. They quoted *Entrepreneur* and the reports we were producing. It gave our sales a tremendous lift.

I started building a media list and sent them complimentary copies of the magazine on a monthly basis. I have always believed in promoting oneself. If you do not, how is the consumer ever going to know you exist?

Although the media looked upon business opportunities as scams, they loved the magazine. The industry's negative image stemmed from the franchise scandals of the 1960s. Unsuspecting consumers were sold every conceivable business opportunity pie-in-the-sky offering.

The scandals caused legislators throughout the country to tighten franchise laws and requirements. But the media could not forget the thousands of consumers who were swindled out of life savings with get-rich-quick schemes.

I hoped to legitimize what we were doing. I stayed away from the get-rich-quick schemes. My reports on new businesses were optimistic (they had to be), but I tempered them with a description of the problems most people would find after opening the business.

As the magazine grew I became more conservative with reports. It was still flashy and intriguing. It promised to show people the way to the American Dream—owning their own business. No other publication even remotely resembled it.

The Los Angeles Public Library kept the magazine on a chain to prevent its theft. A reporter at the *Los Angeles Times* told me he hid his copies in his desk to keep them from being lifted by other staff members.

The graphics were superior as well. The exterior of your goods, in this case the magazine cover, is a calling card. Regardless of what you are selling, the calling card has to look good. Try selling a mink coat with a black-and-white catalog printed on newsprint, and you will get a firsthand lesson in the importance of appearance.

Look at the *Sharper Image* or American Express catalogs. They immediately position their products as quality merchandise because of the slick brochure, four-color photos, and graphic attractiveness. They can charge a premium for the items. Consumers have no trouble believing the items are worth the price.

APPEARANCE AND PACKAGING

In mail order (or, for that matter, any enterprise) if you try to sell something for a high price, make sure the product and the packaging

look the part. Even if you are marketing something that is inexpensive, take care with the packaging. A good-looking package helps obviate any doubts that buyers may have about the quality of the product. In mail order, perceived quality is critical.

To put it another way, there are not many motion picture stars who look glamorous without makeup. How appealing would a Joan Collins or Linda Evans be without lipstick, eye shadow, mascara, and so on? They may still be beautiful, but they may not have the sizzle that is present when they are fully made up.

The same is true of mail order. I always made sure my mailing pieces relayed an image of quality.

Towards the beginning of 1977 the response to "Who's Making a Bundle?" began to diminish—and not surprisingly. It had run more than three years, a phenomenally long period for an inquiry (or any ad) to run.

During that span I had been busy putting together other mailing pieces that would enable us to earn more revenue from our growing mailing list. I had put together numerous catalogs. A catalog usually consisted of our entire library of "how to" business manuals. Within the catalog were capsule descriptions of the manuals we had put together.

One of the first catalogs was "64 Hottest Businesses." I followed that with "96 Hottest Businesses" and every time the response from the catalogs began to diminish I added manuals and reissued it as "—Hottest Businesses."

I used the term "hottest" back in the mid-seventies on a space ad I created in which I named and sold the "10 Hottest Businesses" of the year. It turned out to be a word that had tremendous consumer appeal. It piqued their curiosity. Today, of course, the word has become commonplace. Still, when it is used in a head it attracts attention. It is one of those words that usually helps make a headline on an ad intriguing.

By 1977 our mailing list had grown to the point where we no longer needed an inquiry ad to draw in additional prospects. When a mail order company is young, unknown, and without sufficient capital, inquiry ads are typically the route utilized to build clientele. However, once a mail order company becomes known and its credibility is built, it can look to other ways of generating revenue aside from two-step inquiry ads or expensive one-step ads. One of the most productive alternatives was reworking our list of inquiries and customers with new catalog mailings.

HOW TO INCREASE CREDIBILITY

Our later catalog mailings had something that none of the early ones contained—testimonials from previous buyers who had purchased manuals and done well in business.

There is nothing that offers greater credibility in a mailing piece than testimonials from previous buyers.

Our catalogs did well for reasons other than the testimonials. The timing was perfect. We had gone through one of our periodic recessions, and consumers could see that working for a corporation no longer meant lifetime security. Entrepreneurialism was growing on the college campuses as well.

The media helped, too. Newspapers wrote about cutbacks, television stations spotlighted long-time employees who were suddenly out of a job, and radio stations followed suit. Fear spread and consumers began searching for alternative ways of making money. The "10 Hottest" was packaged well; the cover was two-color, with a heavy stock. I spent more money putting it together than I had on *Insider's Report* when it was a magazine.

I frequently readjusted prices on our manuals. Pricing is a never-ending puzzle. Sometimes you can sell more goods at $10.95 than you can at $8.95. Once again, perceived value is important. Inside information on how to become a success in business had to be worth more than $10 to $15, so I tripled the price of the manuals to $35. Total orders dropped but gross sales rose. (Six years later, when I launched Van Pler & Tissany, I sold our first one-carat simulated diamonds for $15. A year later I raised the price to $25 and saw total orders drop but gross sales rose.)

We mailed additional offers every couple of months. I found it was not unusual for a customer who made an initial $25 purchase to spend six or seven times that amount during the next year if we kept the lines of communications open and made the right offer.

How much will the purchaser buy, and during what period of time will those purchases occur? Every mail order entrepreneur would like to know that answer in advance. I pondered it many times. The truth is you do not know until you have a sales history.

I discovered that a $35 manual buyer would make three purchases during the course of the next year for an additional $100 to $150. That was an important guide in building the company. I knew I could afford to break even on my first sale because the buyer would come back for more, and that is where I could generate significant profits.

GENERATING REPEAT SALES

There is nothing mysterious about repeat business. Once someone buys you know they have the interest. What brings them back—or turns them off—is the quality of the product, service, and satisfaction.

I always gave refunds without question. Also, I never forgot the buyer. Whenever we had information or something of value, I would always let our buyers know. Sometimes it involved selling something to the buyer, but during other periods I would give our customers information at no charge. That is an important principle. If buyers realize you are willing to share information at no cost, they trust you, and trust leads to more sales.

The auto industry was grossly negligent in this area. The Japanese revolutionized the industry's service and communication procedures. Buy a car today and the dealer never forgets. They have seminars, free safety checks, and so on. They want you for life.

In the auto industry not every ad is measurable. In mail order it is. That is another thing I love about the business. It does not take guesswork to determine if your ad pulls; all you need to do is look at the results.

I could also measure the value of the names we generated, and I never abandoned someone who did not buy immediately. When I ran "Who's Making a Bundle?" I received hundreds of thousands of inquiries from people who became customers. Each name went on computer, whether they bought or not. With constant mailings I managed to convert an additional 50% to the buying column.

Buyers, nonbuyers, and prospects are distinct individuals. They do not belong on the same list. I categorized present and potential customers. Manual buyers went on one list, subscribers on another; recent buyers were separated from those who had not bought in a year; and buyers who spent more than $100 were separated from those who spent under $100.

If a buyer bought a manual for a high-investment business, he or she went on one list; purchasers of manuals that required low investments went on another. Not all buyers are the same and they should always be segmented.

List segmentation paid off. It decreased mailing costs and increased profits. I kept our lists clean, and eventually they began to generate enormous sums of money. In 1986 *Entrepreneur* earned more than $350,000 in list rental income with minimal costs. All it took was

a salesperson and a telephone. If a list is good and has responsive names, word gets around and everyone calls to rent it. Our names were the best, which is why we generated so much rental income.

Regardless of how good sales are, I have always felt they could be bettered. With "10 Hottest" and some of the other innovations I introduced, 1977 sales increased dramatically. However, I was not satisfied. *Entrepreneur* had become a formula, and it was beginning to bore me.

EVALUATING A MAIL ORDER BUSINESS

I decided to sell. Selling a business is easier said than done, especially when you talk about a mail order publishing enterprise. Buyers have a difficult time understanding mail order businesses. Many believe a profitable mail order enterprise is a flash in the pan and has no stability. Nothing could be farther from the truth.

Moneymaking mail order operations have a proven customer base, a customer who has already demonstrated his or her affinity for buying through the mail. If a customer bought once, he or she will buy again. This is not true of many other businesses, such as retail. The buyer may purchase a suit at a store in a regional shopping mall but never return because of poor service. The customer's one purchase is evidence that he or she purchases suits—but whether the customer will purchase another suit from the same store is another question.

Buyers of businesses also have a fetish—they cannot keep their eyes off the bottom line, and if net income is not healthy they back off. As I have said, net income means little when it comes to a privately held company. I do not know any businesspeople who would turn down 5% of the gross against 50% of the net. The net is too easily manipulated—and diminished.

Several years before I started *Entrepreneur*, I created "Starving Artists," a national company that sold affordable, quality art on corners throughout the country. I had no trouble selling the business with its assets (paintings) and contracts (for locations).

But *Entrepreneur* was loaded with intangibles, products that few knew how to handle. There were mailing lists, manuals, research information, new manuals about to be released, and a score of other items that meant nothing to a buyer unless they were involved in mail order.

I was stymied. I could not find a buyer. I did the only thing I could do—hold onto the company. I also decided to roll the dice with sev-

eral ventures that had never before been attempted. One involved the most expensive mail order space buy I was ever to make, an ad that would cost more than $50,000 for one insertion.

My thrill has been in risking everything in business. I once bought a bankrupt stereo store in Miami, and that led me to open the first Cuban bar in Miami. I even designed, manufactured, and sold computerized astrological machines. Those were business gambles that meant more than just a payoff in dollars. The gamble I had in mind for *Entrepreneur* was greater than any I had ever tried. It would tie into the new image and name I had created for the magazine.

PRICING

For four years, I had been marketing products to a specialized audience, the executive. At heart, I have always preferred marketing to the masses. I like dealing with Joe Average. My idea was to take *Entrepreneur*—a $7.50 per issue magazine that was only sold via subscription (the business opportunity seeker had to join our Association)—and sell it to the masses. In its heyday *Playboy* could never have generated a following with that high a cover price. Could *Entrepreneur*? Absolutely not.

There was only one way to appeal to the masses. Drop the cover price and introduce it to consumers via newsstands. I decided to drop the price to $2.95. The new price structure would put us in head-to-head competition with some of the other business opportunity magazines that had emerged.

The competition did not bother me. What did was dropping the price. Imagine Cadillac suddenly cutting 50% off the sticker price and trying to compete with Ford. Buyers would automatically assume that something was wrong with the Cadillac. How could the company possibly sell a $15,000 automobile for $7,500? How could I possibly take a $7.50 magazine and sell it for $2.95.

Dropping the price of a product can often be more deadly than raising it. Dropping price without an explanation usually means you were unable to compete at the higher price. It does not mean you are giving your buyers a bargain.

For consumers who had never seen the $7.50 price, that is, the masses who would encounter *Entrepreneur* on newsstands, we were safe. But present customers would have looked upon the change as evidence that we had been ripping them off. They would believe the magazine was never worth more than $2.95.

To make the price palatable I altered the format of the publication, but not radically. Our policy had been to run a complete manual on a new or unique business. Members of the Association got this as a bonus. To nonmembers I sold the manuals through catalogs such as "64 Hottest" and "96 Hottest."

I decided to eliminate complete manuals from the new format. We would still cover new businesses, but I intended to eliminate the details and in-depth information. If a reader wanted it, he or she would have to purchase the entire manual for $35.

This would also enhance the value of the manuals. No longer would they be reprints of the magazine—we were creating a separate and new mail order product.

I still had to soothe the wrath of current Association members. They were used to the complete manuals, and you cannot take something away from a buyer without giving them something in return, if you want to keep them happy and loyal.

To placate existing Association members, we began running between two and four new *condensed* manuals in every issue. I gave them double the information and extended their subscriptions.

I had to revise our covers completely. Newsstand magazines are in a beauty contest. If a publication lacks a good graphic look, people pass it over and never even notice it. Manufacturers of products that are sold in supermarkets are well aware of this fact. They spend millions on advertising and millions more on the package. It cannot be disappointing. It has to have a value and appear as if it is worth the money.

THE LANGUAGE OF MAIL ORDER

In mail order you must describe your product and package with vivid, exciting verbs and adjectives. You must make the product come to life through the written word. In the mass marketing of a product in a supermarket, department store, or similar outlet, active language has to be replaced by dynamic packaging.

Supermarket marketers have an advantage. Customers can pick up the goods and they can feel it. They do not need an imagination. In mail order, stimulating the buyer's imagination is everything.

In repackaging and renaming the magazine, I acted on gut instincts, discarded my normal objective examination, and went for it. I do not advise others to do the same. The only instinct your gut

normally is good for is a stomach ache. As far as a business indicator, it does not rank among the top 10.

But my instinct won out. It said that the name change would not affect sales when it came to the middle manager or corporate executive. They understood the term. The gamble was with the new market I was trying to reach, the masses.

Our first issue hit the newsstands in the late 1977, and it was an instant success in more ways than just newsstand sales. *Entrepreneur* was a catalog filled with our products and people were buying them.

Certainly, it had new product and business news, but it also contained descriptions and order blanks for our manuals. Each issue also contained two or three success stories about people who had purchased one of our manuals and hit it big. Invariably the sales of those manuals would jump once the story hit. An endorsement of one manual meant that all manuals were good.

To coincide with the newsstand introduction of the magazine, I budgeted funds for publicity, or positive public relations. PR is often maligned or overlooked by businesses, but positive publicity can take a mail order business and double it. It is free space that can be generated through the media. PR can be 10 times more effective than any advertisement.

Everyone recognizes a full-page ad when it is purchased by Sears or some other well-known company. Readers know it has been bought. Real impact comes when the local newspaper, a national magazine, or a television newscaster spends time talking about Sears and how good its products happen to be.

A positive story in an automotive magazine dramatically increases sales of a new car. A great review can make a motion picture a box office winner.

I hired a public relations professional to help generate reviews and positive print about our products. There is nothing devious about this. If you are not General Motors and cannot spend millions on institutional ads to blanket the country, positive publicity is the best thing. The publicity we began to generate was a prelude to the $50,000 gamble I was contemplating.

The gamble stemmed from an idea I had almost from the day I saw the response to the "How Much Money Does Joe's Business Make?" ad. I was astounded at how anxious people were to learn about business. The ads I ran later reinforced my feelings, as did the letters I received from subscribers. Everyone was hungry for information.

The acceptance of *Insider's Report* and *Entrepreneur* showed me the

hunger people had. Certainly, to open a business you need capital, but information is more critical. I sold information that people wanted and needed, not what I wanted.

I had an idea as to how to take advantage of that hunger. People were starving for information about business. They wanted practical, "how to" advice, not theory.

I thought about this need and came up with a product that could double or triple our business almost overnight. It was a business opportunity expo, a show that was different from any that had ever been presented.

In the 1960s business opportunity shows were massive, glamorous productions that filled huge halls and convention centers. By the late 1970s the number of business opportunity shows and promoters had dwindled drastically. Shows were held in small halls or hotels, and the vendors peddled obscure distributorships and franchises.

The promoters spent little on advertising, and usually drew a few thousand consumers to a three-day show. Well-known franchisors, such as McDonald's and Burger King, stayed away from these mini-expos. They disliked the quality of the products being exhibited, and they had no need to exhibit because they generated all the inquiries they could handle through classified ads and referrals.

Business opportunity shows had gone downhill because the attitude of consumers had changed and promoters failed to recognize what was happening. They failed to see the difference between the relatively naive buyer of the 1960s, who believed what he or she was told, and the more dubious shopper of the 1970s, who had learned to question and mistrust salespeople.

The old promoters did not heed the new outlook of the buyer, and they watched their audience diminish. No market remains static. I recognized the change and knew what had to be done to turn the shows into moneymaking ventures. I planned to revise the approach, spend $60,000 to $70,000 to promote it, hold informational seminars as part of it, and, if possible, get civic backing.

The seminars would cover the gamut, everything from "how to raise money" and "how to develop a business plan" to "hottest new businesses of the year." I also planned to sell our manuals at the show. I called it a "supermarket of business opportunities and knowledge." You did not have to buy. You could spend your time learning.

It was a new concept. From the feedback I had received from subscribers to the magazine, I knew information and education was a hot seller.

My gut instinct told me to go, but this time I did not jump. I visited

a half dozen business opportunity shows in different parts of the country. I wanted to make sure there were no hidden reasons that seminars were not offered. I also wanted to observe the attendees— were they young, old, dreamers, or doers?

The shows were small with no more than 30 or 40 booths. The impression I had when I entered one of the halls was a quiet, almost tomblike quality. There was no lively chatter or noise as you would expect to find in a major exposition.

The subdued atmosphere of the show worked on the attendees. They showed little excitement of enthusiasm. They were hardly in a buying mood, and their questions convinced me that few, if any, would ever buy.

Most had no conception of the profit or loss potential of a business. They were hesitant and unsure with the questions they asked. The prospects did not lack intelligence, only knowledge, and they were not about to buy without that knowledge.

The salespeople working the exhibit booths compounded the problem with their agressiveness. They tried to bulldoze buyers as they did in the 1960s and ended by turning most of them off.

In every show the scenario was the same. Timid buyers and aggressive salespeople. In most cases few sales were made, if any. What I observed reinforced my opinion as to what these shows lacked, and how a successful business opportunity expo should be structured.

I had definite ideas in mind when I returned to Los Angeles. Instead of going for the small hotel or motel, I rented a huge portion of the Los Angeles Convention Center. If it is big, it must be important. If it is important, it has credibility.

I needed credibility. I had to attract consumers who had not been to a business opportunity show in years, and an equal amount who had never been to one. I needed the size, name, and prestige of the Convention Center.

The cavernous room had more than sufficient space for 100 booths and 2 seminar rooms, which I located in the rear of the hall. My plan was to run seminars concurrently with the three-day show. With the rooms in the back of the hall, seminar attendees would have to walk through the exhibit area in order to get in or out.

Our seminar attendees would be excellent prospects for exhibitors as well. They would all be qualified buyers who had shown their serious intentions by paying anywhere from $10 a seminar to $35 for an all-day ticket. The high price is an obstacle, and only the more serious buyers will surmount it.

QUALIFYING BUYERS

I discovered the obstacle theory through advertising. The least qualified buyer—although he or she still shows interest—is the person who punches a postage paid "bingo" card in a magazine. The bingo card contains a coded number for each ad in the magazine. All the reader has to do is match the number with the ad, and if he or she desires more information the reader marks the postage-paid card and sends it to the publisher. If our ad was number 10, a reader punches number 10 on the card and drops it in the mailbox.

When the publisher gets the card, he or she enters the names and addresses of all those requesting information on computer. The computer operator prints out lists for each number, and the publisher forwards the lists to the advertisers for follow-up.

In theory it is nice. Advertisers, who have their own message in the ad and their own response mechanism, get a bonus from the publisher via the bingo card names. Without exception, the bingo card names are the least qualified prospects. Many punch simply to punch and get free information. Others may be competitors.

A qualified buyer is one who has to pick up the telephone and make a call or write a note in order to obtain information. An even more qualified prospect is one who has to clip a coupon and fill it out. The coupon may have space for name, address, telephone, and several business related questions. In general the greater the effort and time expended, the better the prospect.

Take it a step further. Ask the inquirer to include $1 for postage and handling for information or a sample. The prospect who does is the best because they have indicated a willingness to pay for information.

The number of inquiries diminish as the steps to qualify increase. Prospects who spend the most time and money qualifying will be the best sales prospects in any campaign.

Our seminar attendees would fall into this category. They were willing to spend money to learn about business. They might also be willing to spend on a business opportunity that was on the exhibit floor—once they had learned about it.

I selected 12 seminars, each critical to success in business. I also included a seminar on mail order and one on import/export. Mail order had been our top-selling manual since I opened my business, and import/export was not far behind. Each seminar lasted two hours.

My greatest gamble was yet to come—the $50,000 space ad. Typ-

ically, promoters start advertising three to four weeks before a show with a series of small space ads. As the event draws near, they increase the ad size and frequency. A week or a few days beforehand, a half- or full-page ad is run.

I was convinced that this approach was wrong. I had never advertised a consumer show before but I knew consumers. I had rented them apartments and sold them vacuum cleaners, stereos, and artwork.

Before a consumer buys a major appliance or durable good, he or she plans and thinks about it. Shows and other low cost items are impulse buys, and impulse products, whether they are sold through the mail or at a supermarket checkout counter, are purchased at the last moment.

Show attendees, whether they were going to seminars or just walking through the hall, were impulse buyers. They did not need to make plans any further than a week in advance. Advertising more than a week before I opened would be a waste.

My experience with advertising in the *Wall Street Journal* and buying lists convinced me of something else. Not all buyers are readers, but all entrepreneurs are. It would be a waste to spend any money on media other than print. Television is for the masses, as well as being expensive. Unless you are selling a product everyone can use, it is impractical for target marketing.

Entrepreneurs certainly watch television, but I would be paying an exorbitant price to reach those few. Radio is expensive as well, especially when it comes to reaching entrepreneurial prospects.

THE HIDDEN ADVANTAGE OF LARGE ADS

I was also convinced that small space print ads were a mistake. The argument is, if the entrepreneur missed the first small space ad, he or she might see the second or third.

Do not believe it. The larger the ad the more prospects. A full-page ad will attract many more prospects than four times a quarter-page ad. If a quarter-page generates 100 sales, a full-page may bring in 600 or even 1,000. Why? The greater the size, the higher the credibility and importance in the prospect's eyes.

I have never been one to follow tradition. Shortly after I graduated high school in Chicago, I met a masonry contractor named Bill Riley. He needed someone to sell his services to builders. I had a job with an electronics firm but I was intrigued by Riley's offer.

One afternoon I stopped by Riley's latest project to watch his crew at work. I knew nothing about bricklaying but I was appalled at what I saw. There were bricklayers putting up a wall, and each would stand around and wait for a so-called lead man to put the corner brick in place before they made a move to finish the course. Once he completed the corner, the others would finish the sides, stop and wait the lead man to play his role again.

It was ludicrous. I could not conceive of high-priced labor standing around while the lead man laid his corner. It was union rules, Riley told me. The lead man always went first.

Rules or not, it was a waste of time and money. I had a solution. I suggested putting a pole on the corners and pulling a string across, so the bricklayers would have a guide and could continue laying bricks instead of waiting for the lead man.

Bill liked the idea—as long as the union did not catch us—and I joined his company. We got rid of the lead man, started using the pole, and gave bricklayers an incentive system in which they earned more money without a lead man than with one. Within weeks we had developed one of the fastest, most efficient masonry firms in Chicago.

Builders throughout Chicago were talking about us. That was when the union dropped in, caught us, and fined us. The daily fine was $150, not enough to overcome the savings we offered to builders and the money we were making. We kept our system, the union kept its fines, and before long we were the busiest masonry firm in Chicago.

The lead man rule was tradition; it was also archaic and meant to be broken. If tradition was not meant to be crossed, half the millionaires in this country would not have made it. Never blindly accept the status quo. Look closely at the way anything is done. Think about it, and you can usually find a better way to do it. That better way can often lead to enormous financial gain.

Before founding *Entrepreneur* I introduced a new way to sell an old product—art—on street corners where my mini "art shows" not only helped increase gas station traffic, but also turned into a multimillion dollar business and the forerunner of street corner markets dealing in products ranging from stuffed animals to pottery and peanuts.

When I began selling simulated jewelry in 1983 there was nothing new about the product. It had been marketed for nearly two decades. I took the same old product, added a few twists to it, and sold it to an audience in a fashion that had never been done before. As a result I created another multimillion dollar enterprise.

Opportunity is all around. I felt that way about the business op-

portunity shows. The traditional way of promoting shows struck me as something that was as outmoded as the lead man bricklaying technique. I changed the rules.

I was only going to run one ad. My ad, however, was going to be a knockout, something no one had tried before. I planned to run six full pages, break it the Sunday before the show, and spend somewhere between $50,000 and $60,000 in doing so.

I was going to make the supplement serve a dual purpose. It would promote the show and hopefully draw people to the door, but it would also serve as a one-step mail order piece. I not only included an order blank for those who could not attend and wanted to buy tapes and manuals, but I encouraged readers to use it.

Some said I was cutting my throat, encouraging would-be patrons to mail in money instead of attending. I disagree. There is a vast difference between an audience that chooses to attend a function in person and one that prefers to purchase the material through the mail. There is, of course, an overlap, but generally the two markets are totally different.

My six-page supplement would cost 10 to 15 times what typical promoters budgeted for ads. It was worth it. If it worked, it would pay us back tenfold.

If not, I could always start over.

At the time, it was a revolutionary concept. Today numerous advertisers utilize the supplement approach. Take a look at the boat or auto show when they come to town. All, incidentally, utilize an editorial format.

LAYING OUT THE MAIL ORDER AD

The ad/editorial approach works well in mail order. Did you ever notice the number of mail order ads that are written and laid out similar to a news story. There is good reason. Our eye is trained to read editorial matter, to search for provocative headlines. Ads are secondary. Structure an ad or mail order piece to appear as if it is editorial, and you are ahead of the game.

Consumers often cannot tell the difference between a mail order ad and editorial if the ad is written in news story style. This approach is not meant to mislead consumers, but to get them to read—and it usually does.

I loaded the supplement with stories on hot new businesses, the seminars and the free information that would be available, and the

experts who would be on hand. I also gave myself a page one story, and billed myself as a "millionaire who knew all the secrets to success." The story promised that I would reveal them, along with the hottest new businesses of the year, in a special two-hour seminar.

I took two pages and filled them with capsule summaries of our manuals. Another two pages had details of the seminars and the background of the speakers. There would be no theory in the seminars, the supplement proclaimed, only practical, how to information supplied by speakers who had been through it all. Inside was a telephone number consumers could call for advance seminar registrations. I also had a mail order blank that anyone could fill out who could not be in attendance but would like to purchase a cassette tape on one or all of the seminars. The more you bought, the cheaper they were.

Informational tapes have become a giant industry because of the time they save. People would rather buy a cassette tape and listen to it while driving or at home, than take the time to attend a live seminar. This is particularly true of executives and businesspeople who have schedules with little time.

The six-page ad was a strong promotion piece for the show, but it was also an excellent, one-step direct-mail piece. It was exciting and provocative. It generated enthusiasm and urgency. I had a line that said seminar seating would be limited. In advertising anything that can create a sense of urgency helps people get off their seats and respond. If it is not urgent, they may want the product, but they may never send for it.

That first six-page supplement brought back $44,000 in manual sales and $88,000 in tape orders—more than a 200% return. Los Angeles, however, is a unique city and almost everything goes. But I did extremely well in other cities where I ran the supplement, as well.

For example, in Chicago I spent $28,000 for the supplement and returned $19,000 for manuals. Almost every market paid back at least 50% of the cost of the supplement through the orders we received for manuals.

The returns from each market gave me a good indication of which markets were strongest when it came to mail order response. Those figures also enabled me to plan additional mailings and strategies for months down the road.

I found that if we mailed to a market within a week or two after leaving, our mail order response increased dramatically. There is a synergism in direct mail and other forms of marketing. For example,

catalog mailings, that listed the locations of our bookstores, brought people into those stores even though they could order the same product through the mail. Along the same lines, when we opened a bookstore in a city, and followed with a catalog or other direct mail piece to prospects in the same city, our direct mail sales would increase.

Our bookstores benefitted from mailings and direct mail revenues were enhanced because of the stores. Much of it is name identification. That is, the more often a customer sees a name of a product the familiar he becomes with it. He may see the name on a catalog or a bookstore. Regardless of where he or she saw it, our sales would rise. For example, immediately after a catalog mailing our sales would jump at least 50% in the stores.

Later, when I opened Van Pler & Tissany, I took full-page mail order ads in the *Los Angeles Times*. Although I never put in the hours or pushed the mini-showroom we have at Van Pler & Tissany, our sales in the showroom would double for at least two weeks following the ad.

We never advertised the bookstore, yet there was hardly a day when we did less than $1,000 in sales. Some people prefer to touch and feel the product. This is especially true when dealing with paper. The fact that *Entrepreneur* was headquartered in Los Angeles and had a bookstore there was all the encouragement it took for Southern Californians to visit it.

When I established Van Pler & Tissany, we did more than $1,000 a day in sales in our store despite the fact we never did any retail advertising. Consumers knew the address from the catalog, and from space ads I had placed in newspapers. Often we had customers drop in just "to see what the store was like." They had no intention of buying anything, they just wanted to see the store for themselves.

The newspaper supplement did much to open to the doors for our catalog mailings. In retrospect, it was one of the best pieces I have ever put together. It was also one of the most cost-effective mail order pieces I have ever placed.

I had no idea, of course, what would happen when I ran the first supplement in Los Angeles. Southern California is a melting pot and many things will go in that area that do not sell elsewhere. Still, I was concerned. But I got some unexpected additional help. Months before the show the *Los Angeles Times* had interviewed me, and two weeks before the expo opened the story appeared on page one of the *Times'* financial section.

In addition, a week before the show, the number one radio station in Los Angeles had one of our exhibitors on as a guest for three hours.

The exhibitor, who was touting a voice stress analyzer (a form of a lie detector), was able to plug the upcoming event more than a dozen times during the show.

I needed something else—civic endorsement. City hall was not going to back a profit-making venture; that is, until we came up with an idea that they could not resist. We announced that a portion of the net proceeds would go to the small business or entrepreneurial arm of the University of Southern California. It was a Los Angeles university, and I felt the mayor would endorse our venture if we could tie in the school.

We did, and the mayor proclaimed "investment opportunity week" in our honor. I reprinted news of the mayor's proclamation in the supplement, and at the same time we received the endorsement of the Small Business Administration (SBA). About the only person who did not get behind us was the president of the United States.

With government backing our credibility was enhanced, and when the supplement broke on the Sunday prior to the expo opening, our telephones came off the wall with response.

THE BEST DAY OF THE WEEK

Ads do better on Sunday than any other day of the week. That is the one day people take time to sit down and read. Sunday papers are, of course, thicker than any other days. The thickness sometimes discourages mail order advertisers. They believe their ads will get lost in the shuffle, and they opt for other less crowded days.

That is a mistake. Sunday cannot be beat for any advertiser and product, whether it is mail order, furniture, or advertisements for motion pictures.

The next morning, the part-time operators I had hired began the busiest five days of their lives. They hardly had time for a cup of coffee—that's how busy the telephones were.

When we opened Friday at noon, chaos reigned. The crowd was so great that my staff could not handle ticket sales. The Convention Center came to the rescue. They brought in ticket sellers and supplied staff for our counters.

The rush continued each day. It was an overwhelming crowd that even astounded the Center's personnel. Our 20-foot aisles were jammed constantly. Seminars were sold out, huge quantities of tapes were sold, we ran out of our business start-up manuals, and the exhibitors were ecstatic with the hordes of prospects.

By closing time on Sunday 38,000 had come through the doors, the largest three-day consumer business show in the Center's history.

The expo had the excitement I look for in business. When a project makes you create, wonder, and then gets your adrenaline working overtime, it cannot be beat. That's the challenge and thrill I have always searched for in business. Fortunately, I found it more than once through mail order.

4

Consumer Needs and Repeat Sales

Promoters and opportunists are two different breeds.

A promoter would have looked on the success of my first business show, immediately booked the Convention Center for the next year, and waited patiently.

An opportunist has little patience. He would not only book the Center for the following year, but would search for other ways to use the same concept and make additional money. That is exactly what I did. Taking moneymaking ideas and running with them was an idea I was used to. I viewed the business expos as an opportunity for expansion. My idea was to stage the show in markets across the country.

Although I had tremendous success in Los Angeles, it was far from an accurate test because of the acceptance that people there give to new ideas. Relying on Los Angeles as a test market has misled many mail order marketers.

Los Angeles is too receptive, a conglomeration of open minds and people who will try anything—once. If it plays in Peoria, it may go well throughout the Midwest, but if it goes well in Los Angeles there is no guarantee it will do well anywhere else. Through the years I have seen numerous mail order entrepreneurs baffled by acceptance in Los Angeles and their inability to sell the same product anywhere else. Even today, I never test a mail order ad in Los Angeles. The results can be too deceiving.

Still, even if other markets had been only half as profitable as Los Angeles, my business opportunity expo was a concept that could easily generate several million dollars a year based on the $500,000 I did in Los Angeles.

Los Angeles was a prototype. From there we went to Chicago, Philadelphia, St. Louis, New York, Miami, Phoenix, Seattle, San Francisco, and even Toronto.

My staff screamed when I laid out the schedule. They said there was no way the show could do one show a month in a major city. I failed to see the problem. It took four months to plan and stage the Los Angeles expo, but I told my staff we could do another city in less than two weeks.

How? By simply duplicating what we did. The supplement was already completed. All we needed were a few name changes. Exhibitors were ecstatic and were ready to go with me to any city at any time. Before we hit each city, I utilized both *Entrepreneur*'s list and other business opportunity lists for a direct-mail campaign.

In each city we established small business foundations through a local university. I donated a library of our manuals—worth thousands of dollars—to the university.

With the donation we generated civic endorsement. Not every mayor backed us, but most did. Before we were through, 17 mayors had given us proclamations.

In every city the campaign and the supplement were virtual duplicates of the Los Angeles expo. I did make some changes. I increased the number of seminars and the amount of booth space our company had for manual sales. I also raised prices.

In our initial Los Angeles expo we sold tapes but none existed. The tapes were recorded during the actual seminar and we fulfilled the orders later. That hurt sales. A customer likes to pick up and feel the goods. If they are not available you diminish returns. That is one of the great obstacles in mail order. The prospect cannot touch the product. All he or she can do is see a picture of it or read a description.

DESCRIPTIVE COPYWRITING

When there is no photograph, it is critical that the mail order marketer describe the product in as much depth as possible. To be effective the description of a product in mail order has to be so vivid that the potential customer can see it without a photograph. The high

mail order revenues the supplement generated enabled me to stage expos in markets where the populations were not big, but people were mail order responsive. For example, we went to Indianapolis, a relatively small market when compared to Chicago, New York, or Dallas, and made money through the mail order revenues we generated from the supplement, although actual attendance was low.

Most promoters rely on profits from admissions and booth sales. By the time we had finished our 10th show, gate receipts did not matter. The key to our expos was the average amount of money an attendee would spend once they got in the door.

It was not unusual to see buyers spend $45 for an all-day seminar ticket, $150 on manuals, and another $60 to $70 on tapes for seminars they did not have time to attend. Attendees were all given copies of the supplement and a catalog to take home.

Immediately inside the door, attendees would run into a seminar booth where they could either make reservations or buy a tape. Inside the exhibit hall I often had up to 15 booths selling our manuals.

I hired professional salespeople in each city to handle the booths. When I found people who were exceptionally good, I would take them with us to other cities, pay their transportation, and offer them a draw against commission. In St. Louis I found a phenomenal salesperson who stayed with us for nearly three years. It was not uncommon for him to generate sales in excess of $10,000 during one show.

With that kind of action inside, I kept the admission price low—$2.95—so as not to discourage anyone from attending.

ADVANTAGE OF LOW "ENTRY" FEE

A low entry fee is an excellent technique to utilize in any business when you have additional products that can be sold to a customer. In mail order there is an offer that gives buyers 1,000 return address stickers for $1. The company does not make money, but they have added a name to a list of someone who has proven to be mail order responsive. In time that name may pay for those stickers 50 times over, through list rental. The company can also sell additional products to the respondent.

Do not confuse a low entry fee with no entry fee. Free entry may cause many prospects to wonder if what you are offering is even worth attending. At times I was tempted to even remove the $2.95, but I knew that an open door might increase attendance, but it could

cut down on worthwhile attendees—that is, those who were serious business opportunity seekers.

I was using a mail order principle with a non-mail order product. All I wanted was to get the prospect in the door. There are consumer (and trade) shows held every day across the country that baffle me with high entry fees.

Why charge someone a high ticket price when you intend to sell them something once they get inside that could be worth 10 or 20 times the value of the admission? Cut the admission, get more people in the door, and increase sales.

Auto and boat shows are guilty of high pricing. The argument is that the buyer will be more qualified. Perhaps, but potential buyers are sophisticated today. They resent being gouged with an entry fee when they know they may spend thousands of dollars inside. Consequently, many stay away.

I also captured names. At each expo we had a drawing barrel and attendees could win anywhere from $500 to $1,000 by filling out a form with their name and address, and dropping it in the barrel. Five hundred (or even one thousand) dollars is a reasonable expenditure when it helps generate anywhere from 15,000 to 35,000 potential buyers, buyers whose names can be used repeatedly.

Seminar attendees were given blue drawing slips to fill out, while show attendees were given white slips. Obviously, someone who spent upward of $15 (a seminar attendee) was a more valuable name than someone who just came in the door ($2.95).

I separated seminar from manual buyers as well. Buyers of our mail order manual, for example, had already shown interest in mail order. Their names would be worth a premium to companies that had mail order-oriented products to market.

Each buyer (seminar, manual, show attendee) had a different value when I later created a list company and rented names.

PROFILING DIFFERENT CONSUMERS

Not every seminar attendee in every city was the same. Nor were the manual buyers or the general admission attendees. Every city has its distinct characteristics. People differ radically from north to south and from east to west. Those differences must be kept in mind when marketing mail order products.

Los Angeles was freewheeling and open. It was (and is) full of people who have proven they are willing to take a chance at any-

thing. It is a market that consists primarily of people who pulled up their roots, left family and friends, and came west to try something new.

Florida, with its immigration from throughout the country, has an openness as well, but not to the extent of California's. There is more youth and vibrancy in the west. There is not a great deal of pessimism in the market. It is a melting pot with residents from every state in the Union. Melting pots are excellent cities in which to market a variety of products. The exchange of cultures makes people more open-minded and receptive to new things.

Los Angeles also has a significant number of immigrants from other countries. Most immigrants have been forced to become entrepreneurs because they cannot get jobs. They too are open-minded. Interestingly, many immigrants are not poor, with the exception perhaps of the boat people. Most have come to this country with money. They have been educated.

For example, Florida has had an enormous influx of Cuban refugees, and nearly all are educated. They escaped Cuba when Castro took power. They have money and connections. That is why they have become a force in Miami.

Many found it difficult to fall into corporate life. There are linguistic and cultural barriers. The only ladder they can climb is their own. They become entrepreneurs and open their own businesses. Toronto, Canada, has this same immigrant profile. It is a phenomenal market for business opportunity ventures. Entrepreneurs abound.

Other markets are more conservative and traditional because they do not have the influx of immigrants from other states or countries. The midwest and northeast fall into this category. (New York City is an exception. It has always been a melting pot and is more open to new ideas and products.)

Chicago is traditional and conservative. There are neighborhoods and sections that have not changed makeup for a half century. Indianapolis, Cleveland, Pittsburgh, and Buffalo are eastern cities that have much in common with Chicago. They have changed little over the years. Workers seldom change jobs or look for new opportunities. Trades and professions are passed on from generation to generation. There are few risk takers.

I needed the risk takers. I found them in Seattle, San Francisco, Dallas, Houston, Miami, and New York. These cities are vibrant and energetic. Their mix of people keeps them moving. We did phenomenal business in these areas, but only average in the staid Midwest, Old South, or Traditional Northeast.

In planning shows I realized the difference in each market, and I changed the seminar makeup to meet the needs of the marketplace. In Buffalo, where few would quit a job and open their own business, I offered a special seminar in "how to start a part-time business."

In economically depressed areas, I created sessions built around businesses that "could be started with low investments."

DATA BASE AND MARKET ANALYSIS

Because a market is traditional or conservative does not mean it will not respond to mail order. On the contrary, many of these markets are excellent mail order venues, but you must have the right product and correct approach.

In today's market there is an entire new industry called data base marketing that has developed. Data base is an attempt to analyze and segment people into groups statistically. Some of these data base companies will tell you that certain zip codes, for instance, will not buy through mail order.

The question, however, is *why*? Why won't they buy? Perhaps they would buy if the right offer came along.

Frankly, I do not put much credence into data base. It is an industry where computer-oriented people are trying to put human nature into a computer. It will never work.

Numerous companies, however, are buying this data. They are using it to move into the mail order market. They can afford to drop several million dollars in a mail order venture by using data base. When it does not work they move onto something else and write the expenditure off to R&D, or something similar.

For the small mail order marketer there is no way to drop a few million dollars on a frivolous offer and hope to stay in business. However, the mail order marketer must be aware of the differences in markets. Once again, even if you have not personally visited and analyzed markets, *Editor & Publisher* can give you a good feel for the market.

Those who use *Editor & Publisher* and analyze tests and markets before they "rollout," can make millions in mail order. (Usually mail order marketers rent a portion of a list, e.g. 5,000 names, for a test. If the test portion of the list produces good results then the marketer may rent the remainder of the list and rollout, that is, mail to the remaining names on the list.)

Competition has grown, but there is more opportunity than ever

because most of those in the field do not analyze needs and the market before spending their money.

MAIL ORDER AND THE ECONOMY

Being aware of the differences in markets played a major role in our success. Economics had an effect on our growth as well. In good times consumers are easy with a buck; they do not mind spending. In bad times they close their pockets, become tightfisted, and save. Whether times were good or bad, I never lost with our shows. A change in the economy only meant a switch in marketing tactics.

In business, surviving recessions is a matter of common sense. I found that out the hard way when my partner and I were riding high with our masonry business in Chicago during the late 1950s.

During recessions our manuals that detailed businesses that required high initial capital to launch, dropped in sales. The low-investment and maintenance type manuals flourished. It made sense. In tough times repair and maintenance businesses do well. People do not buy new copiers, computers, or automobiles. They try to save money by maintaining durable goods instead of replacing them. Trying to market durable goods through the mail during recessions is difficult.

The economy changed drastically between that first Los Angeles expo in 1977 and the last one we held in 1982. In 1977 people were upbeat and anxious to examine opportunities and investments. Five years later we were in the midst of one of the worst recessions in our history. There was double-digit inflation, high unemployment, and consumers could not have been more negative.

Despite the changeover in the economy, our sales did not drop— in fact, we grew 1,500% through two recessions. The only thing that changed was our product mix, and the people involved in business opportunities.

We began to sell to people who had never bought a business opportunity previously. Most were forced into the market. They were executives who began to worry about their positions, or workers who were laid off and unable to find anything else in the marketplace.

During those show years I found the greatest influence on good or bad times was not the economy but the media. The media have the power to push us into a recession or create a boom.

If the media concentrates on reporting poor (or negative) economic news, people begin to believe it and their minds dwell on the neg-

ative aspects of the economy. They stop buying and start hoarding. Sales drop, businesses lay off people, and the cycle grows greater as the media continues to report the dire news.

Media reporting becomes a self-fulfilling prophecy. It not only changes attitudes, but buying habits as well. People go to bed feeling depressed and wake up the same way. The media took a multimillion dollar, multilevel company, Herbalife, and with enough negative publicity it dropped Herbalife's sales force from 150,000 to 30,000.

The media thrives on the negative because that is what audiences like to see and hear. That negative preference has dominated the American consumer for more than three decades. It is an attitude that shows no immediate signs of changing.

It is a paradox. Negative ads are disasters, negative news is a winner. How long would a news program devoted entirely to good news survive?

During the show years my experience with the media was primarily positive. I was interviewed extensively on radio, television, and in print. I was looked on as a guru, someone who could accurately forecast trends and what businesses would be hot in the coming years.

I enjoyed the notoriety and the people I attracted. Athletes and musicians are not the only professionals who draw a crowd. At times, however, I took heat from reporters. In several markets I ran into people who were primarily interested in writing an exposé. They could not believe I would supply valuable business information at a low cost. If it was worthwhile, they reasoned, it had to cost more.

Normally I would agree with that premise. But I made money on the back end, the postpurchase selling of products to customers. I was more than willing to give customers free and low-cost advice if they would buy from me later.

Occasionally, I would find an eager investigative reporter at our entrance the day we opened. They were attracted by the supplement and would question the legitimacy of what we were offering. Were our exhibitors offering truly profitable opportunities? Did our manuals really contain the information needed to start and run a profitable business?

As for exhibitors, my expo department checked them as best they could. Before every show, we sent a list of all exhibitors and potential exhibitors to the attorney general in each state.

If they had any legal charges against them they were barred.

However, sometimes we missed. Staging 11 shows a year meant we had to screen thousands of potential exhibitors. On more than

one occasion I paid for an exhibitor's past transgressions with a page one story in a local newspaper that put down our show and told people to stay away.

Once a reporter questioned me as to what redeeming social value the business shows had, what contribution they made to society. I looked at the candy machine across the room and posed the same question. Then I asked if anyone was campaigning to stop the sales of candy, ice cream, and other products that had little lasting value.

The stories did bother me. I have been painted as a loner and a hard-boiled businessman. I am. But I am also human, and enjoy praise and friendship just as any other person does. I disliked seeing something I built and believed in attacked by people who did not know the entire story.

In business you have to learn to live with criticism. I did and the longer it went on the harder my shell became.

Despite the sporadic run-ins I had with the media, our shows grew and prospered. Unquestionably, the best expos we had were held in melting pot cities during good economic times. They were in Seattle, Los Angeles, Toronto, and New York. If there was any show that came close to equalling that first Los Angeles expo in excitement, it was the second one we held there. As was the case with the first, the second broke tradition.

It was early December, and we had just returned from Indianapolis, a quiet, conservative, laid-back area that was nevertheless profitable. My employees were looking forward to a month without travel, as I had agreed to 11 shows a year, with December off. I skipped December primarily because of the holidays and the lack of time to prepare an expo. With me, business has always been more important than a holiday. My family was scattered; my mother lived in Chicago, my grandmother in Tennessee, and I was usually on the west coast.

I had one of my gut feelings. I could see the potential of another show in Los Angeles, this time in December. It would have to be between Christmas and New Year's.

December is a deceptive period. Shopping and holidays are on everyone's mind, but they are also upbeat and cheerful. They also have free time. All I had to do was find three days—the length of our expos—that did not hit Christmas Eve, Christmas, New Year's Eve, or New Year's Day. Usually our shows opened on Friday afternoon and closed Sunday evening. In December we could stage it in the middle of the week, if that week was between Christmas and New Year's.

I ran into a problem. Every major convention center was booked

during the period with one exception, Long Beach. Long Beach was not centrally located, and I knew it would cost us attendees from the northwest sections of Los Angeles, but I decided to go for it.

It was December 11, and we planned to open on December 27 and close on the 29th. That gave me less than 16 days to sell booths, promote the expo, and line up our seminar speakers and sales force. My employees grumbled but even they rose to the challenge of putting on a show in 16 days.

I signed a contract, we sold nearly 100 booths, put our supplement together, and ran it in the *Los Angeles Times* on Sunday, December 24. We opened on Wednesday.

Nearly 30,000 came through during those 3 days. It was one of the highest grossing expos in our history. It proved to me that the holiday week is an ideal time for shows, retailers, and direct mail.

After Christmas and the first of the year, people make resolutions, they vow they will change their lives during the coming year. Mail order products relating to diet and health do well. The same is true of any offerings that fulfill the need consumers have to start fresh.

With our mammoth promotional efforts in each city we visited, we attracted attention not only from the media but from government officials, as well. Our mailing lists grew by the hundreds of thousands, and our catalog was going to more than five million buyers a year.

MAIL ORDER AND CREDIT CARDS

The notoriety the media gave us reinforced the mailing pieces, and *Entrepreneur* became a familiar word and company to millions of consumers. Still, a company in the direct-mail field is not viewed without suspicion. Credit card companies are wary and concerned that mail order entrepreneurs will "burn" customers. Van Pler & Tissany is an excellent example of the suspicion that exists on the part of credit card companies.

At Van Pler & Tissany our customers can utilize a variety of charge cards, including American Express. After nearly three years of accepting American Express—and generating more than $100,000 a month for the credit card company—we were notified that all our American Express charge slips would have to go to Phoenix where they would be processed. Normally, our American Express cards were processed immediately, and the cash was put in our bank instantaneously. Shipping to Phoenix meant there would be a 30-day

delay (American Express takes time to process the orders, issue a check, and send it to us) before we had our money. Shipping to Phoenix is usually not required of non-mail order firms.

Credit card companies are not the only operations that view mail order with suspicion. For years in the advertising field, most direct-mail agencies were looked down upon by the other agencies.

In recent years, however, the larger agencies have come to understand the economic importance and potential of mail order. Many have even established their own direct-mail departments. Much of this was due to the emergence of mail order credit card inserts and the realization by clients that there was millions of dollars of untapped revenues that could be brought in by using monthly billings as a vehicle for inserts.

Shortly after our first Los Angeles expo, I donated $10,000 to a local university, as well as a library of our manuals. The money was earmarked for the funding of a small business department, which would help entrepreneurs in the area. The funds were allocated by the university to help small businesses in the area with marketing problems.

As a result the mayor's office recognized our efforts and presented us with a proclamation while the university had a photograph taken of me with the school's president as I made the presentation.

MAILING PIECE ENDORSEMENTS

An endorsement in a mailing piece by a well-known and respected figure or institution can mean more than a dozen pages of well-written copy.

Non-mail order businesses often have photographs taken with a university or institution president when they make a donation. They use the photographs for positive publicity. Pick up the local newspaper or the university's magazine, and you will find donations publicized by local corporations. Most corporations do it for the publicity, which will ultimately impact sales.

My reasons were similar. The photograph meant credibility for our catalog. We ran the photo with a caption underneath it, describing our efforts to aid entrepreneurial firms through the grant.

The photograph became the lead picture in a new, one-step catalog I called "The Hottest, Most Profitable Businesses of the Year! 96 Small Businesses Covered." That was my cover copy. I used one of my favorite colors as well—blue—for the cover stock.

I use blue extensively in catalogs. Blue is one of the least offensive colors that consumers can receive in the mail. Occasionally, I use warm tones such as maroons, rust, or other earth tones. Warm colors draw a positive response. They are "friendly" and at home.

Some people use red for the attention it garners. I have always shied away from it because it can turn someone off or make them feel and think negative. The last thing you want is someone to have negative thoughts when they pick up your direct-mail piece.

Negative copy is a disaster as well. That is not a theory, but the actual results of many tests run in the mail order field. Taking the negative approach, that is, putting down someone else's offering in an attempt to make yours look better, always loses.

Being positive was critical to success. By positive I do not mean positive thinking. I am referring to the excitement and credibility you want to build in a mailing piece. When potential buyers pick up a mailing piece for the first time, their excitement level may be low. As they read through it, you want to build their enthusiasm so by the time they reach the end they are ready to order.

Adjectives and exaggerations do not build excitement; facts and information do. By the mid-to-late 1970s, consumers had become enormously sophisticated. Old, careless exaggerations and hyperbole were failing. Facts and figures were important. Slap-on-the-back commercials are still used on television, but they certainly do not work in mail order. I doubt if they work on television, either.

SELLING THROUGH MAIL ORDER

Good mailing pieces sell by building excitement. Excitement is developed through fact, information, and education, not hype or exaggeration.

I sell with fact, information, and education. That was the basis of "96 Hottest." On the back cover was a reprint of the *Los Angeles Times* story that had been written about me.

Inside, aside from the picture of the university professor, the school's president, and myself presenting the check, there were quotes from newspapers, a copy of the Los Angeles proclamation, nine success stories, and a capsule summary of the "96 Hottest Businesses," which was a description of each of the manuals we had in our catalog.

Above each summary was a boldfaced subhead. Most of us are lazy readers and dislike struggling through copy that runs together. Subheads break copy up and help the reader. They reiterate the body

copy and sales points. If a person scans the subheads, they get the message.

The catalog was prepared by the International Entrepreneur's Association, our nonprofit research arm. On the inside back cover was a coupon that enabled someone to join the Association and order the manuals.

I also gave readers numerous options. They could join for one, two, or three years. The longer the membership, the more it cost, but the greater the benefits and bonuses they would receive. The more manuals they purchased, the greater the discount.

THE PERFECT MAILING PIECE

The catalog was filled with offers. A reader could spend up to $750 in the 20-page catalog, and we had a number of buyers who did. The catalog was one of the most successful I ever put together, because it contained all the right elements. It was visual, easy to read, loaded with credibility, and had an offer that people could respond to. There was also a toll-free number for ordering. I accepted credit cards for the first time, as well. It increased response by 10%.

The perfect mailing piece—if there is one—contains a combination of credibility, clear, crisp, succinct copy that is easy to read and understand, is repeated more than once so the message gets across, contains a definite offer (discount, free goods, money back, etc.), and makes it easy for buyers to respond.

I also set ourselves apart from competitors. I never compared our products to anyone's. I found the elements within our products that were outstanding and different from all others, and I stressed those characteristics. Today, *Entrepreneur* has at least 100 competitors and I still do not compare or acknowledge them.

Why should I? Does McDonald's ever compare itself to Burger King? Of course not. If you are number one, never bring up the competition. When you do, all you accomplish is to bring attention to a lesser-known competitor or product. Follow the smart politicians. If they have a comfortable lead, they never refer to their rivals. It is only when they are number two in a race or neck-and-neck that they sling the mud and offer to debate.

With the exception of two pages toward the back of the catalog, I wrote all the copy. Copywriting is not tough. Some people, of course, are more verbal, while others may be math-oriented. The key, of

course, is sensitivity: understanding your potential customers and what their needs are.

A good portion of my verbal skills came from my early years on the farm when I read everything I could get my hands on, and rewrote ads for fun. I was not a born writer; few people are. But I developed the skill through practice and work.

Writing is no different than developing an athletic skill. Most of us have the raw ability, but not everyone will dedicate themselves to it. Those who do become outstanding athletes, just as those writers who work and practice become proficient.

That does not mean everyone can become a Hemingway. On the contrary, there is a world of difference between fiction writing and copywriting, and it is certainly more difficult to become an accomplished novelist than a copywriter. On the other hand, I do not want to belittle mail order copywriters. The good ones are certainly talented, and they have an understanding of human nature equivalent to a Hemingway.

COPYWRITING AND STORYTELLING

Good copywriters do have a great deal in common with novelists. Like novelists, successful copywriters must be storytellers. They must have the ability to speak to one person and tell their story slowly, clearly, and carefully. Much as novelists must weave a fascinating plot, mail order copywriters have to build an interesting story (and case) for their product.

Storytelling is critical. In high school, for example, I played football. I was a halfback and linebacker on the varsity team. Don't let the dual positions throw you. Those were the days before school athletes specialized and most of us played two or three positions, as well as both offense and defense. I also happened to be a third stringer, which gives you some insight into my ability in the sport.

My one fond memory goes back to my junior year and a game we played on another school's field. Our star halfback had inadvertently left his cleats at home, and I was the one person who had the same size shoes. I loaned him my cleats, never expecting to get in the game or need them.

I settled down on the bench, and watched the game progress. By the end of the third quarter, we were six touchdowns ahead. The coach began cleaning the bench, and late in the fourth quarter my number was called. I was so frustrated and anxious to get out on the

field, I did not even get my shoes back. I ran barefoot across the field and immediately took up my position as linebacker.

I was pumped up, the adrenaline was flowing. On the first play the opposing quarterback faded back to pass. I shot through a hole in the line, blocked his attempted pass, and the ball went straight up in the air, and landed in my arms.

Barefoot, I took off for the goal line 80 yards away. By the time I hit the 10-yard line, my pack-a-day cigarette habit had paralyzed my legs. I could hardly breathe, and I felt as if I was moving in slow motion instead of running.

Out of the corner of my eye I could see a tackler from the opposing team desperately racing toward me. He had an angle on me as we approached the goal line. He put his head down as he prepared to make the tackle. I did not have the strength—or the wind—to run through him. I could see my one chance for glory vanishing in a puff of cigarette smoke.

Just as he came in for the kill, I summoned the last of my energy, leaped high in the air, cleared him by a foot as he shot under my flying body, and fell into the end zone for a touchdown.

I laid there for what seemed to be an eternity. In reality it was only a few seconds, but I had to be helped off the field. If the gun had sounded and we had won the game by a point, it would have been a tale I could have told my grandchildren. But we were 40 points ahead, and my touchdown only served to bring comic relief to a game that had gotten out of hand.

My high school tale is an example of storytelling. It has a beginning, middle and end, and is designed to hold a reader's interest.

WRITING FOR THE LOWEST COMMON DENOMINATOR

My football anecdote illustrates another point: always write in conversational tones when putting together mail order pieces. Do not look in the dictionary for four or five syllable words. Remember, you have to write to the lowest common denominator. That is, make sure everyone can understand what you are saying.

You will never insult consumers' intelligence by using a term in a copy that they know. They will never think you are talking down to them. But you will lose customers if you use terms that they fail to understand.

There is a rule I go by that is extremely important. Forget it, and

you will lose your audience: write your copy so that an 8-year-old can read and understand it.

By no means does that denigrate the consumer, nor does it mean that mail order buyers are simpleminded. It is, however, an important guideline and a precaution that all mail order marketers should follow. Keep it simple and your chances of succeeding are much greater.

Think, too, about how the average person is going to respond to a word or term. I try to judge words by the impact they have on a consumer, not necessarily the meaning that the dictionary contains. For example, when I was in high school "hot rod" referred to a souped-up, fast-moving automobile. The two words had nothing to do with the dictionary definition of the two words.

You do not want to use a word that may be commonplace but not understood. Lately, the media have gone overboard with ubiquitous. You see and hear the word everywhere, but how many know that it means existing or being everywhere at the same time? I would guess very few. It is not the kind of term to use in a mail order ad.

I lost interest in sports by the time I graduated high school. I have not been to a game since. I do not enjoy doing the same thing over and over, and athletics make that kind of demand on you. My tolerance and patience wear thin, and I see no point in concentrating on something forever in order to perfect it.

I never work out, either. Unless, of course, you put dancing in the physical category. Four years of push-ups, running laps, and sit-ups in high school were enough. The closest I get to exercise is sitting in a jacuzzi. I have been able to keep my weight within 10 pounds of what it was in high school.

I am fascinated by the physical penchant we have developed in this country. It is all part of the "me" generation; a desire to not only feel good, but look good as well. Thin is in, as is ego.

This is not an attitude fostered and present primarily in young professionals. It goes far beyond that group. It is in the group that is still in college, and those who are just entering high school. It is an attitude that will carry into the twenty-first century.

Consumers are interested in things that are good for themselves, not anyone else. Later, I will discuss attitudes and the importance they have when it comes to marketing through the mail.

I am neither for nor against the fitness craze. I am content to sit in my jacuzzi and watch the joggers and cyclists go by. But I am an opportunist, and I view attitudes strictly for their moneymaking potential. I am not, incidentally, the only marketer who thinks that way.

Take the obvious, personalized license plates, which tell everyone "who I am." *Sharper Image* catalogs sell a variety of ego ingratiating items, ranging from electronic talking scales to 14-carat gold nameplates for your desk.

In the nonbusiness area there is everything from Jordache to Puma. Commercials for both products do not just sell the quality of the item. They sell status and ego as well. Americans are into themselves and anything that will enhance their image is saleable.

Some businesspeople use exercise as a relaxation, a technique for getting rid of tension and getting the creative juices refreshed and flowing again. I take vacations. Any businesspeople who think they can continue to be effective managers without one are kidding themselves.

I usually pick an isolated spot—Mexico, the Caribbean, a cruise ship—and prefer to go alone. If I meet someone, fine. If not, that is alright, too. Emotionally, I have always been cool, detached. That does not mean I lack feelings, but that I can control them.

I have never had a need to be surrounded by people. I am content to read and think alone. I prefer the companionship of one or two people to a group. That is why I am thought of as a loner. Most successful businesspeople are loners. They may be surrounded by people but, ultimately, final decisions belong to the owner or chief executive. They have the responsibility; it is never a group or committee. If business dips, the shareholders always point the finger at the executive in charge.

When I needed a new idea, a fresh ad or approach, I usually went on vacation. We were in the midst of monthly shows, but there was no need for me to oversee each one because I had a complete expo organization in place.

I hired an exposition manager who sold booths and was responsible for booking convention centers in major cities. I had a publicity person who was responsible for promoting our company as well as the expos. The supplement drew in thousands, but publicity swelled our attendance and was critical, especially when it came to television coverage. We needed it opening day to ensure traffic for the weekend.

I usually had some gimmick that would attract television cameras. Television crews do not just come to speak to an entrepreneur, businessperson, or personality—unless they happen to be the President. They want something that is visual and will interest viewers at home. So I gave it to them.

At the first show we had an indoor skateboard park built, with

continuous demonstrations. I also had a vendor with a voice stress analyzer, a vocal "lie detector," that could tell when someone was under a great deal of stress and was probably lying. A number of television field reporters and anchorpeople took the test and had fun with it.

In Chicago we had our best gimmick. It was a live chicken that played tic-tac-toe. The chicken was an enormous hit, and we carried him for nearly a year before the appeal diminished. He was in a cage that was mounted on a four-foot high box that was actually a computer. On the box was an illuminated tic-tac-toe board that lit up when you punched an "X" or "O."

As soon as you made your choice, a computer inside the box would read it and light up the proper box for the chicken to hit. With the computer, the chicken could never lose.

The chicken was a challenge for every television reporter. They would drop a quarter in the machine, mark an "X" or "O" and wait for the bird to make his move. Without fail, the chicken hit the right "X" or "O" and never lost. That is because it was not the chicken that played the game.

The chicken learned that when he hit the right box (the one the computer had lit) he would be rewarded with a kernel of corn.

To ensure the bird's appropriate response, the owner always kept him hungry, at least when we did shows. It was perfect until we hit a city with a softhearted janitor.

It was the night before we opened, and the chicken was perched inside the cage, waiting for the red light to go on so he could punch the button and get his reward. The janitor took pity on the poor bird and fed him corn until he nearly burst. The next day when the cameras showed up the bird refused to play. He was, of course, too full.

Television stations loved the bird. When they arrived the camera crews would go up and down the aisles, shoot footage of some of the more interesting exhibits, and at the last minute the reporter would arrive. He or she would play the game with the chicken, spend a few minutes talking to me about hot new businesses, and leave.

Television covers most events in the same way. They move through rapidly and run to the next news story. It is not an in-depth medium (with the exception of the television news shows such as "60 Minutes"), but it has incredible impact. A one- or two-minute shot on the nightly news would bring in thousands of additional patrons the next day. For attracting people to an impulse event, television cannot be beat.

Not all our publicity was staged. I found the media were fascinated with my ability to forecast trends and hot new businesses.

I discovered that radio had the same immediacy as television when it came to impact from positive publicity, except that the numbers were not as great. Print, of course, was not immediate but could influence buyers through reprints long after the television and radio shows had aired.

I was soon to find out firsthand that the media had even greater impact when it came to reporting negative news.

5

Catalogs and Selling Products

I penned my first "autobiography" nearly a decade ago. It never ended up on the bestseller lists, but it turned out to be one of the strongest direct-mail pieces I have ever written.

It was my J.C. Revel letter, the follow-up piece I sent to those who answered my "How much money does Joe's business make?" inquiry ad.

A few years later, I followed with another "autobiography," only this one ran six pages and was part of "Confessions of a Hard-Nosed Millionaire," a one-step direct-mail piece that turned out to be one of the most successful I ever produced.

To this day, "Confessions" remains embedded in my mind, and for good reason. It was the first successful *subscription* mail order piece I had put together. My catalogs—"64 Hottest New Businesses of the Year" and "96 Hottest Businesses"—were designed to sell manuals, and they did.

However, once someone bought a manual (or manuals), he or she often felt that there was no longer a need for more business information. Hence the buyer would not subscribe to the magazine. Ideally, the way for us to go was to initially get consumers to buy the magazine, and then sell them manuals.

"Confessions" was designed to do exactly that. It was a straight subscription piece. Aside from talking and writing about myself, it was a piece in which I put my storytelling ideas to the ultimate test.

I was hopeful that "Confessions" would reach as wide a business opportunity universe as possible. I used our own list and rented

others. Any list I rented I tested. Few things can be more disastrous in mail order than purchasing 50,000 names and rolling out with a mailing piece that dies.

TEST BEFORE "ROLLING OUT"

As basic as it may sound, renting the right list is not the easiest thing to do. There are two ways to find a list. Either use a broker to help you find and screen lists, or go through Standard Rate & Data Service's (SRDS) book on direct-mail lists. By utilizing SRDS you can bypass a broker (if you choose) and rent directly. There are disadvantages, however, in not having a broker.

It is a must to consult SRDS before renting a list. It contains the names of almost every company that offers a mailing list. The lists are broken into categories. There are women's (i.e., lists of women who buy through the mail), general merchandise buyer lists, men's lists, business to business, and dozens of other categories.

If, for instance, you are marketing a product for business and you need business lists, by consulting SRDS you can find all the business lists available and the companies that are willing to supply them. For example, if you were trying to reach businesspeople who had purchased personal computers because you had an accessory you wanted to market through the mail, you could find the names of numerous computer companies that were willing to rent PC buyer names.

SRDS provides the mail order marketer with information on the type of list, number of names on it, price per thousand, and so on. It also shows the list source, which is often overlooked but which is critical to success. List source simply explains where the company renting the list obtained the names.

MAIL ORDER RESPONSIVENESS—WHAT IS IT?

At *Entrepreneur*, for example, we had lists of seminar attendees, manual buyers, cassette buyers, people who bought products from us through space ads, and people who bought products through the mail. If you were a mail order marketer interested in selling something to business opportunity seekers, you might rent *Entrepreneur*'s list. It would be important to determine which of the *Entrepreneur* buyers bought through space ads and which utilized the mail. Remember, the person who has already purchased one item through

the mail has proven he or she is mail order responsive. A space buyer has not, as yet, proven whether he or she will buy through the mail. A list made up of buyers who purchased through space ads is not nearly as good as a list of buyers who purchased through the mail.

Space and mail order buyers are two different breeds. Mail order buyers have proven their responsiveness to mail order, whereas you do not know if space buyers will purchase through the mail.

Some companies play games and merge space buyers with direct-mail purchasers. If they do so, the SRDS listing should break out the percentage of buyers on the list who bought through the mail and the percentage who purchased through space. For example, you might find a list source that says 90% space, 10% direct mail. It is, of course, possible that the list may be good for mail order; however, only 10% of the names on it have purchased through the mail. That is a factor that should be considered before renting the list.

Another important consideration is to determine how much the average buyer paid for the product(s) he or she purchased through the mail. If you are marketing a $90 direct-mail item, and those on the list average $14 a sale, you may be renting the wrong list. The buyer may not be in your league.

Try to get a copy of the last mailing piece that was sent to those on the list. It will give you an idea of the type of offer that has been made to them.

By examining the last mailing piece you will get a feel for the type of market that is buying the product. Are they buying high-end products? Low end? Paper or merchandise?

Another consideration is when the buyers on the list last made a purchase through the mail. As a general rule, the more recent the purchase, the better the prospect. The older the buyer, that is, the longer the time span that has passed since the last purchase, the less likely the prospects are to buy.

THREE THINGS THAT LISTS SHOULD HAVE

I look for three things when renting: recency, frequency, and price (RFP). How long has it been since the list was used and the buyers purchased an item? How often do the buyers buy? What amount of money do they spend (on the average) when making a purchase?

I buy 5,000 names and "walk" through the list. That is, I mail the first 5,000 and wait. If the response is good, I take another 5,000,

mail, and wait. I never rush. I make it a practice to walk through every list.

Mail order is tough to begin with, and I never piled the odds higher by buying lists and mailing without testing. You have to be a copywriter, storyteller, businessperson, and marketing person all rolled into one, and it never made sense to put more risk into the business than necessary by treating lists and names in a cavalier manner.

Many mail order entrepreneurs have obtained exceptional results on their initial 5,000 mailings, rolled out without walking through the remainder of the list, and suddenly found themselves on the losing end.

Unfortunately, as well as the direct-mail business is policed, there are still some companies and brokers who will load the first 5,000 names with great respondents, and have no qualms about sticking the list renter with 95,000 poor respondents once the test is over. The business has become more sophisticated, but the fast-buck artists remain.

One way to ensure quality with a list is to ask for "nth" name selection, which requires the broker or company renting the list to provide the renter with a wider selection of names. For example, if a list is 200,000 and you order 5,000, then instead of getting the first 5,000, you get every 40th name. If a list is 100,000 and you order 5,000, you get every 20th name.

The total number of names ordered is divided into the total number of names on the list. If, for example, you order 10 names from a list of 100, your "nth" name selection will be every 10th name because 10 goes into 100 ten times. Without any additional effort the mail order marketer can sample an entire list with his or her first test.

Nth name selection can be utilized on any size list. If the list is national, nth name selection will provide a profile of the entire country.

With computers, selection from mailing lists has become more scientific. If you know your product works better in certain sections or states, you can pick nth name selection according to geographic area or state.

Regardless of the list or offer, there are things that have not changed in the business since it began. Compiled lists are not, in most cases, good for direct mail. A compiled list is simply a listing of all the dentists (if you rented a list of dentists), doctors, nurses, drivers, and so on. It does not mean the names on the list are mail order responsive.

COMPILED VERSUS SUBSCRIBER LISTS

Compiled lists are usually good for business-to-business offers. That is, if you are selling a business product to businesspeople, a list containing names of all the people in a particular city who are in business would be a compiled list. The trick, however, is to get your envelope through the secretary who sorts the executive's mail. In Chapter 8 we will discuss envelopes and how to get them by secretaries.

A subscriber list is definitely better than a compiled list. A list containing all the subscribers to *Time*, for instance, proves one thing—they all sent for something in the mail. That is a plus.

With all the variables in list rentals, it is safer and more economical to get a broker when you are looking for lists.

Brokers have knowledge of everyone's experience. They know which lists have pulled well, which have not. Brokers are not anxious to simply sell you a list, either. They want to find you a good list so you will become a repeat customer. That is the only way they can make money. There is little profit in renting a list of 5,000 names. Brokers want to rent you hundreds of thousands.

Incidentally, brokers are not paid by the list rentor. They are compensated by the list company, which gives them a commission for the rental.

HOW TO FIND A LIST BROKER

To find a list broker, open SRDS, turn to the general merchandise section, and see who manages what kind of lists. The brokers' names will be listed. You can examine every category, see who manages the most lists, and use that as a guide. If a broker handles a number of different lists, that is evidence that he or she is doing a good job. Brokers would not be successful at renting unless they steered mail order marketers down the right path. And they would not be handling many lists if they did not generate sufficient rental monies for their clients.

SRDS runs about $150 a year, or it can be found at most major libraries. The only problem with many library copies is they may not be updated due to a library's limited budget.

With SRDS you will find publications and lists you have never heard of. If you are trying to market to a specialized audience, you may find dozens of publications that go directly to your market that

you never see on newsstands. SRDS is a tremendous guide in that area.

Even with a good broker you will find that only one out of four or five lists will be profitable for your offer. That is, incidentally, an excellent percentage. Do not expect every list to be a winner.

WHAT PERCENTAGE OF RETURN IS NEEDED?

As for the percentage of return that is needed for a list to go beyond the test stage, much depends on the cost of your goods and your package. At *Entrepreneur* I always looked for a minimum return of 200% on investment. In other words, if I invested $3,000 in a mailing, I looked for $6,000 in orders. If I just wanted to acquire a name, I could go lower. Often, if you just want names, a sweepstakes or contest will suffice.

Renting the list is only the first step. Next comes the direct-mail piece, which may run $250 or more per thousand, by the time you finish printing literature, renting the list, and mailing. Rather than list rental a more economical way of marketing is package inserts. A package insert, in which your mail order piece is one among many that is being mailed, may run $50 a thousand.

The effectiveness of a package insert depends entirely on the interest the reader has—will he or she read the inserts or not? That is unpredictable. Do not, incidentally, confuse package inserts with the 3 × 5 or 4 × 5 card decks that are mailed. They are usually only good for name generation, and seldom return orders.

Regardless of what list I bought, the pull of "96 Hottest" and "10 Hottest" was extraordinary. Despite the returns, I thought constantly about our need for a subscription piece. In mail order never rest on your laurels. A piece can die quickly, and if your business is to continue, a follow-up should always be in the wings.

The approach for my subscription and follow-up piece came to me one day while I was sitting on the penthouse balcony of a beachfront hotel in Hawaii. I was staring at the crystal blue, clear water and cloudless sky. It was idylic; a setting that only a millionaire could afford.

A millionaire—that was it! A millionaire's secrets to success. Without even knowing what I was going to put inside the brochure, I picked the title: "Confessions of a Hard-Nosed Millionaire."

Creating a mail order piece is not like writing an article or putting

together a report. I have never been able to force it. I relax, and let my mind wander. That is usually how I develop the approach.

The best thing about the title was its curiosity factor. It would be hard for most people to ignore a title with such a revealing promise. There was another aspect to it. Most people, especially those who respond to business opportunity offerings and dream about their own business, want money. They would love to be a millionaire, especially if it could happen overnight. Look at the lotteries that are held throughout the country. People play to win $1 million, not $5 or $10.

WORDS THAT NEVER LOSE APPEAL

Certain words are buzzwords and never seem to lose their appeal when it comes to mail order, generating interest and curiosity. Buzzwords are evident is successful mail order ads; that is, ads that are constantly repeated in magazines and other publications.

In this business, if you coin a word and it is successful, you can expect to be copied. I coined the term "hottest." Today, it is commonplace because it still sparks curiosity and intrigues the buyer.

"Secrets" is another one of those words. It is a term that has been overused and abused—but it works. There are other equally positive words that generate interest on the part of the buyer. There are few words, however, that can compare to secrets. You can hardly pass a newsstand without seeing it on the cover of the *National Enquirer* or *People*.

I make it a practice to study successful mail order headlines. Obviously, the successful ones are those that are repeated. After examining a dozen or so you begin to see a pattern in the headlines and a tendency to use certain terms. Those terms may vary from product to product.

"Confessions" had another intriguing term in the title—"Hard-Nosed." Millionaires are tough-minded and have to make difficult decisions. They do not always make friends while making money. They *are* hard-nosed and a brochure with that term in title fits the perception the typical buyer has of the millionaire.

KEY ELEMENT OF THE BROCHURE

The headline or cover copy can be 70% of a brochure's appeal. I usually spend more time creating a title than the body copy. Create

the head, and the remainder of the ad should flow. That's what happened with "Confessions." The title was the key. All I had to do was write the copy, decide on the offer and, of course, describe the secrets.

The head may be the toughest part of the brochure or ad to write, but that does not mean the remaining copy is unimportant. On the contrary, heads are teasers but they should never be misleaders. I have seen many brochures that made promises and failed to deliver. If the mailing piece (or catalog) does not give the reader what is promised on the cover, the recipient will quickly put the piece aside and not buy. If the consumer detects deception, money will never be put in an envelope.

"Confessions" ignored our manuals. The plan was to generate subscribers, and then (hopefully) turn them into a manual buyer. I had confidence in *Entrepreneur* and its inherent quality. Seldom had I ever seen anyone pick up the magazine and put it down without praising its editorial style and the information that was packed into it. With that kind of introduction, I felt sure we could sell manuals.

This is a marketing technique that is utilized all the time. Sell something to buyers that meets their general, overall needs, then come back and market something to them that meets their specific needs.

Later, I used the same technique when I created my simulated jewelry company, Van Pler & Tissany. I did not try to sell rings and pendants. Initially, I only tried to get mail order buyers to purchase a simulated diamond through the mail. Once they obtained the stone, it was evidence of the quality of the product as well as our rapid fulfillment time. Along with the gem came a catalog showing the many settings and other items that could be purchased.

The quality appearance of the stones and the rapid service usually resulted in 80% of the gem buyers returning the stone for a ring, pendant, earring, or other piece of jewelry. Typically, we might sell somewhere between $25 and $100 worth of stones to a buyer. He or she would follow with an additional purchase (of jewelry) worth anywhere from $100 to more than $1,000.

The investment for *Entrepreneur* was low (as little as $18) as was the initial price a consumer paid for my simulated diamonds (as little as $15). But the quality of both products led to those same buyers coming back and spending 10 to 20 times more.

Mail order marketers are not the only businesspeople who practice this art. Automobile dealers are superior in this tactic. They interest the prospect in the car, determine the exact model, then begin to add

in the specifics—radio, air conditioner, electronic locks, and a hundred other extras that generate additional revenue.

I credit the success of "Confessions" to the story it told. Centuries ago, history was passed down to succeeding generations through stories. The indians were master storytellers, and the best mail order marketers have mastered the art as well. My story was simple, easy to believe. It was the tale of a self-made millionaire, and the secrets he learned.

The cover was a departure as well. Instead of the usual copy, (e.g., "96 Hottest" or "64 Hottest") there was a photograph of me in my office. I was leaning against a credenza, wearing a rumpled suit. I looked worn out.

It was the most serious picture I had ever taken. I could not have looked meaner, and the photograph was intended to portray me in that manner—and for good reason. People believe millionaires are mean. How else could they have earned their money? So I gave the consumer a portrait that was believable.

That, however, was not the first cover for the piece. Originally, the photograph was of me leaning up against my customized Cadillac Seville Opera Coupe. In the background was a Lear Jet. The photograph depicted all the trappings of a millionaire, and the copy reinforced it.

The rumpled suit cover outpulled the Lear Jet by 30%. Why? The first appeared too slick and staged.

Inside was the usual testimonials, including two dozen success stories, proclamations, a certificate from the White House Conference on Small Business, plus a photograph of Boston's mayor presenting me with a proclamation.

To everyone who became a subscriber, I promised a copy of my 14-point formula for success. The piece did not miss. It appealed to Mr. and Ms. Average and their basic desire to make money.

I understood that appeal well. As I have often said, relating to the masses is critical in mail order. Although I have made a great deal of money, I never had a desire to live in a mansion in Beverly Hills. Most of the time I rented.

I finally bought a rundown house on an acre of valuable land in Pacific Palisades, California. It was not the first home I have every owned, but I put more work and effort into it than any of the others.

I gutted the house, and completely redesigned it. It gave me a chance to use my architectural creativity. I spent more than a year rebuilding it, and used tons of redwood both inside and outside. I worked on the house every afternoon and weekend. Some days I

would spend an entire day supervising the hired crew. I did most of the planting and landscaping myself.

When you use your mind to create, manual labor is a relaxing diversion. My efforts resulted in a piece of property that has gone from $300,000 to $1.5 million in less than two years.

There is a sloping backyard that builds into a 50-foot hill behind the house. Between the rear of the house and the hill is a swimming pool, waterfall, jacuzzi, and Japanese garden. From the back door I can look beyond the yard and pool to the sloping hill. At the top of the hill is a 1,000-square-foot teahouse and office I built.

Oriental architecture is peaceful and relaxing. There is no better atmosphere for creating ads or sculpting or painting. I can sit in the backyard for days on end without ever having to leave the house.

From 1977 to 1982, everything I did worked. It was not only the catalogs, but the venues I picked for the expos and the forecasts I made. I nearly always followed business rules and principles, which is one of the reasons I did so well during that period.

I have always believed that anyone with reasonable intelligence can be a success in business.

11 RULES FOR SUCCESS

I put together 11 rules that would guarantee success if followed. They apply to mail order as well as business, although mail order is the one business in which no one can guarantee success. The 11 rules are:

1. *Know the basics of accounting.* You do not have to be a CPA, but you should be able to read a profit and loss statement and determine whether or not you are making money.

2. *Know the basics of law in relationship to business.* You do not have to be a licensed attorney, but you should be capable of reading an agreement and understanding it. If it appears to be complex, take it to an attorney.

3. *Know how to get money to operate your business.* Know how to finance customers who buy your products—if you have to. Sooner or later, every businessperson needs money.

4. *Know how to promote and advertise your products and services.* You must be able to draw people in the door or get them to respond to

your advertisements. If you are unable to promote or advertise, get a professional to give you a hand.

5. *Understand the basics of selling.* Be sensitive to people and their needs.

6. *Understand distribution in your business and industry.* If you are a retailer, distribution is not a problem; you get products from a wholesaler and sell them to consumers. But if you are a manufacturer who deals locally or nationally, it can be a problem. Know how it works.

7. *Know how to hire the right people, and how to fire, if you must.* I am good at the latter, but not too hot at the former.

8. *Know the tricks of handling money.* Do not just put cash in a checking account and leave it. Understand the advantages and disadvantages of certificates of deposits, special accounts, and so on.

9. *Know how to motivate people, to get them to believe in what they are doing for the firm—and you.*

10. *Understand government regulation and how it may affect your business.* In mail order, fulfillment is critical, and you can run afoul of the post office as well as the Federal Trade Commission.

11. *Most important, be sensitive to the public and their needs.*

I was confident that anyone who followed these 11 rules would be a success. At one point, we took our business expo to Atlanta, and while I was being interviewed on a local radio station I impulsively made that comment. I said I could guarantee anyone success in business if they followed my rules.

The challenge had been issued and it was one the station could not ignore. The next day we met with the station's management and worked out a "guaranteed success contest." I put up a $10,000 bond as a guarantee that I would make someone successful in business, and the station created and ran a contest to find a candidate.

Out of 8,000 entries, Dean McDonald, a young man who had never been in business won. Dean had worked as an auto body man for repair shops since he was a teenager. He did not have a college degree or any business background. Then, neither did I.

I liked Dean. He was a country boy with a lot of common sense. He was not a mathematical genius, but he understood profit and loss, just as I did. He was also a hard worker and had plans. He not only wanted one auto body shop, but he had dreams of opening a second within a year. Dean knew the one thing that would make his

business stand apart from all others; a concept that everyone in business preaches, but few practice—service.

With my guidance Dean succeeded. He not only opened one auto paint and body shop, but within a few years he had his second. I spent four days counseling him and the next year I consulted with him via telephone. I also assigned several staff members to check on his progress.

Dean had a remarkable understanding of accounting. He knew if he manufactured a product for $1 and sold it for $2, he did not always make money. There are the hidden costs that sink so many businesses—postage, insurance, taxes, and so on. That $1 item may eventually run $2.50.

Mail order has an equal number of accounting problems. Suppose you are selling a paper product. It may cost under $1 to produce, but before it is sold there are significant advertising costs. For example, a $40 inquiry ad may generate 100 responses. Those 100 people have to be sold. The follow-up mailing piece that is designed to sell the inquiries may cost 56 cents in postage. It could also contain sales literature worth another 40 cents.

Amortize the cost of the ad ($40) among the 100 responses and that adds up to another 40 cents per package. Before you know it, there is a $1.36 investment in each of those inquiries.

If 20%, or twenty order, and an average order is $10, gross income is $200. With a 20% cost your gross profit is $160. The cost of the mailing ($136) has to be subtracted. Now the net is $24. Hardly worth the effort unless you deal in volume or have a solid back-end program.

The most common mistake is to view the $200 as gross profit, and $40 as the cost of product for an adjusted gross of $160. Many novices, in their excitement to do well, forget to figure in all the costs. In mail order you can go broke with that slip.

Nearly everyone in the industry is enthused about selling paper. It can be copied or duplicated cheaply, and stored without fear of spoilage. Those are nice thoughts, but there is an interesting paradox. Paper may be the least expensive product, but it is also the toughest to market. Paper products have the lowest perceived value on the part of the consumer or buyer.

A buyer can see a bicycle, pair of shoes, watch, piece of gold, necklace, or exercise machine. These items can be depicted graphically in a mailing piece and may appear as if they are a bargain at twice the price.

Paper, however, is paper. Books are books. They may be easier to

store and cheaper to produce, but customers must be convinced of the value of the information before they buy. The appearance of the paper does not have the impact of a catalog that features a fur coat, expensive perfume, model car, or executive toy.

I marketed tons of paper through *Entrepreneur*, and later tried more tangible items. I was surprised at the amount of credibility a tangible item has as compared to one that rolls off the presses. A nonpaper mail order product can be marketed for less than half the marketing costs of a paper item.

At *Entrepreneur* we upgraded our manuals from a package that sold for $3.50 to one that eventually generated 10 times that amount, and I needed every bit of the increased revenue to make a profit. By the time we had raised prices to $35, a manual was costing $7 to produce, and that did not include the marketing expenditure (i.e., ads, direct-mail pieces, etc.).

Aside from catalogs, we took space ads in almost every publication imaginable. Weekly newsmagazines were educational. Despite large circulations and the huge numbers of business-oriented readers, they were poor vehicles when it came to consumer-oriented mail order products. They often, however, are good for business-to-business sales (i.e., IBM selling computers to business readers) or generating prospect names.

At the same time, there are some weeklies that are phenomenal for consumer mail order products, such as *Parade* and *Family Weekly*.

WEEKLIES VERSUS NEWSWEEKLIES

There is one important difference when looking at the newsweeklies (i.e., *Time* and *Newsweek*) and weeklies, (e.g., *Parade*). *Time* means work. That is, it is work to read the publication. *Parade*, on the other hand, is fun; it is entertainment. People enjoy reading it.

Time subscribers receive the magazines but do not necessarily read them. The magazine may sit on someone's desk for a week. Eventually, the subscriber might glance at it. Suddenly the next issue arrives and there are two magazines on the desk. The former copy is discarded and the process begins again.

The summer is especially poor for newsmagazines. When the weather turns warm, people go outside and read less. That phenomenon hurts almost all phases of mail order.

A magazine that sells more copies on the newsstand than it delivers at home is a better buy for the mail order entrepreneur. When

someone goes out and makes an effort to buy the magazine from the newsstand that implies a greater interest on his or her part than someone who receives it as a subscriber. The newsstand buyer is after something specific in that issue. They will read it. That means they may also see your ad.

Magazines that have a high newsstand circulation have a high turnover of readers. There is a difference between a magazine that has one million subscribers and one that has 100,000 subscribers and a newsstand circulation of 900,000.

On the surface both reach the same number of people, but the readership differs. In the case of the publication with the heavy subscription base, it is the same million who see it each month. The magazine is delivered automatically to their home or office. Also, there is no guarantee that subscribers will read it. They have not made a conscious effort to go out and buy it.

Take the publication with 900,000 newsstand sales and 100,000 subscribers. The 100,000 are the same each month, and once again, there is no guarantee they will read it. But the 900,000 newsstand buyers are usually a different 900,000 each month. They make an effort to buy, therefore they have a reason, they want to read, and they may see your ad.

With a heavily subscribed magazine, you may only have to run a mail order offer once or twice a year to reach the entire audience because the same readership is there every month. With one that is big on the newsstands you may be able to advertise monthly (or weekly) and find new prospects each time.

Of course, the turnover in readership means little if the audience is not responsive. But what if you find a magazine that does have a responsive audience with a high turnover? It can be a bonanza in mail order.

Mail order marketers should also be aware of "controlled circulation publications." These publications usually go to a specialized audience free of charge. The reader does not have to pay, but receives it because he or she is in a certain field, occupation, political persuasion, or the like. But being free of charge means the person may have no interest in the publication, or may not even open it. There are numerous controlled circulation books; some are good for mail order, and some are bad.

WHERE INQUIRY ADS GO WELL

I have always found it safer to use inquiry ads in controlled circulation publications, rather than large space ads. The inquiry ad enables

you to test the readership response to mail order and your offer, and to conduct the test at a low cost.

Consumers who subscribe to daily newspapers do not always read them, either. They pay for the paper by the month (or every three months), and get it whether they have time to read or not.

Once again, when someone consciously spends money at a newsstand and purchases a publication, they intend to read it—that day. That is what I like about *USA Today*. Nearly all of its circulation is through newsstand, not subscriptions. When people buy it they want to read it. That means they are going to see the ads. It is an excellent vehicle for the right mail order product. (Remember: *USA Today* readers are primarily businesspeople.)

For one-step mail order ads, there are few publications that can match or beat the daily newspaper, especially the large metropolitan publications such as the *Los Angeles Times*, *The New York Times*, and others of similar size. This is especially true of Sundays, when almost everything is put aside (yard work, paperwork, etc.) in favor of reading the newspaper.

I tried other business-oriented publications aside from the *Wall Street Journal*, such as *Barron's*, *BusinessWeek*, *Forbes*, and *Fortune*. Sales from the business magazines did not even come close to what I generated from the *Wall Street Journal*. The reason: the others are in the news weekly category.

When an ad did not work, the publication's sales representatives were always around to explain why it failed—and why the ad should be placed again.

RESPONSE TIME

I never went for the sales representatives alibis. In mail order, response does not improve with time. If a space ad fails the first time out, forget it. Each ad should stand on its own, pay for itself, and show an adequate return. That is one of the things I like about mail order; the responsibility and measurement you can assign to each ad.

In television and radio, repetition sells. The first time a person sees or hears a spot, a slight impression is made. No one spot counts more than another. The impression increases the more the spot is heard, but few mail order advertisers can afford the exhorbitant cost of these media.

Television takes three consecutive weeks of at least two spots per

day to have an impact. It is fast, and people cannot turn it back to see the 800 number or the address where they should respond. By the third time they see the spot, it has made an impression on their thought patterns. By the fourth time they may get a pencil out and write down a telephone number or address.

Television may be an excellent vehicle for retail products, but it is not for every type of mail order product. Merchandise sells well, but paper products or information (reports, newsletters, manuals, etc.) do not.

Television was demonstrated as a direct-response media long before the "home shopper's network" made its debut. Remember the famed Ginsu knife in the 1950s and 1960s? At the time, sponsors were able to air a two-minute spot in excellent time periods, and in two minutes you can do a lot of selling, enough so that the viewer would pick up a telephone and order.

The television announcers who sold Ginsu knives and similar products were performers. They were entertaining and could talk as fast as the knife would drop.

Trying to prompt that buying decision in 30 seconds is impossible, however. Anything less than 60 seconds with a mail order product is difficult to sell. Mail order advertisers have found they cannot get spots of more than 60 second duration in highly desirable time periods, such as prime time or adjacencies to prime time (7 PM to 10 PM). Mail order ads have always been restricted to late night or afternoon because of their length.

HOW TELEVISION AUDIENCES DIFFER

Late night audiences consist of people who are single, live alone, or are young. They are the people who watch television after 11 PM. Early afternoon and mornings belong to older people and retirees, while the afternoons belong to women.

The most effective mail order television spot is going to be 120 seconds. It will outpull a 90-second spot by a considerable margin and a 60-second by almost 5 to 1, instead of 2 to 1. The "120" is akin to a full-page ad in a newspaper. And full stories can be told (and sold) with that kind of space.

In order to get your "120" played you have to settle for time periods that may not be the best for your product. Usually, you are restricted to late night, with the exception of cable. Mail order ad-

vertisers will pay less at night but the question is, is that audience the buyers you want?

In mail order you cannot always choose the program you want because you are buying time at the lowest rate. Marketers must carefully analyze what they are buying and who is watching. There are numerous variables when it comes to television that go far beyond the type of product you are selling.

For example, the after 2 AM television viewer is not a great user of credit cards. Yet, most direct response ads require credit cards (or C.O.D.) Therefore, most direct response advertisers use 2 AM (or later) time periods for per inquiry (PI). The spot is designed to generate an inquiry (PI), not a sale.

Credit cards enhance mail order sales. Without them there is pressure on the viewer to copy the address, put it away, hold onto it until they have cash or can send a check. A lack of credit cards indicates a lower economic bracket as well. Afternoon viewers differ. They have credit cards and use them.

Another problem in selling mail order items via television is the differences in the impact of a spot on male and females. Women buy more than 50% of the products offered via direct response on television, and they are motivated by different buying patterns and desires than men.

Women respond to emotional spots. Men require a spot that is crammed full of logical reasons and facts. It has nothing to do with intelligence; rather, it is because men are more cynical.

My first space ad for Van Pler & Tissany is evidence of that. It is crammed full of logical reasons to buy a simulated diamond. As a result, more than 55% of our respondents were men. This is in contrast to most merchandise ads, which definitely have a majority of women as respondents.

My first Van Pler & Tissany space ad (see Chapter 10) pulled strongly for more than three years before it ran out. I followed it with another, entirely different one-step space ad that sold the same product but was highly emotional. The headline read "What are Nancy, Liz, Jackie and Joan Wearing? And Prince Phillip, too??"

It was an emotional, highly charged appeal that was designed to increase Van Pler & Tissany's female customer base. That's not the way to sell men, but it works with women.

Aside from the direction of the message (i.e., romantic for women and factual for men), television's effectiveness varies with the time of year. Spots for mail order products during the summer are a waste. People are outdoors and their television viewing is cut. Networks

know this, and that is why they place reruns in the summer months. Once snow falls and the consumer is indoors, daytime spots come back to life.

PI AND PO TIME—CAN THEY BE OBTAINED

Television spot buying did not intrigue me but I did contemplate a PI (Per Inquiry) or PO (Per Order) arrangement. PIs and POs are spots aired without cost. A commercial is put together by the sponsor and the station airs it without any fee. For every inquiry, in the case of PIs, and every order, in the case of POs, the sponsor pays a fee to the station.

K-Tel, the record marketing company, nearly ruined PO time for mail order companies. They made deals giving stations up to 50% of the retail price. K-Tel set the precedent and every mail order company that came along afterward ran into those demands. Later, K-Tel bought time and found they could purchase it for 10% to 15% of the price of the product instead of the 50%.

There are independent stations that will go for the PO or PI arrangement. The real opportunity is in the cable market. Cable is hungry for revenue, and open to deals. Cable, however, is fragmented, and the number of claimed viewers is open to suspicion.

The production cost for a commercial can be reasonable if done completely in a studio with only one or two cameras. I made a deal with a cable station, rented their studio, camerapeople, and editor for $250 an hour. I scripted the spot, hired an AFTRA announcer for $300, and we had a 30-second television spot cut for less than $1,000.

I was convinced print was the best media in which to reach entrepreneurs, but I was curious to see the impact of television spots. Television news generated substantial numbers of convention attendees; perhaps spots would do the same.

I cut a series of 60-second commercials, and designed each in an editorial format. I had an actor standing in front of the convention center where we were going to appear, and his lines gave viewers the impression that he was actually a newscaster doing a remote report. I ran the spots the week the expo opened. I bought late night and daytime, and tallied the results through a printed survey sheet we utilized with attendees.

We spent an average of $10,000 in television time in three consecutive markets, but I saw no appreciable increase in attendance. We did market surveys within the shows and found that those who came

from television and radio comprised less that 5% of our attendance. Those that were drawn from the spots were not big spenders, either. They seldom attended seminars or bought tapes, and rarely purchased a manual.

We generated $2.95 attendees from commercials; people who were there to look. I analyzed this attendee carefully because I had thought about using television to sell manuals. The results from the spot commercials confirmed what I suspected. Entrepreneurs are information seekers, readers. They do not watch much television or listen to the radio. They read the newspaper, which is the best vehicle to use to reach them. If I was selling a product that was entertainment-oriented, television and radio might be another story. People listen to radio and watch television to be entertained. Those commercials fit.

I abandoned television and returned to print, where ads are cheaper and the respondents more predictable.

When a mail order ad does not work, it is too late for research and analysis. Before I ran my six-page supplements, I spent time analyzing the market. I had been selling entrepreneurs manuals and magazines for four years, and I knew they read. I had written letters and sent them lengthy mailing pieces. I knew length did not discourage them. I also knew most suspected the legitimacy of mail order offers. I knew that through the letters I received from many buyers who questioned the authenticity of the manuals, and the accuracy of the magazine.

Research takes patience. I am not a patient man; I never have been. I take shortcuts, but when it comes to mail order and spending my money, I am extremely patient. I will spend hours in the library, and days researching trade publications and other books so that I know the marketplace well before I even write a line in an ad.

I had patience when it came to uncovering new businesses and trends, as well. Despite our rapid growth, I kept close tabs on the business research and editorial departments. I wanted to make sure that what was being reported was worthwhile and salable. At times I had to delete fluff from the magazine and throw out three or four stories because they either missed or were not thoroughly researched.

I am not (nor have I ever been) a benevolent manager. I am an owner and boss. No one cares more about a business than the owner. No one has put in more than the owner. Employees can be excellent, but in the end if there are problems, the only thing they lose is a job.

That does not equate with losing a home, life savings, and millions of dollars.

My management tactics hurt me in the long run. There were people within *Entrepreneur* who knew of our growing problems in 1982, but they did not want to say anything to me. I never realized it until it was too late. If I had, I could have saved myself many sleepless nights and many more monumental problems with an open-door policy.

I thought little about employees. I was concerned with building the company. I started a series called "fraud of the month." Each month we would investigate and expose a current business opportunity scam on the pages of *Entrepreneur*. We explained to readers how the con game worked, and how to avoid it.

The attack on frauds generated enormous favorable publicity but that was not where it ended. I ran the series for 18 months, and decided to take all the frauds we had detailed, combine them in a book, and offer it to consumers at cost.

I packaged a 74-page book called *Business Opportunity Frauds* by Chase Revel. It was a softcover, black-and-white, and inexpensive to produce. We sent news releases to major newspapers across the country telling of its availability. Consumers could purchase it for 50 cents, which was the cost of postage and handling.

Within weeks media throughout the country were writing about it, and where it could be obtained. We received thousands of orders for the pamphlet, fulfilled them, and retained the names. They were excellent prospects. Anyone willing to spend 50 cents for a booklet on frauds was clearly demonstrating their interest in business. They were excellent prospects for one of our manuals, tapes, or subscriptions to the magazine.

Many companies use the same technique to generate prospects. Almost every industry has one or two examples. For instance, the insurance industry has several pamphlets. One they give away is called "The Facts about Life Insurance" and the other is titled "Least Expensive Auto Insurance."

Prospects for non-mail order type products may find themselves on the other end of a telephone conversation with an insurance salesperson, or they could receive a postage-paid response card (for more information) when the booklet arrives.

FREE OFFERS AND INQUIRY ADS

Free offers are similar to inquiry ads. They are one way to generate qualified leads. Regardless of the industry, free and consumer-ori-

ented booklets are lead-generating devices. As soon as the names arrive, the product is mailed and the prospect goes up on computer. The offers and literature follow.

The response for the fraud booklet was so good that I decided to structure an ad and give it away for the same 50 cents. I designed one that had a mayor presenting me with a proclamation. As usual I tested the ad in a publication.

The test return was disastrous. It puzzled me at first, but after giving it some thought I came up with the reason. The media endorsing the product and giving it editorial exposure was one thing. The media can sell the negative; negative news works, and the booklet was negative. But people do not buy a negative product through mail order, and that is what our booklet was—we were selling information on frauds, which was certainly a negative topic.

Adding to the names on our mailing list became one of my prime goals. One technique I developed was to offer prospects a counseling service via the telephone.

Every week we mailed postcards to previous manual buyers. The postcards were handwritten and had tantalizing lines on them that read "it is important you call as soon as possible. We have valuable information on (the name of the business)."

If the buyer had purchased a manual on computer stores, the copy on the postcard would mention computer stores; if they bought a manual on restaurants, the tag would relate to the food business. At the bottom of the card was a toll-free 800 number, and beneath that was the name of a counselor.

When the prospect made the call, he or she was greeted by the counselor, who supplied updated information pertaining to the buyer's previous purchase. That opened the door for the counselor to talk to the buyer about another manual in a similar field. We increased manual sales by almost 25%, the prime reason being we *gave* previous buyers valuable, updated information. Their gratitude translated into additional sales.

The free information technique is a potent sales tool. Mail order professionals use it in a variety of ways. The premise is to supply information and education to the prospect on a regular basis. The prospect becomes indebted and ultimately makes a purchase.

This method is particularly effective when dealing in a competitive mail order field where everyone is selling similar products. What separates one mail order offer (and firm) from another is the "extra mile" they are willing to go, the additional service they are prepared to give.

Professionals nurture the prospect. Even though someone may have turned down the first offer, they expressed an interest. That means at some time in the future there is a chance they will buy.

There is no better example than one involving a young man who was my marketing director for several years. Eventually he went out on his own, and one of his first clients specialized in selling precious metals through the mail.

During high inflationary periods, when everyone was buying gold and silver, this firm had little difficulty. But inflation abated and investors abandoned the collectible market. Along with that exodus went numerous gold and silver marketers.

My former marketing director refused to panic. He calmly continued mailing information and educational pieces to previous customers. He spent money buying reports that discussed the future of collectibles, and sent the reports to both present and previous customers. In some cases the reports even contained negative projections for the collectible market.

As a result, he developed a trust and credibility among the prospects. Inflation continued to drop, but his client's sales actually increased.

When you are in business, you have to utilize every method imaginable to generate customers and sales. Business is a war. Not everyone does what is fair. The entrepreneur who believes differently will not last long. You have to be able to dance with creditors, cajole irate customers, and keep the happy ones satisfied.

Not all consumers are honest. Some order things and claim they did not get them. Or they order something, copy or read it, and return it for a refund. Not all competitors are ethical. Many ordered our manuals, copied them, made slight changes, and sold them under different titles with a slightly altered approach. Others jumped in and copied the format of our magazine.

There are mail order marketers that make a living out of duplicating successful ads and products. They change a few words, devise a similar product, and run a revised ad. That is human nature and I learned to expect it in business.

Mail order entrepreneurs are not the only ones who copy. Any time there is a product that hits and does well, other companies jump in and come out with similar versions.

Don Kracke, a marketing professional and inventor, lectures on the subject. Years ago, he designed, produced, and sold a fad product called a "ricky-ticky-sticky" during the hippie years (late 1960s).

Kracke's product was a flower with adhesive on it that could be

stuck on any surface. In less than two years, it swept the country and grossed nearly $20 million. Kracke's sales accounted for $2 million—the rest were copies or ripoffs.

To survive copying and all the other obstacles found in business, you need street smarts, especially when it comes to mail order. Never underestimate what a competitor will do, and never believe your product will remain exclusively yours forever.

NUMBER OF PRODUCTS AND RELATION TO SALES

The more products or items in a catalog, the greater the sales. The imitators could duplicate one or two of my manuals, but they had a difficult time conjuring up the vast number our catalogs contained. One reason "96 Hottest" did well was because of the diversity of businesses in it. I found the more manuals I had in a catalog, the greater the response.

It made sense. If a mailing piece went out and it concentrated on selling only one manual—a computer store, for example—only those prospects interested in a computer store would respond. But when a catalog went out with 96 choices it was like a smorgasbord. Prospects might not care for computer stores, but they had 95 others to choose from and there was a good chance that there was at least one business in the remaining number they would order. Usually, the more manual choices a prospect had, the greater the order.

Sharper Image and many other mail order catalog marketers use the same approach. They mail to business executives. If *Sharper* sent a catalog that only offered electric pencil sharpeners, it would have limited appeal. Instead it not only offers sharpeners, but dozens of other gadgets executives might buy. Buyers who have no use for the sharpener may see two or three other items they prefer and order all of them.

That approach is used by retail-oriented stores, too. Take a fast-food restaurant. The secret of success is not selling a hamburger to a patron, but in getting the same customer to add to his or her order and buy french fries and a malt at the same time.

Fast-food restaurants expand menus so consumers will add to their orders. The more offered, the greater the individual's order. Product mix can lead to greater sales without an increase in prospects.

I did the same with our business opportunity shows. We started with a dozen seminars and gradually increased the number to more than two dozen. Initially we had two seminars competing against

each other. With two dozen sessions we had three battling for attendance at any one time. Instead of splitting the attendees, we increased the total number.

Upping the number aided our mail order sales. If we were in a market where live seminar attendance dropped for a particular session, invariably the sales of the tape for that session were up. Overall, tape sales climbed as I added seminars.

I had profit centers at our corporate offices, as well. I had developed telephone sales, tape sales, subscriptions, list rental, and even entrepreneurial book sales. I was not interested in competing against the major book chains, but business publishers came to us in an effort to sell us products that we would take to expos for resale.

I saw an opportunity in buying and marketing closeouts that related to business, and selling them in our bookstores as well as at our expos. We bought the books at a fraction of the original cost, and turned the area into another profit center.

The company had settled into a steady, predictable growth pattern, and as the expos became more routine, my restlessness increased. I did little aside from come into the market a few days in advance for media interviews, give three seminars, count the money, and leave.

I was bored. That is when I came up with another idea. I could see a rising interest in fitness, health, and sports. I saw this interest in sports as a chance to stage another expo—an "exotic sports" expo.

I planned to take every obscure and oddball sport, put them under one roof, demonstrate them hourly, and take in $500,000 in the process. The demonstrations would take place in one corner of the hall. Outside I planned to have midget Gran Prix auto racing demonstrations.

Inside, the demonstrations would range from Korean martial arts to "mountain" climbing. We hung ropes from the center of the hall so climbers could demonstrate the techniques they used in scaling. There were even hovercraft demonstrations. (A hovercraft is a vehicle about eight or nine feet long that is suspended about six inches above the ground by a force of air. It moves rapidly across the floor, attaining speeds of up to 30 miles per hour.)

I saw the expo as the perfect vehicle to use in order to take advantage of the health, fitness, and exercise craze that was sweeping the country. I described the idea to people at the company and friends. Without exception, they thought the concept was a sure winner.

The unanimous praise for the idea should have been a clue that something might be wrong. Instead I took it as a signal that the idea was so appealing, unique, and original that it could not miss. Before

our expo department had even sold a booth, I had them book halls in Chicago and New York for the following months. I fully expected to have both a business opportunity and sports expo traveling across country, with each visiting one city a month.

The prime market for the show would be the health and fitness devotee, the 18- to 30-year-old. I planned to use print, radio, and television to reach them. However, I did not rule out other segments of the market. I expected to draw everyone from 8 to 80. In fact, I thought the crowds would be so heavy that I not only put in 20-foot aisles, I increased the show days from three to five. We would open Wednesday and close Sunday night.

I spent $10,000 on radio spots with the top rock stations in town during the week of the show. I also worked several promotional tie-ins with one station. They used tickets as giveaways, and plugged the show.

I planned to sell 500 to 700 booths at $300 to $600 each. I also looked for 75,000 general admissions at $3.50. I had visions of a $500,000 gate, and thought I could hold expenses at about $250,000.

The first sign of trouble surfaced through my booth sales department. Our exhibitor prospects were primarily small retailers. Most equipment manufacturers for these oddball sports could not afford to buy booth space. They were still small and undercapitalized.

Hacky-sack, for instance, a volleyball game played with a small sack full of sand which is kicked over the net, was created by a family. It was a sport that had not yet caught on and obviously there was not much profit in the thousand or so bags of sand they had sold.

The mountain climbers were all entrepreneurs; independent contractors who did not get their equipment from any one or two sources. White water rafting was an exciting sport, but it, too, was run by independent contractors.

My expo sales department was trying to sell booth space to individual operators of stores or independent contractors. They put in an exorbitant amount of time selling vendors, but they were still only able to sell 150 booths. Occasionally they landed a major exhibitor who would take three or four booths.

My expenses had no end. The convention center rental and costs ran close to $50,000. The newspaper supplement cost $60,000, radio and television time $25,000. I also had to pay commissions for booth sales.

Costs far exceeded my projections, but I had hopes that the crowd would bail me out. The day we opened, I anxiously awaited the hordes of attendees. At noon, when the doors swung open, a few

hundred people drifted through. They drifted through the rest of the day, too.

The demonstrations were media hits and we attracted coverage from every television station in town. One reporter even climbed the "mountain" while another rode around in the hovercraft. Visually the show was fun.

The crowd started to build but not in the numbers I anticipated. By weekend it was apparent we were not going to jam the aisles, and I was going to lose a bundle.

Sunday night when I tallied our gate and costs, I had dropped $250,000.

It was the first time in years that I had flopped—and it was an indicator of the trouble that was on the way.

6

The Cycle Ends

My uncle was a boisterous Baptist minister who spent a good deal of time slapping people on the back and preaching the gospel. In Tennessee that is not unusual. Neither is going to church two or three times a week.

Baptists must, at one point, confess their sins in front of the congregation. Also, they are not members of the church until they are baptized.

I was not enthused about doing either. Whenever my uncle was around he would try to pressure me. Try haranguing kids; nothing turns them off faster, especially if they are teenagers. I was, and I was not going for it.

One day I decided to have a little fun and get even with the bore. One of my chores on the farm was to plant and work in the garden. I had accidentally cross-pollinated bell peppers, by planting hot and mild species too close together. I knew it because I tasted several.

My uncle was visiting and he wandered into the garden. As usual he was preaching and I was resisting. He scanned the vegetables and asked what was good. Without hesitation, I recommended the bell peppers.

With one of his huge hands he scooped up a hot pepper, and almost devoured it with one enormous bite. I could hardly control my glee as he ran screaming to the house, searching for water and my grandmother. I laughed for days, and it was a long time before he ever bothered me about religion.

TWISTING ARMS FOR THE SALE

The incident stands out because religion played an important part in my early development. I am not a devout Baptist, nor for that matter am I a devout member of any religion. Pressure to conform taught me a valuable lesson that I carried over into my business career: if you want someone to do something, if you want them to buy a belief, or for that matter, a product, do not twist their arms. Give them rational, logical reasons to buy. That is the way to sell.

Pressure or hype may sell a product once, but it does not generate repeat or loyal customers.

Education and information are two other ways to get people to buy. When someone knows all there is to know about a product, when all their objections have been overcome, there is only one alternative left for them—buy.

Consumers require a subtle, soft sell. The more belief they have in a product, the more likely they will buy. That was one reason why I agreed to do a small business column for the Los Angeles Times Syndicate.

From the *Times'* standpoint it was not just another column. We were mailing 5 million catalogs a year, and doing 11 business shows a year. We had the ability to promote the column—and the newspapers that ran it—in every catalog and business expo.

There is not much money in syndication, unless you happen to be Art Buchwald or Abigail Van Buren (Dear Abby), personalities who go to hundreds of different newspapers. But for a mail order company, there was a more important consideration than the fees.

In fact, there were two: lead generation and credibility. Editorial coverage in established newspapers helped me garner more credibility. Readers assume that anyone with a byline knows what he or she is talking about.

It was not easy to get the column going. Editors held back, afraid if they ran a column that touted a business, they would be responsible if an anxious reader jumped into it and went broke. So I changed the approach. Instead of devoting a column to the positive aspects of a business, I spent half of it detailing the pitfalls and risks. It enabled the syndicators to sell newspapers.

I changed our catalogs and mailing pieces so that each carried the names of newspapers that carried the column. Frankly, I doubt if we generated additional readership. That was not the intent. What we accomplished was to enhance my credibility among catalog readers.

The names of the newspapers had a positive impact on catalog recipients. If I was good enough to write a column in a major newspaper, perhaps our products were good enough to purchase. It was that simple.

At the end of each column I always offered readers a free booklet or brochure. With one column it was the fraud book; with another, a list and explanation of the 10 hottest businesses. All the readers had to do was drop a note to the newspaper, and the editor would forward the names to our offices for fulfillment. It gave the newspapers a chance to monitor the interest in business, and it provided us with thousands of new prospect names.

I took pride in the column. I made a special effort to fill it with new ideas and concepts. I described the key to making money in business: get into something before everyone else does. When I first reported on video stores, they were an opportunity; today they are high risk ventures that no longer present the individual with opportunity.

The same is true of computer stores. When I initially wrote about them, there were under two dozen in the country. Anyone who opened a store could not help but do well. Today, the market for computer stores is saturated and the industry is going through a shakeout.

I used the column to show people how they could spot trends and find new ideas or noncompetitive, in-demand products that could be sold through mail order. I recommend readers study the *Los Angeles Times* and *New York Times* daily, as well as the London *Times* and *USA Today*. I also suggested adding the *Wall Street Journal* to the list.

HOW TO SPOT TRENDS

Those publications subscribe to major wire services. The wires have thousands of reporters in the field who file reports and news items daily. The newspapers also have sizable staffs of their own.

These reporters pick up on the latest business and product news. The papers are filled with them, and each day those pages have to be refilled. They are a storehouse of knowledge and opportunity.

At *Entrepreneur* our research department spent two hours a day, five days a week, scanning those publications. Anything different or unusual was cut out and put in a file. At our weekly editorial meetings I went through the file looking for unusual items. If I found one, I assigned a researcher to follow up.

Years ago, I was reading the London *Times* and saw a two- or three-inch item about a nightclub called a "discotheque." Discos had lines outside the door, and were doing turnaway business in cities such as Paris and London. The story did not even describe a disco, what it was, or how it operated. It referred to it simply as a nightclub.

Worthwhile ideas that you find in print seldom have details. In the editor's mind, they do not have the importance of a summit conference, drug bust, or political election. But to the opportunist it is a clue that must be followed.

I called the editor, and it took me more than one call to get him on the line. I asked for the name of the reporter who turned in the story. Eventually, I got the reporter on the line—he was in Paris—and he explained discotheques to me. It was nothing more than a club with a disc jockey playing the latest records accompanied by flashing lights.

I thought it an ingenious idea. It may not seem so today, but think back to the initial entry of discos into the United States. They caused a sensation, and for good reason. They solved two major problems, one for the bar owner and one for the public.

When consumers go into a bar and hear the same group night after night, they eventually get bored. Some nights the band is good, others it is not. If a consumer hits the bar on an off night, he or she may never come back. That, of course, creates a problem for the bar owner.

The disco provided the most popular music, music that had already proven appeal. This prevented the consumers from going elsewhere and the bar owner found himself or herself with a steady audience.

I saw discos becoming a major trend. I made that prediction, and within months, one opened in New York. Two weeks later another popped up in Washington, DC. Before long they were in every city.

Forecasting the emergence of discos was relatively easy. It cost me $200 in telephone calls. *Entrepreneur* was hailed for its forecasting ability, yet anyone could have done the same thing if they had been reading and studying those publications.

Discos were a proven idea before they came to this country. For anyone marketing products, it is important to stay away from revolutionary concepts. Consumers are slow to accept change. Let someone else blaze the trail, as they did with discos.

With mail order the problem is if someone else comes up with a good idea and you try to adapt it for your own use, it may be too

late by the time you see it. Good mail order ideas sweep the country rapidly, and once they do there is little room for imitators.

There have, of course, been exceptions. Most notably, the dieting industry. The need to diet was on every consumer's mind. They had to diet. Dieting was a major trend and fad, and anything that becomes as commonplace and popular as dieting will work repeatedly.

For example, there was not just one or two diets that sold well through mail order. There were dozens, and they are still being sold today. In mail order, people who bought one diet, bought at least two or three others.

If the market for a product is as broad as it is for dieting, then the mail order marketer can risk introducing another similar product through the mails.

I find an effective way of finding a need and a product to fulfill it is to scan newspapers and magazines. Study the attitudes of consumers. Look at the ads that are running. Search for products that catch your imagination and fill a need. Try to find something that not only sparks your interest, but appears to be underpromoted or poorly promoted. When you find one, try to rewrite the advertisements that are selling the products. Look for a new approach. Try to say it and sell it better.

USING GIFT AND TRADE SHOWS

I also make it a practice to go to gift shows and read trade publications for a variety of industries. At a gift show you will often find new and unique products that fulfill a definite need but have not been marketed. Many of the creators of these ideas do not have the money to market products nationally, so they go to a gift show in hopes of picking up a representative or distributor to handle their product.

Gift shows are an excellent way for mail order marketers to find potential products. I found this to be especially true when I started Van Pler & Tissany. Most jewelers would go to jewelry trade shows, as I did, but I also felt that gift shows, which were large expos, might be the place to find small manufacturing firms that had been unable to get national distribution because of a lack of capital.

Many had excellent products that I felt the public would buy if they knew about them. Regardless of how enamoured I was with a product, I would never pick one because I liked it. It had to have a potential market and answer a need for the people within that market.

When I started *Entrepreneur* business opportunity ventures were underpromoted, yet there was a major interest in the market. I took an old idea—selling information—and gave it a new twist.

I did the same with the Van Pler & Tissany, the simulated/synthetic diamond company I developed. I was intrigued by the product, but thought it was being sold the wrong way to the wrong audience. I changed the approach. Although the product dated back 20 years, there was a recent breakthrough in the industry and none of the mail order marketers were taking advantage of the superior simulated diamonds that had been perfected. I was the first to do so. I simply put a new twist on an old, but improved, product.

The difficulty is letting go if it does not work. Unfortunately, one of the most difficult things for a creative person to do is let go of a bad idea. A product is developed, an ad is tested, and it does not pull. I have been in those situations. The tendency is to hold on, revise the ad, try again, and spend more money.

Gamblers suffer from the same addiction. They believe they are psychics and will win. Many entrepreneurs with new ideas are the same way. They throw good money after bad.

HOW OBJECTIVITY MAKES AND SAVES MONEY

In mail order, determination is not nearly as important as objectivity. In fact, positive thinking can be a mail order entrepreneur's worst enemy.

Patience and determination are admirable traits, but they have to be tempered with objectivity and logic in business. Thomas Edison tried over 100 variations before he created an electric light that worked. He was determined. However, every time you miss and try the same thing again, it costs money, valuable capital that you might be using on newer, more productive ventures.

I disagree with the positive thinkers. Positive thinking is supposed to make you a winner. I am not knocking the concept, but it is not a cure-all. Nor is it the secret of success.

I believe in negative thinking. I use negative thinking to see the faults, the problems, and the pitfalls in every idea and product. Negative thinking kept me out of trouble for a long time. It helped me anticipate all the things that might go wrong with a project.

I am positive, and I temper my enthusiasm with negative possibilities. By developing the negative and analyzing it, I avoided many

disasters. It is only when someone ignores the negative implications of a business or product that they fail.

In mail order a winner possesses ideas and a loser is possessed by ideas.

Before entering a venture, I put rules down on paper. There is a time line, a formula that is predetermined. If my idea does not meet the criteria, I drop it. I set the rules in advance. Once the game has started, it is too late; it is difficult to remain objective. I never second guess myself, either. What is done is done; go on to the next project.

I leave my ego out of business, too. When I was living in Chicago, a used car salesperson told me I could obtain actual invoices that were given to dealers for their new cars. These were the prices to the dealer from the manufacturer. I could even obtain the true cost of accessories.

What a coup, I thought. That information would be incredibly valuable to anyone shopping for a new car. I decided to put the information in book form and sell it through direct mail. This was in an era when people bought a new car every two to three years.

I bought a list of consumers who had purchased automobiles in one city during a two-year period. The numbers were staggering. I was excited about the possibilities. I could see redoing the book each year and reselling it. Ten million automobiles were sold annually. I did not even need 1% of the market to make a million dollars.

I structured a direct-mail piece describing the manual, the benefits, and how it could save hundreds, perhaps thousands of dollars on a buyers next car purchase. I mailed it to a portion of the list.

I needed one half of 1% to buy my $10 product. Only 5 orders per 1,000. That is a low profitability number. To my consternation, I drew one-tenth of 1%; only one out of a thousand purchased. Did I lose!

I had a fantastic product; why weren't people buying it? I could have revised the mailing piece and tried direct mail again, or I could drop the idea.

I dropped it. I did not let my ego get the best of me. I had spent enough on the project. A few weeks later I met a publisher and explained the book to him. He liked it, and worked out an agreement in which I recovered my development costs and received a royalty per book sold.

Two weeks after he bought it he put it on the newsstand. That was more than 20 years ago, and the book is still selling. It is updated yearly, and he has five competitors, but he continues to do well.

Why did it work on the newsstand? Credibility. No one believed that I could deliver that kind of information. On the newsstand they

could pick it up and browse through it. They could see it was for real. With mail order they could not.

Consumers may read things they get in the mail but they do not believe every piece that arrives. They do not automatically assume that the mail order firm is honest.

The auto book was my initial effort at marketing a text (or information) through mail order. Since that time, however, I have sold hundreds of thousands of books-or manuals-via the mails. I was confident that with the right title and subject, I could turn a hardcover into a bestseller through the mail. In 1981, I came up with the concept. It stemmed from the time I spent in singles' bars, watching both sexes hover over each other, struggling to strike up a conversation and say something clever.

It made me see a need. Despite a sexually liberated society, both men and women had awkward moments when they met. What do you say? Should you be funny? Serious? Regardless of how liberated they were, the initial encounter was always trying. What they needed was a technique to break the ice, some clever lines that would get the other's attention.

My answer was a book with clever pick-up lines, one that could be used by either sex. The lines would be garnered from college campuses across the country. I came up with an idea for a national contest that would be run at the college level. I would advertise for entries in college newspapers, and give prizes for the best lines.

Lines that were winners and runners-up would be inserted in the book. I was convinced I had a captive audience among college students. Every student who submitted a line would buy one. Winners would tell their friends. It was a book with enormous word-of-mouth potential. I could see it becoming a rage at fraternity and sorority houses. I had a product that would appeal directly to 10 million people—the number of students in colleges across the country.

Based on the experiences I had in singles' bars, there were many people beyond college age that were potential customers, as well. It was a "can't miss" idea. There was a need, it was targeted at a specific audience, and the entries, if clever, would also generate publicity.

I decided to call it "501 Best Pick-Up Lines." College students are creative, and I was sure we would have at least 501 entries. We might even have enough for a sequel. I did not, incidentally, pull the 501 out of a hat. I planned it, as numbers are an important ingredient in mail order.

501 VERSUS "HUNDREDS"

In many mail order ads a specific number is mentioned. "Ten ways to get rich," "Eight tips that cannot miss," and so on. There is a reason for the numbers. In mail order, being specific sells. People are sending money through the mail, and they want to know what, and how much, they are getting in return. In mail order the marketer should try to be as specific as possible. Avoid broad generalizations. Give people an exact number to bite their teeth into. It sparks interest and motivates the prospect when they know exactly how many of this or that they will get.

"Best Pick-Up Lines" does not say the same thing as 501. "Best" says they are the best, but it does not say how many. There may only be three or four, or a dozen. The number 501 says there are plenty.

I also use odd numbers whenever I can. That is, I never use a number in a title or brochure that is rounded off such as 500, 25, 100, and so on. Numbers such as 501, 23, 68, or 96 are more believable to the buyer.

I placed the ads and waited. The response was phenomenal. I generated thousands of entries. Before I even sorted them, I had a full-page ad written and designed. It was a one-step with a photograph of the book's cover and testimonials from "users" of the lines.

I put other numbers in the ad as well. I had a line that said "212 girls and 289 boys won $10,000 in prizes contributing the best lines they used or heard." I stressed the fact that girls had submitted entries. To the male, if a girl submits a line she thinks is clever, other girls would probably believe it to be clever as well.

There were subheads that reiterated the sales message. The heads ranged from "girls really love interesting pick-up lines" and "pick up those hard-to-get girls" to "get those beautiful girls that other guys are afraid to approach" and "lines that capitalize on your awkwardness and shyness."

The ad was loaded with sizzle. In fact, I thought it was one of the best I ever wrote. It promised benefits and answered needs. Buy this book and you can make off with the best looking girls, be the life of the party.

I had to be careful with the copy. Everyone needs help, but you never want to say it overtly. No one wants to admit they are incapable

of doing something, especially striking up a conversation. We like to think of ourselves as outgoing, charming, and likable, We do not want to be told that we are not. That approach would have doomed the book.

My copy sold success and sociability. It never implied that the purchasers might be misfits (that's negative, and negative ads do not work in mail order). Before the book was even completed, I tested the ad on the sports page of a large metropolitan newspaper. It was ideal placement for a product designed for urban individuals. A good percentage of college students are sports fans.

The ad drew miserably. I brought back just over 25% of the cost. I tried publications that were geared to the single man; magazines such as *Chic*. I lost there, too. I tried the college market. Another bomb. The only ad that returned successfully was one I placed in a business opportunity journal. It brought back 140% of the ad's cost.

Why? What was wrong? The idea, of course, was not entirely new. Several years before I published my book, there was another that sold more than one million copies with a similar editorial thrust. Why didn't mine work?

I never found a definitive answer, but I had several ideas. (In mail order, it is always easy to find a dozen reasons why your ads do not work—after you have spent the money.)

At first I thought the market was saturated. That was not the case, because although I could not sell the book through the mail, it became a bestseller at our expos, where consumers could actually pick it up, browse through it, and prove to themselves that the lines were indeed, clever. It was an impulse buy at the shows.

There were other possibilities. One of the most critical aspects when it comes to succeeding with a mail order offer is the audience; they must be mail order responsive if the offer is to succeed and bring in profits. People who are not used to buying through the mail will not purchase as readily as someone who is mail order responsive.

I had the right product and addressed the correct audience, but they may not have been mail order responsive. On the other hand, when I went to the business opportunity journal, the readers were used to purchasing through the mail.

That may-or may not- have been the answer. When you miss there is not always a logical answer. My automobile book failed because it was not a mail order item. It is possible that "501" could have had the same problem. Perhaps the audience read the ad, and did not believe there were 501 lines that they had not heard. Perhaps they felt they knew all the lines, and did not need help. Or maybe they

believed the lines were clichés. Perhaps it would do better in a college bookstore where kids could browse through it and prove the worth of the book to themselves before they bought it.

I have never beat failure to death. When an ad misses, I do not spend months agonizing over reasons. I go on. I know a good mail order average is one hit in five trips.

Experiences such as 501 bring you back to reality. Everyone misses. I never assume everyone will buy my products. I only want a small percentage. That is all I need. That is all anyone needs in a nation of 230 million people.

I was still intrigued by book publishing and the possibilities I thought it had for enhancing business. I felt there was a way to load commercial books (i.e., those that are sold in bookstores) with information and have them act as a catalog at the same time.

Entrepreneur was a catalog. Of course, it had the latest business information, but each magazine carried mail order ads for our products. I always had a double-truck (two pages facing each other) ad for our manuals in each issue. Our stories on new and unique businesses were designed to arouse a reader's interest in the complete manual. The draw was phenomenal.

A paperback book, sold on newsstands, could do the same. I approached Bantam Books with a unique proposition; a proposition that has brought *Entrepreneur* back more than $1 million to date.

I proposed that we print a paperback for drug stores and other Bantam outlets. It would contain capsule summaries of the hottest businesses. Each summary would run approximately two pages, enough to pique the interest of the buyer. At the back of the book would be an order blank for the in-depth start-up manual that corresponded to the summary.

Initially, I would supply condensed versions of 186 of our manuals for the paperback. We would call the book *186 of the Hottest Businesses in the Country*, by Chase Revel. The orders would come directly to Bantam. They would turn them over to us for fulfillment.

We gave Bantam a 7% royalty of everything (manuals) that were sold through the book, and they gave us a $25,000 advance plus a 7% royalty on all the paperbacks. To date, the first book has brought back $1.4 million and is in its fifth printing. There is a second book out that is doing equally as well.

We not only sold hundreds of thousands of manuals, but we were able to use new outlets (drug stores, supermarkets, convenience stores) through which we could introduce products. The names of customers

who bought the manuals through the paperback proved to be qualified additions to our mailing list as well.

Realistically, Bantam is selling a catalog. It is close to 200 pages of advertising. This concept is growing. There is one east coast company that has set up "catalog racks" in major bookstores. The catalogs in the racks, which are normally given away free, carry a price tag ($1 to $3). The bookstore generates sales, the catalog distributor generates dollars from the catalog companies, and the mail order catalog firms reach a new market.

The Bantam venture is an example of what I mean by being an opportunist. Many businesspeople might be content to sit back and let the company grow at its normal rate. An opportunist is always on the alert for a new and better way to make money.

KEEP MOVING

In mail order you cannot rest on your laurels. Once you have created a product or idea and it sells, the most important thing is to develop other ways to market it or other products to add to the line. Sit still and you die in this (or any other) business.

Shortly after I graduated high school I went into the masonry business in Chicago. We were phenomenally successful until a recession hit, and the construction business went under. I could have given up, but in business you learn that setbacks are part of life. To succeed you have to keep searching for new opportunities. I found one in the door-to-door vacuum cleaner sales field.

There are few things tougher than door-to-door sales, but I had a gimmick. I trained and convinced sales applicants who wanted to work that they were demonstrators, not salespeople. All they had to do was get in the door and demonstrate the vacuum.

If the consumer liked it they could have one for free; all they had to do was set our demonstrators up with appointments with their friends. For every appointment that turned into a sale, the consumer would receive $25. With nine sales, they received a vacuum for free. Consumers bought on the premise that they would pay for their vacuum through referral sales.

It seldom happened. Setting appointments with friends sounds easier than it is. Check your rolodex or telephone book, and add up the number of people you could convince to sit still for a demonstration. Generating nine was not easy.

Years later, when multilevel marketing became the rage, distrib-

utors discovered the same thing when they tried to enroll friends and relatives in selling schemes.

Just when the vacuum cleaners were rolling, my former partner in the masonry business called. He was a hustler, and when the business went down, he kept banging on doors looking for another opportunity. He found one through a group of rental property owners. They had built numerous apartments in the Chicago suburbs, and had a high vacancy rate. They were frantic. There was nothing wrong with the units, but Chicagoans were accustomed to renting in the city. The suburbs were alien to them.

The owners told him if he could rent the units, they would give him an exclusive rental and management agreement for all their buildings. It was a plum worth thousands of dollars every month if he could pull it off. He called me, knowing I had a talent for copywriting.

I asked for copies of their ads, and immediately saw the problem. They were trying to rent apartments, not answer needs. The ad failed to communicate the advantages of the suburbs. It failed to stress how close they were to the city, and how the amenities that existed meant only a few extra minutes of commuting time. The ads they ran contained few facts. They were mostly hype, and failed to generate any excitement among prospective buyers. To get someone to buy, you have to move them and get them excited.

ANSWERING NEEDS WITH FACTS

In less than two hours, I wrote an ad and placed it in the *Chicago Tribune*. I pretended I was a real estate salesman talking to a prospect. I used virtually the same dialogue in the ad. I explained how close the apartments were to downtown, how reasonable the rents, how beautiful the area. I also wrote about the advantages of bringing up kids in the suburbs. I did not use adjectives and exaggerated statements. On Sunday, applicants poured in and we were back in business, this time with a real estate management company.

The real estate management company was another opportunity I did not miss. Years later, when Entrepreneur started getting proclamations and recognition from the government and media, I continued to look for opportunities to maximize impact. Boston's Mayor Kevin White was a true fan of small business. Every time we came to town he proclaimed a day in our honor, and our gate went up 20%.

During one presentation I had a photographer snap a picture of the mayor giving me the proclamation. I structured a full-page, one-step ad and used it to sell a new manual we had created—"How To Get SBA Financing." The headline was a good one: "Best Source of Expansion or Start-Up Capital Usually Ignored." It had appeal for both new and established businesses.

The mayor's picture did not hurt. I positioned it in the center of the ad with a caption that identified the mayor, the city he came from, and myself. It drew extremely well, especially along the east coast. It returned 300% in the eastern edition of the *Wall Street Journal*, and 300% the first time I ran it. I tried other *Wall Street Journal* editions and it never failed to pull that 300%. There were only six subheads in the ad but they told the story.

1. Most accountants not aware of new procedures.
2. Red tape reduced to less paperwork than most banks require.
3. 93 out of 102 applications approved.
4. Approval within three weeks.
5. 33 things that could get you turned down.
6. Free bonus manual.

It had about as much sizzle as I could pack into an ad. The first subhead automatically posed questions in the reader's mind, even if he or she had a competent accountant.

The next addressed an issue which every businessperson dreads when they face the government or banks and ask for money.

The third showed the incredibly high success rate people attained by using the techniques in the manual.

The fourth answered another question most businesspeople have—yes, the paperwork may be easy, and the technique right on the mark, but will it take us a year to get our money?

The fifth represented inside information that could help them, and the sixth item was a bonus we were offering if they bought the package.

Those six subheads addressed every possible question and objection a prospect could have. Make sure people know what you are selling and how much it costs.

I used the mayor's picture on another one-step. I was selling a 291-page booklet called "Who's Making a Bundle and How Much?" It was a takeoff from the ad I had been running for four years. On

this one I got fancy. I buried the title of the book in the copy, even though it was in boldface. The headline was difficult to read.

"I quit thinking status quo and made a million dollars before I was old enough to vote. . ."

Terrible headline. There is nothing wrong with long heads as long as prospective buyers can read and understand them. I ignored an important rule; keep it simple and understandable.

The ad barely broke even in the *Los Angeles Times*. In mail order, breakeven is sufficient if you have capability for a back end. We did, but when a quarter-page entrepreneurial ad pulls poorly in a first-class Los Angeles newspaper, I hold back and reevaluate where I am going. If it did poorly in a good vehicle, it will probably be a disaster in markets where the audience is not heavy with entrepreneurs.

I was not finished with the "Who's Making a Bundle" booklet. I created another gimmick which I was proud of for the impact it had on whoever received it. I wrote a review of "Who's Making a Bundle" and had it typeset in the same style as a newspaper. I then had it printed on newsprint, which is the stock that is used by newspapers.

On the flip side of the review, I printed stock tables. The name of the newspaper was not visible, but there was a reviewer's name above the article about the book. The name was fictional. On the review, I wrote—in longhand with pen—"thought you might be interested in this. . .J."

I used the letter "J" because more names begin with "J" than almost any other letter in the alphabet.

I tested the impact of the review with a list. Not surprisingly, it drew well in some places and poorly in others.

The reaction of the prospect was one of puzzlement when they received it. They would rack their brain to identify the "J" who signed it. Almost all of us know at least one or two "J's." So did my prospects. I followed the review with a one-step mailing piece for "Who's Making a Bundle?"

One mail order ad that gave me problems was a two-step offshoot I created from the "Who's Making a Bundle?" head. I was offering a book loaded with information on 140 of the current and best businesses around. It was my usual ploy.

I sold it for $8, and ran the ad in the national edition of the *Wall Street Journal*. I listed nearly every one of the businesses covered, and

even featured a shot of Mike Douglas interviewing me on television. The ad failed. It did not even make back 50% of ad cost.

I pulled back and reexamined the offer. I could see several problems. There was a laundry list of businesses but no details to get people excited. I would have fared better to feature a handful and say something about each, instead of creating a lengthy list without any sizzle. I believed listing as many titles as I could would cover a wider market.

A money-back guarantee would have helped. Mail order firms always return money, but there is not an ad that does not benefit from that line.

During that five-year span, I created dozens of ads and hundreds of combinations of offers. I found I could never predict what a prospect would do. Consumers buy for a variety of reasons, some of which require extensive analysis.

For instance, I saw hundreds of thousands of people come through our expos, sink their life savings into a venture, and never bother to research the viability of the business.

They did not have to go far to research, either. I had put together a manual and seminar titled "How To Buy a Business." It detailed all the underhanded methods sellers utilize in order to get someone involved in a business that may not be profitable. It only cost $15 but few people would take the time—or spend the money—to see if their judgment was correct.

That is human nature. Once we buy something we do not want anyone confusing us with facts or telling us we are wrong. Most of the time we do not even want advice. Our seminars were a good measure of this attitude. Most were geared to help the existing small businessperson, but attendance normally consisted of 20% present entrepreneurs and 80% potential ones.

It is tough to convince businesspeople that they do not know everything. Many believe that even if they do not know something, they will soon discover it without help.

It was a hectic, fast-paced five years. We grew out of our Wilshire Boulevard offices, and moved to West Los Angeles where I leased a two-story building that had space for our bookstore on the ground floor.

Business was booming, and we began to add employees. I hired several relatives and regretted it later. Never hire relatives. Eventually you have to fire them and you make an enemy for life, although I did not need to fire relatives to make enemies. I generated a sufficient number with minimal effort. Our shows brought out the best—

and the worst—in people, especially the ones we staged on the east coast.

New Yorkers took the prize. They scrutinized our seminar ads, and when they attended they would check each point off as it was covered. If the speaker failed to cover one area because the questions on previous topics ate up all the time, there was an immediate uproar and demand for refunds.

One year, I took our show to New York and held it in two venues, the Hilton Hotel, which housed our seminars, and Madison Square Garden, where we had the exhibits. We could hardly handle the crowd.

At one seminar a speaker ran out of time before he could cover an area mentioned in the ad. One or two people in the audience grumbled. He offered to talk to them afterward and answer their questions. One got so excited he almost punched the speaker. The police eventually had to escort the belligerent entrepreneur out of the show.

Every time we came to New York we ran into the same problem. I loved it. New Yorkers are wild but stimulating. I was never lulled into complacency at a New York expo. They spent a ton of money at our shows, as well. After a three-day event at Madison Square Garden we usually came out with our highest grosses. Follow-up mailings were especially effective in New York after we left.

Despite the invigorating atmosphere, I was always glad when we left the Big Apple and got away from the potential harassment. Although I had problems as a youngster and wound up in gang fights, I never sought out trouble—it usually found me.

In the midst of our expo successes I began to think of other ways in which *Entrepreneur* could generate dollars. Taking a company public is one of the fastest ways for a firm's owner to become an instant millionaire through the sale of stock.

I had sufficient funds, but had always been bothered by my inability to get a high enough selling price from buyers who were interested in the company. Publishing and business opportunities were hard to evaluate. With stock issued, valuation would no longer be a problem.

We went public, and when the stock issuance was completed, I owned approximately 75% of the outstanding shares. My plan was to spend another year or two building the business, and then sell my shares.

I put a management team in place that I believed to be extremely competent. I had confidence in the group and would take off for three and four weeks at a time. I traveled with the business show,

did interviews, plugged our products, and supervised the opening of bookstores in selected markets.

The time away gave me an opportunity to create new ads and mailing pieces. Occasionally when a show ended I would take off for a week in Mexico or the Bahamas.

The first signs of trouble came after I returned from a vacation to Mexico. My chief executive officer (CEO) had been desperately trying to contact me, but when I go on vacation I usually disappear. I do not leave a number or call in.

I have a recorder on my telephone, and when I returned home I received the message. It was a frantic call from my CEO that briefly explained we had trouble. The trouble was in the form of $250,000 we owed the Internal Revenue Service (IRS). That did not bother me. You could always bargain with the agency, and as long as you made an effort to pay—and eventually paid—they would not close you down.

IMPORTANCE OF REFUNDS

Never play around with, or argue about refunds in mail order. Aside from incurring the wrath of your customers, who represent much of your future business, there are numerous agencies that can not only make things difficult, but close you down as well.

There were more disturbing signs. I was told we owed $400,000 in refunds to customers. That was an astounding figure. My policy had always been to refund immediately without question. It may not have been the best policy, but it was the wisest.

We sold manuals, tapes, and other paper products that were easily copied and duplicated. It was no problem for someone to copy the materials and demand a refund. We fell victim to that game on more than one occasion. But if you are in the mail order business, a solid refund policy is a must.

The $400,000 was accumulated during a six-month period. I never held a refund longer than 30 days. Beyond that you invited scrutiny from the Federal Trade Commission (FTC). If they take a disliking to your operation, they can close you up within 24 hours. We were also running the risk of alienating our bank. Banks are not fond of mail order accounts that use charge cards because of refunds and the time they take to process. When you store those refunds for months, and then hit the bank with them all at once, you create an uproar, with many objections and problems.

The $400,000 had even more dire consequences. If we had that kind of obligation built in six months, it meant I was looking at close to $1 million for the year, an exorbitant amount of refunds for a $15 million a year company. It could mean our salespeople were using too much pressure on the telephone.

The greater question was, why hadn't we paid the refunds? *Entrepreneur* was a cash-based business. We never had receivables. For some reason, money was not being paid. I thought about our mail order program. Ads can be volatile, and those that draw well can suddenly cool. If they are not closely tracked, a company can lose hundreds of thousands of dollars before anyone knows it.

That could have been the case except we were not buying that much in space. Most of our ad dollars were going into catalog mailings. It was February, our prime catalog mailing period. There was another possibility. Our lists could have cooled, or we might have bought lists that had poor response. It was a long shot, but it could have happened.

I spent an entire morning going through marketing records and accounting. There were no signs that the mailings or ads had gone flat, but there was an indication the company had gotten out of hand. The number of employees had doubled in six months, and quadrupled during the past year.

I questioned the management group I put in charge, but could get no satisfactory answers. By noon I had fired two of the three, and by early afternoon the third resigned. The extent of my problems did not become apparent for weeks. I brought in two CPA firms to ferret out the mess.

The bookkeeping system was in disarray. More than $500,000 worth of checks had not been mailed. Whether we had the funds to even back the paper was another question. The bank statements were in a shambles.

I started a list. At the top was the $250,000 we owed the IRS. Next was the $400,000 in refunds. Then came the creditors and two pages of items that were hard to believe. They related to payroll and the number of employees. Our staff had gone from 65 to nearly 240 in less than a year.

Mail order is not labor-intensive. That is one of the beauties of the business. Sales could double and we would need less than 10 additional people. It takes no more personnel to mail 1 million catalogs than it does to mail 10,000. In shipping I found an increase of 11 people. There were 29, up from 18 the previous year. Most were managers.

That was only the beginning. Salespeople were being paid commissions plus a salary instead of having salaries as draws against commission. We owned six bookstores in various cities. The overhead of each was budgeted at $40,000 a month. They were running at $80,000.

The new computerized accounting system which cost more than $100,000 was not functioning. No one knew how to utilize it, and payables were not being tracked.

We were going to printers and instead of negotiating a good price, we were paying higher fees for more liberal credit terms. After 90 days, when we fell behind in our printing bills, we would switch printers and the cycle would start all over.

I pared staff and readjusted salaries and commissions. In two weeks I cut 30% from our payroll. By the end of the month, I had a grasp on the problem areas.

Our obligations totaled $3 million.

The $3 million was the end product of only six months of mismanagement. In the hundreds of hours I spent scouring the books, I found there was no one place where the money went. Salaries, overpriced printing, and foolish shipping procedures. We were mailing books, which have a special rate, first class. With that one swift move, we more than doubled the cost.

In business, when you are on top you never believe you will tumble. I experienced the fall on previous occasions when I became overconfident and did not properly research mail order ads and products. This was not a matter of an unsuccessful ad. I was faced with a situation where it was questionable as to whether *Entrepreneur* would survive.

Four weeks later, I was in the midst of triumph and crisis. Interest rates were coming down, the economy was on the way up, and we had just set a monthly sales record of $1.7 million. Profits were at a record high. Our mail order response was extraordinary. It was February 1982 and we were entering another five to six months of strong sales.

With one excellent month behind us and another coming up, I thought we would be able to reason with creditors, bargain with the IRS, and get the refunds rolling.

Just when I thought everything was going well, I ran into trouble. Creditors began to badger us and threaten legal action. Then I received a call from a friend in Washington, DC. The FTC was about to put a lock on our doors if refunds were not paid immediately.

I could not the meet the refund obligation because I had paid some

of the creditors. I searched for a possible solution. If Lee Iaccoca did it, why not us? I was wrong. With our poor record of payments, we had destroyed our good credit. In business, credit is your most important asset. Get as much of it as you can when you do not need it. Once you need it, no one wants to give you any. Everyone can smell a dying fish.

Even if we had good credit, $400,000 would not be easy to find. I realized we were not going to be able to pay refunds and satisfy creditors at the same time. The IRS was beginning to grumble, too.

I had spent nearly a decade building the company, and I owned 80% of the stock. There was only one alternative: figure what 80% of a company is worth that nets $1.5 million on a gross of around $14 million.

Do you throw 8 to 10 times earnings as a selling price out the door? Do you start all over again with the $44 ad? Not if you do not have to.

There was an alternative. Earlier in the day I had talked to my attorney about it. It was a radical move, one that we might never recover from, but it was our only chance.

The alternative was Chapter 11, bankruptcy. There is a difference between Chapters 7 and 11. Chapter 7 represents a hopeless situation; Chapter 11 says there is a chance. It gives the company protection while it reorganizes. Reluctantly, I opted for Chapter 11. For me, there were both advantages and drawbacks.

On the plus side, we could continue to operate and rebuild with the court's protection. On the other side was the way the media would handle it. I had been riding high for five years, the subject of hundreds of interviews, television appearances, and radio shows.

I had been a small business preacher, telling everyone how to make their businesses more profitable. The only trouble was I failed to heed my own advice. That is how the media would play it.

Once the media got the story, would anyone buy our products? How do you convince someone you can make them a success in business when you have just declared bankruptcy?

I pondered that one for some time before I made the decision. Then I called my attorney.

As I left the office, I was resigned to a day or two of broad, negative media coverage. After that we would be on the road back.

How wrong I was.

7

Attitudes/Products for the Future

Within days after I filed for Chapter 11, I was a media celebrity. I expected it fully. I had been on page one before, but never did I experience the mammoth negative news coverage that seemed to hit at the same time.

During one 72-hour period, I made all three national television network news shows, every local television news broadcast, and for good measure I hit both the Associated Press and United Press International wire services, which guaranteed exposure in newspapers across the country.

I knew "60 Minutes" could ruin a company or topple a president, but I had no idea as to the potency of the rest of the media. It did two things to my company and affected buyers and potential buyers in different ways. First, the network news coverage increased—instead of decreasing—magazine sales, and there was a good reason.

In each of the network news stories, the cover of *Entrepreneur* was displayed. People have short memories, and those who were not familiar with our company completely forgot why we were on television. What they retained was the visual impression of the magazine.

The networks had planted a solid, two-minute commercial and image of the publication in their minds. Consumers did not remember whether it was positive or negative. When they saw it on the newsstand, they remembered the cover and in many cases bought a

copy. March 1982 was one of the best newsstand sales months in our history.

Obviously, a 20-minute segment on *"60 Minutes"* would not have been as fortuitous. You would remember why the topic was covered, and whether it was negative or positive, the impression remains.

Frankly, I think the networks did the only thing possible. It was a good story; a company selling advice fails to heed its own. The guru of small business sinks. I could see the appeal in the headlines and on the evening news. I would have played it the same way.

ABC and NBC developed tongue-in-cheek spots. CBS allocated more time and gave me a chance to try to explain. Actually, what was there to explain? I was the chairman of the board, the man with the responsibility, and the disaster was my problem.

I smiled throughout it, but on more than one occasion I thought about chucking the entire business and retiring to the ranch I had recently purchased in central California.

When a businessperson seemingly goes broke, it affects people in strange ways. The maitre'd's I had so frequently tipped eyed me with suspicion. I was always a generous tipper and usually ordered the finest wines, but the evening after I had become coast-to-coast fodder for the networks, I detected a distinct change in their attitudes.

Instead of accepting my credit card as always—without delay or question, regardless of the size of the bill—there was now a delay. I recognized that someone was verifying the card's validity via telephone.

The landlord, who had never questioned or called us even if our rent payments were a week late, was there in person to collect his money on the due date. The bank called and wanted to have a conference, as did several of the credit card companies that did business with us. Newspapers either cut our credit limit or insisted on cash up front.

I had been the recipient of praise and adulation for nearly five years. Now it was time to accept the fact that I was on the hot seat.

To buyers and consumers familiar with the company, the coverage was devastating. Consumers construe bankruptcy as being broke, closing your doors and going out of business. They do not distinguish between Chapters 11 and 7: to them, broke is broke.

That implication single-handedly destroyed our manual sales and almost forced us out of business. We were in the height of the mail order season, and millions of prospects had received our catalogs.

THE "HOT" MONTHS FOR MAIL ORDER

At *Entrepreneur* our biggest sales period started in winter and ran through spring (January through May). Inclement weather aided our sales, as it does for most mail order companies. During cold weather people are more apt to stay indoors and read. During good weather, they get out in the sunshine and reading declines.

The network blast hit in early March and most of those who saw the network exposure did one of two things. Either they discarded their catalogs, believing we were out of business, or decided not to order because it was not worth buying goods from a company that could not follow sound business practices.

That was only the beginning. Word of mouth took over, and anyone who did not see me on television or read about our misfortune, heard about it from a friend. In 72 hours we made contact with almost every prospect on our list and every business opportunity seeker in the country.

I had failures before, but this took the grand prize. Most of the time, if you miss in business, no one knows but you, your family, and a couple of friends and associates. I shared my failure with 100 million Americans.

My mother was concerned, and called from Florida wondering if she could help in any way. It was the first and only sincere call I received. She was used to me being in the spotlight, and the sudden television coverage did not perturb her.

I had a list of minor disasters that I ranked as failures. None even came close to approaching the impact of Chapter 11. My fame had opened a great many doors, and brought me to the attention of many people. They had asked for advice and even autographs. Now it was payback time.

In the past I had seen the media's influence help build us. Now it almost destroyed the company. In one week manual sales dropped 60%. We were moving nearly $5 million dollars worth of manuals a year, and in seven days that figure was more than halved.

The greatest difficulty was with creditors. Within weeks following the media blitz, we were in a precarious position. Our sales the previous month had approached $2 million. They should have hit $2 million in March, but they dropped to just over $500,000.

Our cash flow was hardly sufficient to pay the day-to-day bills.

We were not a company in the throes of recovery. There were rumblings that the creditors might ask the bankruptcy court to liquidate and distribute whatever proceeds there were among them.

Some have the wrong impression of Chapter 11. It protects you from creditors, but not forever. If there is no progress, no recovery, the court may listen to creditors who cry for liquidation in hopes of salvaging some of their debts.

In the eyes of the court, the creditors are king. What they want, they get. If a company is healthy and making profits, the court is not going to liquidate. But if the firm shows terminal signs, the court will often appoint a trustee and follow with liquidation. Most Chapter 11s end in this fashion because the creditors demand it.

We had plenty of creditors who were making demands, and not just because I owed them money. They disliked me. They felt the debt was my fault, and many of them were owed substantial sums, enough dollars so that their companies were in jeopardy. I also had several former employees who spent a good deal of time talking to creditors and reinforcing their belief that I was responsible.

TWO KEY INGREDIENTS IN BUSINESS

My idea was to cajole the creditors. The bankruptcy attorney I hired had other thoughts. He insisted I stay away from them, and I listened. I should have questioned his judgement. Instead I acquiesced, and failed to use common sense and logic, the two most important ingredients in business dealings.

Common sense told me to visit the creditors, explain the situation, and calm and reassure them. Instead I stayed away. It was one of the major business mistakes of my life. It not only alienated me from the people who had control, but made it appear as if I was trying to dodge the issue.

There was another problem. Outwardly, I am not an emotional person. Not may capricorns are. I have always kept my feelings and emotions inside. On the road at the expos, whether we did good or bad, I never said anything to the exhibitors, nor did I socialize with them to any great extent.

If I ran into one in the evening, I would buy them a drink, chat for awhile, but I never discussed my personal life or feelings. As a result I was considered aloof, and after a time some exhibitors even believed that I thought I was too good to associate with them.

I treated creditors the same. My behavior, coupled with the drop

in sales, brought us to the verge of a court liquidation. The tighter our cash reserve became, the more difficult it was for the creditors to reach me. Occasionally, a creditor did manage to get through on the telephone, and despite my attorney's advice, I talked to them.

My temper got the best of me on more than one occasion. It is one thing to chew out employees, but you never get angry with creditors who have influence with the court. I did. In fact, I told more than one where to go. But arguing was never going to get me out of the mess, only increasing sales would. If I had it all to do over, I would have hired two, not one, attorneys. The first would have represented the company, and the second me personally. Utilizing the advice of both might have kept the creditors in a more congenial mood.

Instead, I stopped taking calls and started thinking about what I could do. More than once I have said desperation is the mother of invention. I was desperate; that's when I came up with the lifesaver. My idea illustrated the importance of businesspeople reading, studying, and storing information.

THE POSITIVE EFFECT OF A RECESSION

Credit for the company-saving idea belongs to my knowledge of recessions and how they affect business and consumers. Chapter 11 was filed during the waning days of the recession. Recessions may have a negative effect on most businesses, but they have a positive effect on some.

For example, the repair business thrives because people do not want to risk their funds on new items. They would rather hold onto their capital and get it fixed. Do-it-yourself stores boom as does low-cost entertainment such as records and motion picture videotapes. People do not go to expensive movies or shows during bad times, they stay home and watch television, listen to the radio, or rent a movie.

Analyzing recessions is relatively easy. What happens when people do not have money (or if they hoard it)? They cut discretionary spending and only allocate funds for necessities. If they cannot fix the plumbing, they have to call a plumber. If they can, they buy parts at a do-it-yourself outlet. There is nothing mysterious about it.

The entrepreneurial urge is still there, but people who contemplate opening their own business have their motivations changed during bad times. Instead of being driven by optimism (a product of good times) they develop a negative attitude, and are plagued by fears;

fears of losing their job, their house, and so on. They look on their own business as a security blanket in the event they lose their job, or as a second income, particularly if interest rates soar along with inflation.

Instead of taking the plunge, entrepreneurs tiptoe. They look for a low-investment business. Among the low-investment enterprises that thrive during recessions is multilevel marketing. Multilevel does exceptionally well during good times, as well.

It is a much-maligned industry, and some call it a pyramid scheme. It is however, legal, and for those willing to work at it there can be rewards with minimal cash outlays.

Multilevel is really a distribution technique. It is the way Shaklee and Amway sell products. Companies get independent distributors to sell products to others. Those distributors sign up additional distributors and if the new distributors sell product the old ones get a piece of the action.

The appeal of the business is that someone can build extra income through his or her efforts as well as through the efforts of others they have signed up. And they can do it with minimal investment.

It has another benefit. It is not a full-time job. There are some who have made it a full-time occupation and they have done extremely well, but for the most part the typical multilevel entrant works no more than 10 to 20 hours a week.

Multilevel thrives during inflationary periods. Families find they need additional income, and in a tight job market one way to increase income is by working on the side and selling products.

It is not unusual for an entrepreneur to build a multilevel business and generate monthly income in the four- and five-figure range with investments of less than $100.

However, there are disadvantages to the business. There is a high dropout rate. Nine out of ten distributors that sign up fail to do anything aside from buying a starter kit. The multilevel distributor has to find new distributors constantly and keep the old ones enthused if he or she is going to make money.

In early 1982 the U.S. economy was still struggling and multilevel was thriving. Stories about multilevel were not usually part of our editorial thrust. I stuck to new business opportunities, distributorships, and sometimes even wrote about franchises. But with the economy tight I increased editorial coverage in the multilevel area. In most issues we had at least one or two stories covering the industry and the latest opportunities within it.

When you depend on the mails for business as I did, you must be

cognizant of subtle changes in the audience. The most accurate barometer for me was our manual sales. At least once or twice a month I checked them to see what businesses were being purchased. Without fail mail order was always number one, but our multilevel offering had come close to matching the mail order sales figure.

Multilevel was on my mind, as was a business page story I had seen about a new company in the industry and how fast it was growing. To someone who was not an opportunist, those two items might never connect, but to me they were the signs of a way out of our financial crisis.

MULTILEVEL MAIL ORDER

An idea began to crystallize. There had been hundreds of different multilevel products introduced during the time I studied it. However, the distribution system remained the same. I decided to try something unique—multilevel mail order.

Our manuals could be sold through multilevel. We had 200 products, a nice selection for any distributor to sell. Over one weekend I developed a multilevel program aimed at our readers and subscribers.

In multilevel a prospect has to be sold on the worth of the product before he or she ever becomes a distributor or signs another one up. That is why it takes new multilevel enterprises a long time to get off the ground. They have to recruit, sell, and continue recruiting. It can be months, sometimes years, before a firm gets the number of distributors needed.

I did not have the time or the problem. The subscribers to *Entrepreneur* were already sold on us, and they had one other thing in common—they all wanted to make money.

TODAY'S TOP BUYING MOTIVATOR

They might read *Time* for the news or *TV Guide* for television information, but when they bought our publication there was only one motivation—greed. There is nothing unusual about greed and numerous advertisers appeal to it. That is why brokerage houses, savings institutions, and other types of investment offerings do well. They, too, play on one of man's basic emotions, although they may use other terms—"providing for your future," "earning what you

deserve," and so on. Beneath it all, however, is one of modern man's basic needs.

My plan was simple. For a registration fee ranging from $32 to $150 we would make someone a distributor. For the fee, they received a quantity of our catalogs. The catalogs were addressed, and all the distributor had to do was mail them. If the recipient ordered product (other manuals) the distributor would receive a piece of the action. The distributor's name was on the return card inside every manual.

It was a nice, clean deal. Distributors did not have to worry about carrying manuals as inventory. All they had to do was mail and wait. They could earn additional money by signing up friends and relatives to do the same thing. One of the prime selling advantages—and the reason the program did so well—was that distributors did not have to make any personal contact. In typical multilevel operations, distributors, if they are to be successful, must spend countless hours making contact with other potential distributors. In our multilevel plan, they did not have to spend any time recruiting. Everything was done through the mail. Typically, we mailed five million catalogs a year, and our mailing costs were astronomical. This would not only lessen the costs, but it would enable us to reach more people and, most important, generate the income we desperately needed.

In seven months I signed up more than 30,000 distributors. Some multilevel companies that have been in existence for seven years do not have that many.

We were swamped. I have never had a mail order piece pull as well. My first test mailing to potential distributors pulled 2,100% return on investment. I averaged 1,800% return on every mailing.

The response was so heavy that within a short period of time we ran out of our five million names and had to obtain others to satisfy the demands of our new distributors who were mailing our catalogs almost as fast as we could print them. In nine months I bought every list of present and potential opportunity seekers I could find. I wound up with 15 million names, the broadest audience I had ever addressed—and it would not have been possible without the multilevel idea.

We generated $1 million in distributor sales alone during that period. It was one of the best ideas I had ever come up with and I could see it becoming a major profit center. I could also see us raising the capital to pay off the creditors within 12 months.

Slowly, we began to climb out of our financial crunch, and we started putting money in the bank. But it was not long before the lists of opportunity seekers began to shrink, and I could no longer

send distributors catalogs and names. Eventually we had to drop out of the program, but before doing so the program saved the company. By the time we did, I had more than $1 million in the bank, and manual sales had returned to normal.

I credit most of the return to normalcy to two things. First, the short memory of consumers and the return of an upbeat economy. Consumers who received our mailings had forgotten the bankruptcy or considered it unimportant as long as we continued to supply the information they sought.

Second, and probably equally as important, our 30,000 distributors had mailed 15 million catalogs, and probably contacted another 100,000 prospects in person. Their energy kept us going and out of the grasp of liquidation.

Bankruptcy, however, is more than a game of earning money and paying off creditors. People who believe that still put their teeth under the pillow in hopes that the tooth fairy will arrive. Bankruptcy is a dirty game; a process that makes money for attorneys and accountants, takes power away from the shareholders of a company, and puts undue burdens on a company's management.

However, in business attorneys are a necessity. If you are going to incorporate and have a complex agreement, you need one. If you issue stock, you need one. If you enter into any kind of complex agreement, you need one. If you run a magazine, you need one to inspect the editorial content for libel or slander.

Business and bankruptcy attorneys are difficult to evaluate. It is hard to decipher how good a job a business attorney does until a problem develops. It is almost impossible to determine the worth of a bankruptcy attorney because you have no previous experience to compare them to, and not many firms go through bankruptcy more than once.

If you need a criminal, estate planning, tax, or another attorney who specializes in an area, there are thousands to pick from if you live in a major city, as I did. But if you need a bankruptcy specialist, you quickly discover there are not that many. They all know each other, and the bankruptcy judges know them, as well. It is, as one attorney friend suggested, a well-oiled club.

In one action a bankruptcy attorney might represent the company, in another the creditors, and in a third he or she might even be the trustee the court appoints. They jump from side to side. A criminal attorney always represents the defendant. That is not so when it comes to bankruptcy.

I found bankruptcy judges to be a breed apart as well. They had

one viewpoint—do what is best for the creditors. In some ways I cannot fault that attitude because it is the creditors who have been burned and they are the victims. But bankruptcy judges are short-sighted. They fail to consider the entire picture, and what might be best for all parties instead of just one.

It was disturbing to see the familiarity of the court's judges with several of the attorneys. It was even more so to see their disdain for others. Bankruptcy judges run a dictatorship, and in the midst of our case, when funding for the judge's salaries was temporarily cut off by Congress, I breathed a sigh of relief.

Chapter 11 was a three-ring circus. Everyone had an attorney—us, the creditors, and the shareholders.

Bankruptcy creates an unusual situation. When you put yourself in the hands of attorneys, you listen to them and take their advice because you are paying them. I never questioned our attorney because bankruptcy was alien to me and it was his domain. I thought it best to do what he said and keep my mouth shut.

Bankruptcy makes a business owner fearful. I knew the court could pull the plug at any time, and I did not want to make anyone angry. I should have.

To survive Chapter 11 a company must formulate a plan, submit the plan to the court for its approval, and that of the creditors. To put the plan in motion we had to rely on our attorney. It took almost two years to get a plan written and approved. During that time I experienced frustration, anger, and arguments with attorney and creditor representatives.

There is no greater boondoggle than the bankruptcy courts. Companies in bankruptcy can become money machines that feed a never-ending stream of attorneys and accountants.

While we were in Chapter 11 we spent more than $1 million in attorney fees. It was money that could have gone to creditors if a reorganization plan had been approved promptly. Bankrupt firms could develop payback plans in half the time if every judge required that no fees be paid the attorneys until a reorganization plan was submitted. Unfortunately, that is not the way it is. In most cases, attorneys are compensated as the case progresses. There is no time element, and the only possible pressure comes from the creditors. The system encourages abuses.

As the months went by, the creditors became more impatient and angry with me. I was the culprit, the delay. They began to believe that I would never pay their money, and if a plan was submitted I would unquestionably have a caveat within it.

I could not afford to devote all my energy to the bankruptcy proceedings. I had a company to run, a company that had been slimmed-down and was in the throes of once again becoming a moneymaking machine.

I no longer had the ability to do as I pleased. When I had shareholders to answer to, I could still run the company, and expand in the manner I chose. I owned more than 65%. But with bankruptcy, I no longer had that option. Major decisions that required capital outlays required court approval, which usually meant a hearing in which the creditors had a say. It is a cumbersome way to run a company.

I phased out the business opportunity shows despite the continued upbeat nature of the economy. Nothing lasts forever, and I could see attendance beginning to dwindle. We had burned out most of the markets. Most entrepreneurs had been to our shows once, sometimes twice. They had seen what they wanted, and bought what they needed. The third time we came into a city they started to stay away.

There may be 13 million small businesses in the country, but there is not an unlimited source of potential entrepreneurs. After a decade in the field, I had thoroughly analyzed the entrepreneurial market. With the lists we compiled at the shows, the inquiries we received, the lists I purchased, and the responses I generated, I calculated that the total number of potential entrepreneurs in the country was somewhere around five million. I also felt that it would regenerate—that is, replace itself completely—about every 10 years.

THE GROUP THAT SHAPES BUYING ATTITUDES

A good portion of the business opportunists had come from the 18- to 30-year-olds. As previously stated, it is this age bracket that shapes the attitudes for the entire country. The 18- to 30-year-olds develop attitudes and preferences for some products or particular designs. When it spreads throughout this age group, the older consumer begins to look at it.

Those 40 and over know they are "going over the hill" and try to emulate attitudes and preferences of the younger consumer in an effort to recapture their lost youth.

This does not, of course, happen overnight. For example, take the hippie attitudes of the 1960s. The hippies fostered peace and love. They abhorred stress caused by jobs or conditions throughout the world.

By the early 1970s a number of things happened because of the hippie influence. Executives in companies (those 40 and over) started emulating hippie dress. They wore raggedy clothing and jeans, discarded ties, and grew longer hair.

Clothing manufacturers saw this attitude change, and they took advantage of it by making jeans for "those over 40." Today, it is a jean with "a skosh more room."

Some executives went far beyond the clothing and hair change. They quit their jobs and dropped out of society. They went to mountains and farms, where they hoped they could escape stress and the pressures of a modern world.

None of this happens overnight. The percentage of those accepting the change grows as time passes. Some, of course, never adopt the change and remain the same, but there is a much larger percentage that eventually follows the lead of the 18- to 30-year-old.

Interestingly, many of the so-called yuppies of the 1980s are really the hippies of the 1960s. They are the hippies who found their attitudes changing when they had to go to work and conform to society. They have done a complete reversal from what they were in the 1960s, which is not unusual. But yuppies do not influence or create new attitudes. They are simply adopting the standards that have been out there for years—they work for a living and seek material rewards.

Yuppies have abandoned their hippie leanings, and not surprisingly. The young (18 to 30) are more idealistic. As they get older, reality sets in and they find that idealism does not work too well. Consequently, they change. They become more conservative.

Certainly, a percentage of the hippies have never changed. They remain in rural areas, they may live on farms or in small towns, and they retain their liberal ideas.

But Abby Hoffman is certainly not one of them.

Hoffman, the hippie turned businessman, is an example of how attitudes modify as one gets older. There is less rebellion and more of an attempt to get along with society.

TAKING ADVANTAGE OF ATTITUDES

To sell products, the mail order marketer has to look at today's 18- to 30-year-olds and their attitudes, because those attitudes will soon be adopted by older consumers.

Unlike the hippies, today's 18- to 30-year-old is not trying to make

an impact on society. They are, for want of a better term, the "punks" and the punk attitude is "we cannot do anything about it (society), so we will just make fun of it, laugh at it." Outrageous hairdos and hair colors are examples of a young person laughing at society.

The punk attitude, which started in the late 1970s, is one of the most fascinating to come along. There are significant ramifications for the mail order marketer.

The punk attitude probably developed because of a frustration over the youths' inability to change anything. They are the first generation of Americans to realize they live in a mass, computerized society in which they can do nothing.

They see all the negative news and feel they cannot change it. This is in marked contrast to the hippie who wanted to change things and made an effort to do so.

The hippie was also nonviolent and nonmaterialistic. The punk movement has an underlying theme of violence, but punks also realize that anything violent will hurt themselves.

In other words, the rebellion is more internal than external. From a marketing standpoint, the punks have affected several areas. Obviously, clothing is one; many in the 40-year-old bracket (and above) have already adopted the punk dress code.

Punks have also affected entertainment. They are into the 1950s, and we see a host of music and entertainment programs (e.g., "Crime Story") that have made an impact.

Beyond clothing and entertainment, however, the punk impact is minimal but there are some implications on the horizon. In Europe the violence has become overt. College students are demonstrating as they did in the 1960s, only this time it is a violent, not an antiviolent demonstration.

The demonstrations are all part of a frustration that youth has in which they feel governments cannot answer their problems. Terrorism is on the rise, nuclear weapons continue to proliferate, and the younger person is frustrated. Eventually, the European-type demonstration with its violence may make an appearance on American campuses.

Now, what does all this mean to the person in mail order? The punks want to achieve, and they are after goods and status. They are an acquisition-oriented market, not a market that will save for the future. They want the goodies now so they can show them off to friends.

The punks will continue to be a heavy purchaser of goods and will

dominate the marketplace until the mid-1990s when, perhaps, there may be a change in attitude.

Until then, however, those marketing (and especially those marketing through the mail) will prosper. The range of products that are acceptable through the mail has been broadened, as well.

HOTTEST TRENDS TODAY

For example, technological goods are accepted in stores and through the mail without question. Computerized toys will grow by leaps and bounds, along with other high tech items. Mail order firms in the area have a phenomenal future, particularly those that will be marketing items that relate to "war games" or "survival games."

These games are two of the hottest new trends around today. War games enable the consumer to become a participant outdoors in a sport that certainly has a violent underlying theme.

Consumers run around 20-acre plots of ground, shooting paint pellets at each other and representing different armies. The winners are those who come out with the least pellet marks. The game stems from our growing fascination with violence. Television, with its tremendous number of police-oriented programs, has not satiated that need.

We want more, and war games are it—for now. Upcoming is another hot business called "photon." It is a game that can be played in a studio and participants shoot lasers at each other. Each person wears a hat, and when they are "hit" by a laser, a light goes on in the helmet and they are out.

It can be played on the streets with photon equipment that is already on the market, or it can be played in 10,000-square-feet of space. It has already become the rage in Japan, as in Toronto. It will not be long before it becomes one of the most popular activities in this country. Christmas 1986 saw a dramatic demand for the photon guns and hats in this country. It was the sleeper of the toy season.

By the time this game does become the rage in the United States, we may be looking at variations ranging from people sitting in model airplanes to running a "synthetic" war. These games and activities represent the consumer's desire to be more actively involved. There is a movement away from spectator and toward participant.

Obviously, photon equipment and accessories are mail order opportunities for the future, however there are others.

We live in a society where it can take 20 minutes to drive 2 miles.

People have to stand in line and put up with clerks and salespeople who know little about the products they are selling.

TIME AND CONVENIENCE MOTIVATORS

Catalogs are a convenience. People will opt for mail order rather than wait in line and waste time. Time and convenience are critical motivators today—and will be tomorrow.

This change is already obvious in the number of television shows that are being aired in which consumers can pick up a telephone and order merchandise. In the future most of our shopping will be done from the home.

The home market will not escape retailers, either. Most will branch into it, and the reason is the revenue that they see through the mail. Twenty years ago, if a company such as Texaco was told they could pick up $100 million in revenue through package inserts being mailed to their customers, they would have been insulted. Today, however, no one scoffs at the value of inserts. Mobil generated $375 million last year through billing stuffers, and every mail order company is into the same thing.

Mail order has gained a new respect, and will grow rapidly because of the success of statement stuffers and catalog mailings. This does not mean mail order entrepreneurs are going to be crowded out of the market. On the contrary, they are going to find more willing and believable consumers on the receiving end.

The key, however, is for the mail order marketer to carve a niche for himself or herself. The major (or mass) merchandisers are selling the common, ordinary items—the radios, stereos, televisions, ladders, air compressors, and other materials that can be found without trouble in a store. They have no creativity and are not interested in pioneering a new product. They make enough off the existing items they offer.

The mail order marketer has to pioneer and find something different. The market that shops in the store is not the same as the one that buys through the mail. The mail order market grows yearly, and that means opportunity.

Consumers also have more confidence when buying through the mail. Twenty years ago, if they were burned through the mail, their money was usually lost and there was no place they could go to complain. Today there are dozens of agencies and policing tech-

niques. They know they can get their money back and are not afraid to order.

But to get that order you must market something unique, something consumers cannot find without problem through their local retailer.

IMPACT OF CYCLES ON MAIL ORDER

Whatever you market through the mail, beware of cycles. They come and go, sometimes quickly. When a cycle ends there is nothing that can be done to extend it.

After five years my business opportunity expos had come to the end of a cycle. I could have continued putting on smaller productions in hotels and/or motels, but the effort was not worth the potential rewards.

My expos were not the only enterprises that had cycles. All industries do. Sports have cycles that run 10 to 12 years. Bowling was a rage for a decade, then it died for almost 15 years. Now it is back.

Roller skating came back after 20 years. The exercise craze brought it back. Tennis and golf are interesting sports that have had peaks and valleys. Tennis, for example, was a giant sport in the 1920s, and then it died down. Neither sport died out completely because they are activities that can be taken up by both the old and young. They can be played throughout one's life.

Professional football is starting a down cycle. It will not die out but it is going to wind down slowly during the next five to six years due to a combination of boredom and fan disenchantment with high salaries, exorbitant ticket prices, and outrageous player behavior.

Exercise is another activity that is fading. The 18- to 30-year-old dropped jogging long ago. Older consumers, that is, those 40 and over, are still into it, but not the younger market. It is on the way out. People have discovered that getting up every morning and running around the park or in circles is not fun. Consumers do not continue for a long period of time with any activity that is not fun.

Studies show that Americans are more cognizant than ever of weight and exercise, yet there are more overweight people in the United States than at any time in its history. People do not always do what is best for themselves. Exercise is boring. Certainly there will always be the hard core that continue to cycle and jog, but exercise is losing its appeal.

I would not plan on trying to sell any products that relate to exercise or fitness for at least another 10 years.

The exercise craze was, in reality, only an excuse for young people to meet young people. Now, the 18- to 30-year-old has found another way to meet people that is less strenuous and more fun. I'm referring to the diners and cheaper restaurants that have developed over the past few years.

They are places that sell hamburgers, some health food, and some even have discos. None are expensive dinner houses. A typical meal is $4 to $5 (dinner). They are loosely run and the customer can get up and walk around and socialize.

At the same time, bicycling, roller skating, aerobics, and health foods restaurants are slowly dying. Once again, it was the 18- to 30-year-olds who brought life to these ventures. Those who were over 30 felt awkward in the health clubs. Now they do not because the younger people are not in them anymore. In time the older generations will abandon these activities and will look for some other new activity—an activity they will copy from the younger generation.

REASONS PRODUCTS "GO"

Convenience has been one of the prime reasons for the success of new products during the past decade. It will continue to be a key determinant in forecasting whether a new business or product will be a success or failure.

Cycles are all around us. Forty years ago, one of the biggest businesses was the mom and pop grocery store. Supermarkets emerged and wiped them out. A decade ago we saw a resurgence of a store that was similar to the mom and pop operation—the convenience store. They charge up to 50% more for the same products you can purchase in a supermarket, yet they are incredibly successful. Why? Convenience. They are time-savers. We have become obsessed with saving time.

The old hardware store has died and in its place is the huge Builder's Emporium, Ole's, National Lumber, and other similar super-hardware operations. The old ones died because they could not carry the growing number of products that were being sold to consumers in the home remodeling and do-it-yourself field.

Television stores of two decades ago have given way to the video store of today. Instead of a small mom and pop operation where an entrepreneur sells a few televisions and fixes your set, the video

store, with its gadgetry and diverse selection, has taken root. Repair has become secondary, but it has not disappeared. Should the economy suffer another recession, the repair business will make a swift comeback.

Trends and cycles. I reported on all of them during those early Chapter 11 days. I structured special mailing pieces on some of the hot new glamorous businesses we researched.

Computers had captured the imagination of the public, and we developed eight computer-related manuals to take advantage of the trend. They ranged from computer consulting and desktop publishing to computer repair and opening a software store. Most of those businesses are commonplace today, but in the early 1980s they were new and unique to the public, and thousands of them were sold.

Business was booming, but I was having more problems with our bankruptcy. The best way to get out was to submit a plan. We delayed, and problems began to emerge in late 1983.

It had been more than a year since our Chapter 11 filing, and our situation had come to the attention of several companies that eyed *Entrepreneur* as a takeover. Naively, I did not worry at first. How could any company takeover us when I owned more than 50% of the outstanding stock? However, in Chapter 11, normal business rules do not apply.

Shareholders are last in the pecking order when it comes to bankruptcy. Whether I owned 65% or 95% of the stock meant little. A company could come in, buy the obligations owed to the creditors, become the new creditor, and petition the court to dissolve or liquidate *Entrepreneur*.

If liquidation took place, the firm that owned the creditor obligations would be the recipient of the proceeds. There would be no company for me or any of the other shareholders to own.

It was devious and outrageous, but no one ever said business was fair. The offer was presented to the creditors. The suitor would give them approximately 70% of the funds owed and become our new creditor. I was in a vulnerable position. My new CEO had suddenly resigned. Our controller passed away, another board member resigned, and the firm was without any officers and had only one director.

There was an additional problem. Our accounting department discovered that we were due funds from our list rental subsidiary. The subsidiary was a firm I had established several years previously. I put an old line employee in charge, and gave him a percentage of the profits in addition to a salary.

Whenever the list was rented, *Entrepreneur* received an invoice with the amount due on it. Over a period of several years, we had received numerous invoices, but apparently there were funds generated from the rentals that were never paid to us. As owner of the list rental company, the responsibility fell in my lap. The matter was ultimately resolved, but before it was the creditors had one more reason to view me with suspicion.

The chaos at the company almost sealed our fate. I was angry and frustrated. I was sitting on top of an investment worth $3.5 million and was about to lose it.

When there is trouble in business, rules and ethics seem to disappear. At one point a former executive proposed a deal. He would give me $100,000 a year for 10 years if I would turn my shares over to him. I was ready to bodily throw him out of the office.

I realized that if I did not move quickly, everything was going to fall apart. I found another president, put him in place, and named two additional directors. It was not enough to appease the creditors. They were seriously weighing the offer they had received.

We countered with a payback plan that would give them 100% of their money over a three-year period. To sweeten the offer, I also offered them one share of stock for every $1 in debt we owed to them. It meant issuing two million shares of additional stock, and it would dilute the shareholder's interest, but it was better than liquidating and coming out with nothing.

The shares won them over. Our stock had dwindled to less than 25 cents, but the thought of owning a piece of the company intrigued them. They agreed and we began negotiating the plan for formal submission to the court and the creditors.

The conditions were stiff. There would be a seven-man board. I could name three directors, three others would come from the creditor's committee, and a seventh member, the chairman, would supposedly be a neutral member agreed to by both the creditors and management.

It took weeks of delicate negotiations to put the final plan together. Finally, however, the creditors approved it, and the court gave it its blessings.

It would take nearly three more years before *Entrepreneur* paid off its debts, but the debts were paid off—and the $15 million a year company I had started with a $44 ad a decade before would be saved.

8

How to Find Opportunities

During the decade that I ran *Entrepreneur* there was one thing that became obvious to me about those who search for a niche in mail order or any other business—they miss opportunities because they fail to see the connection between two seemingly separate events.

For example, shortly after launching *Entrepreneur*, one of the forecasts that earned me national notoriety was my prediction that bicycling would become a national craze.

It happened one day while reading the morning newspaper. I saw a small item in the newspaper that said the import of foreign bicycles was up 4%. I called the Department of Commerce and asked where the bicycles were coming from and what kind they were. They said the imports were primarily 10-speed bikes. That sparked my curiosity. Ten-speeds were rarities in this country. I started checking local bicycle shops, and although few were selling them, 80% of the dealers I checked said they were getting more and more requests for the foreign bikes.

I decided to check back in a few months to see if there was a trend. When I did, I found the orders for 10-speeds had increased dramatically, and nearly every bicycle shop had them back ordered. That's when I made a prediction that the bicycles would become our next big craze.

I wrote a manual on how to open and operate a successful bicycle shop. It was one of the first I authored and sold through *Insider's*

Report, and it was one of our best sellers. It was easy to see why. Within a year after I had made the prediction, the bicycle industry hit an all-time high sales figure of more than 15 million bicycles.

LENGTH OF CRAZES AND WHAT THEY ARE

Crazes, however, do not last forever. Three years later I came up with another forecast that was equally as accurate as my bicycling prediction.

It was no wild guess, either. I came upon it while walking along the Santa Monica pier. I saw a dilapidated shack that was being overrun by hordes of anxious young people. As I moved closer, I could see what the owner was doing—he was renting roller skates!

Four weeks later I saw a small item on the business page of the *Los Angeles Times*. It described a company that had shown a phenomenal increase in sales and earnings primarily because of its sales of roller skates. The shack on the pier immediately came to mind.

That afternoon I called a trade association to which most of the roller skate manufacturers belonged. I obtained the names of several firms in the industry, called each, told them I was writing a story about the growth of the industry, and began to ask questions about their sales.

HOW CRAZES START

The most significant item was that most of their skates were being sold to stores in and around college campuses. When I found that college students had discovered roller skating, I knew we were onto the beginning of a new trend, because colleges, high schools, and younger kids are usually the first population segment to pick up on new ideas and trends. I made the forecast and within a year it became a fact.

There was nothing ingenious about it, but I was hailed as a seer for a prediction that seemed to come out of my hip pocket. I had simply put together two events, a crowded roller skating rental store and a small item in the newspaper, and came up a winner.

Be curious and ask questions. To be a success in mail order you must be aware of what is going on around you and what people need.

The exciting thing about observation and uncovering trends is that

they almost always bring new business (as well as mail order) opportunities with them.

For example, roller skates opened the doors for the skate rental and repair business. The 10-speed bicycle demand created enormous opportunities for importers, retailers, and service shops. Those businesses created mail order opportunities as well. I sold manuals on both roller skating and bicycle shops. Others saw the trend and began to sell bicycle and roller skating accessories, ranging from seat covers and custom tail lights to helmets and gloves, through the mail.

About the same time that roller skating entered the market, computer stores began to appear. Today these stores are commonplace, but look at the hundreds of computer-related products that are sold through the mail today.

HOW TO CASH IN ON TRENDS

Cashing in on trends is a matter of observation. My ability as an observer goes back to my youth in Tennessee. I spent time playing mind games. I would see a leaf fall, and try to imagine how dead leaves could be put to use. Far out? Perhaps, but that is the type of mental process it takes to get ahead in the mail order field.

There are, of course, other ways to develop ideas for new products and markets aside from watching leaves fall. As a youngster I would read items about new products in a magazine, and would then try to imagine how the item could be used on a farm or in the city. Was there a use for it? Remember, there are untold numbers of products; the key is to find a use and a need.

Shortly before I founded *Entrepreneur* I sold furniture for a company in Los Angeles. I saw an opportunity by putting two seemingly unrelated developments together to create a new business and an opportunity.

Salespeople worked hard when they dealt with customers. They not only had to find the furniture and correct color preference, but they had to have credit applications filled out and approved also. On more than one occasion, I saw salespeople close a deal and lose a sale because the financing fell through. This was especially true in our store, which had strict credit standards.

I pondered our lost furniture sales and the stores that would be anxious to have the names of the customers we had to turn down because of insufficient credit. I took a half dozen of our rejected contracts to a store in another part of town. I explained that we could

not handle the paper, and asked if they would be interested in the business if I could deliver the customers to their door.

They were excited about the thought of having presold customers delivered to them. We worked out a financial arrangement in which they agreed to give a me a 25% commission on all the "turndowns" that we delivered to them and they sold.

I began to make calls to customers who had been rejected by the credit screening. I never told them their credit fell through. Instead I said everything was fine; however, we were out of the furniture (or model) they had ordered, and it would be some time before we could restock the item. Would they mind going to one of our other affiliated stores? There would be no change in price.

The "affiliate" was, of course, the store we had "wholesaled" the paper to. When the customer arrived, the store simply sold them either the same furniture (if they carried it), or switched them to something similar.

It worked perfectly. During the next four months I sold paper to other furniture stores and earned our outlet more than $40,000 in commissions with below par credit risks.

Opportunities. They are all around. The furniture outlet I worked for was called "Living Rooms, Inc." A salesman I knew wanted to open a store next door to Living Rooms and call it "Bedrooms, Inc." His ingenious idea was to let Living Rooms do the advertising and his customers would be supplied by the marketing efforts of the store next door.

He theorized that if people came in to buy living room furniture, there was a good chance they needed bedroom furniture as well. The concept was good. Was he devious? Was he taking advantage of a former employer? Not really.

Today you see the same approach taken by people in dozens of industries. Did you ever notice how many Burger Kings are located within a few blocks of McDonald's, or how many Kentucky Fried Chickens are located within a short walk of Wendy's?

USING SOMEONE ELSE'S MARKET RESEARCH

One is taking advantage of the market research the other has done. If there is enough traffic to warrant the placement of one fast-food restaurant, why not two? In the heyday of cheap energy, gasoline stations used the same premise. Having gas stations located on four corners of the same intersection brought more business to each. A

gas station that shared a crowded intersection with three competitors did better than if it had the intersection to itself.

Market researchers say it is a matter of "consumer psychology." I disagree. Consumers prefer choices. They would rather go to a location that offered two, three, or four similar products than to an area that had only one. That principle is especially true when it comes to mail order *catalogs*. The more (related) items you have in a catalog, the higher each sale will be. I'll illustrate that point in Chapter 9.

Understanding the mail order buyer's desire to make a choice and not be restricted is nothing more than common sense. All of us like to choose. Having common sense is critical in mail order. If you have it, the business becomes much easier to master. Without it, there is a tough road.

Fortunately, I was blessed with common sense. My first mail order venture succeeded because of it. I was a teenager, and I had saved money while working at a Christmas tree lot. With the funds, I bought several hundred electric motors at a bargain price. The amount I paid was so low I could afford to sell the motors for $9.95, which was about half the normal price. I purchased a one-column, one-inch ad in *Popular Mechanics*, which has a large number of do-it-yourselfers as subscribers. They were perfect prospects for bargain-priced $9.95 electric motors. I had never written an ad but that did not stop me. I thought about a headline. The price was the best feature of the product, so I put it in the head. But price alone is not good unless it is accompanied by the item that is being sold. So I structured a simple head:

"Electric Motors $9.95."

The price combined with the item sparked the reader's curiosity. The remainder of the copy told how much horsepower each motor had and how to buy one. I also put in a money-back guarantee. I used the guarantee because everyone else did the same thing, and because common sense told me that people would wonder about the quality of a motor that was so cheap. I alleviated the doubts with a guarantee. I sold every motor within three weeks.

Common sense and observation were responsible for my involvement in my first multimillion dollar venture. It was during the late 1960s, and for years magazines that covered the furniture field had promoted wall paintings to consumers. There was a problem, however. Other than cheap prints that sold for $9.95 at the drug store, a

consumer could not buy a good print for under $100 which, at the time, was a significant investment.

During the 1960s, Mediterranean style furniture was the rage. Every specialized magazine was pushing it, and every tract home, apartment, and condominium was furnished with it.

The artwork featured in the magazines went along with the furniture styles—there were Spanish galleons, conquistadors, and similar prints. The average consumer, however, could not afford the high-priced art, so furniture stores carried replicas.

In the midst of this I ran into a manufacturer who produced actual oil paintings that could be sold for under $30. Amazingly, the paintings were painted and produced on a production line. He had developed a system whereby there was a silkscreen outline for each picture. The design was put down on the canvas so the artist could follow it and fill in the colors through a process similar to "paint by numbers."

If there were 10 colors on a painting, he might have 10 artists on the line. Each artist would only paint one color, and with a few strokes he or she would be finished. The painting moved down the line to the next artist. As a result, oil paintings could be cranked out in six minutes.

At first, I did not see the potential of the paintings. To me they were just another product, and as I have said, there is no scarcity of products in this world. I should have immediately recognized the potential, but I did not. Instead, it took hours of convincing by the manufacturer and my partner.

I was an art afficionado. I was far from pleased at the array of paintings the vendor brought with him. He tried to convince me of their marketability by hanging some on the back wall of the furniture store where I was working. I could not imagine them selling.

Snobbery? It was. That can be a fatal disease in business. Reluctantly I studied the paintings. I was convinced we would need a unique marketing gimmick in order to sell them. I did not believe people would come flocking into our store to buy replicas. I had to get the paintings to the people. Without saying a word to my partner, I hurried to the local building supply store, bought some oil cloth, 2 × 4s, and c-clamps. I took the canvas home and painted a message on it.

Oil Paintings . . . $5.95 Up . . . Must Sell . . . Artist Starving

The next morning I loaded a station wagon with the paintings that had been left, drove to a nearby vacant gas station, rolled out the canvas, mounted it, and waited. In the next five hours I sold 15 paintings, nearly every one for more than $5.95 (most for over $25) and I became a believer in the product.

PSYCHOLOGY AND SALES

The sales did not happen simply because of the location. There was psychology involved, just as there is psychology in every sale.

I put all the large paintings (3 × 4s and larger) out front. The $5.95 paintings were small, and were all in the back. I used the large paintings, which sold for $25 and more, as traffic stoppers.

My basic colors were the current, most popular hues—orange, avocado, blue. I never put two similar colors next to each other because they would blend together and would never stop the consumer's eye.

Initially, I had no idea what price consumers would be willing to pay for the paintings. If a shopper came through and did not buy, I trained our salespeople to let them almost walk off the lot, then pursue them, say they "really needed the sale" and would they take it for $25 (or whatever). If not, the salesperson would let them almost get to their car, then he or she would run up and offer to drop the price another $5.

To make the product more appealing I developed a story about each painting; its background, and so on. The salespeople were trained to relate the story, and the tale gave the paintings more character and warmth.

The stories also gave consumers something they could take home—in addition to the painting—and relate to friends who came to their house and saw the painting. Oftentimes it was the story that became the sale's "closer."

The success generated through these tales is another illustration of the importance of stories when selling people products. It does not matter whether they are being sold furniture, paintings, or a mail order product. Stories intrigue people. They pique the curiosity level. I have used them effectively in dozens of mail order campaigns, and they are one of the most important ingredients in an ad.

During the next month I sold paintings as fast as we could buy them. We averaged 30 a day, and the typical price was $25 to $30

each. As the Christmas holidays approached, I added two additional locations.

My partner was convinced that the demand was a result of holiday gift-buying. I believed something entirely different. I had analyzed the appeal and had my own theory. The specialty magazines were pushing paintings that no one could afford. We offered an affordable alternative that looked as good as the expensive oil paintings.

"Starving Artists" was a gimmick, too. Today, selling goods out of a gas station is commonplace, but when I originated the idea in the late 1960s it was new and caught everyone's attention.

Despite our success, my partner was concerned. We had accumulated a growing inventory of paintings, and he could see us eating hordes of cheap replicas once the holidays had passed. He suggested we curtail our art purchases, and start moving the remainder of the paintings into the store where they could be displayed and sold after the Christmas season.

My feelings were the opposite. I believed we were sitting atop a multimillion dollar fad. I countered with another offer. I would give up my interest in the furniture store in return for Starving Artist ownership.

It was one of those gut-feeling decisions. I had made them several times in the past, and I would do the same in the future. Sometimes they paid off, and other times they did not.

In this case my partner jumped at the proposition. He could not believe his good fortune and neither could I mine. We parted company just before Christmas 1967. It was the last time I would ever worry about a partner.

My first move was to buy my supplier's business. He had been at it for years and never did much more than eke out a living. He was tired and ready to give it up. For $900 I took title and had access to his artists and production people.

Starving Artists did not afford me the luxury of a four-hour work day. I was constantly running from production line to retail outlets. I knew three locations would never be enough to develop a business that paid well.

The moment I had our art production line straight, I went to a local Exxon representative. The way oil companies work, they have reps for every gas station, and a gas station cannot do anything without its rep's approval.

I convinced the rep that we could bring in a lot of traffic—and we did. Selling paintings at open stations increased our sales dramati-

cally. Our average went to 40 paintings a day. The Exxon dealer increased his business by 22% in less than two weeks.

That was all I needed. The representative arranged for us to make a presentation to a regional manager and other representatives. The regional manager went back to headquarters to tell national managers about the effect the artwork had. He even took movies of the crowds at the station. When he came back, we had national approval to set up Starving Artists at any Exxon station in the country.

I took the Exxon permission letter and went to other oil companies, where I was given almost immediate approval. Before long we had the rights to exhibit at virtually every high-volume station in the country.

The business mushroomed at an incredible rate. I had the proverbial tiger by the tail. Despite working 16-hour days at the production facility, we still had a problem keeping up with the demand. I rented a huge warehouse, five times the size of the original production facility. Within two months I was looking for more space.

IMPACT OF A FAD

Starving Artists was a fad. I was realistic about that. Each year as we came back to display our wares, sales dropped. The impact of a fad such as Starving Artists is good for a year, perhaps two. I sold in the third year.

The demise of the business was due to several factors. There were competitors, and consumers have a saturation point. It was a unique concept when they first saw it but after passing stations for a year, it lost appeal—but not before it had made me a multimillionaire.

Today, Starving Artists has changed to Starving Artist Galleries. The concept has changed, the paintings are higher quality, and are sold via auction. The idea of upgrading the operation had occurred to me before I sold; however, I was only interested in marketing to the masses. I have never been fond of concentrating on a specific economic bracket.

Although many mail order marketers prefer targeting a group (this is the age of specialization), I recommend marketing to the masses. *Entrepreneur* was limited to a specialized group, those interested in opening their own businesses. After 10 years, I realized the largest universe (customer base) we could reach was 5 million people. Develop a product for the masses, and your universe is unlimited. I'm talking about 200 million versus a few million.

Starving Artists was for the masses. At the same time, it was a fad. When you jump into an enterprise it is important to understand whether you have started a fad business or one that has longevity.

Fads die quickly. They are short-lived and difficult to take advantage of unless you are the first to see them coming. Remember skateboard parks? When I forecast the emergence of the parks through *Entrepreneur*, I made it clear that the business was a fad—and an expensive one.

If you are marketing a product to a sports fan, study the difficulty of the sport. Is it something that is easily mastered? Does it bore people after a short time? If so, get in and out—quickly.

HOW LONG DOES A FAD LAST?

Fads may last 18 months, perhaps 2 years. Skateboard parks lasted around a year, but people were carried away by the popularity of the skateboard. They thought as long as there were skateboards there would be skateboard parks. Limited partnerships raised $500,000 to $600,000 to construct the parks, and for two years the owners of the parks pulled in the dollars.

Fads can die quickly, often without warning. When the interest in skateboard parks waned, it happened almost overnight. Owners and investors in the parks found themselves with incredible amount of debt, and the only thing they had to show for it was a cement park, complete with curves and jumps, that could not be used for anything else. They became financial disasters.

Those problems could have been avoided if investors had been more obj.~tive. Learn to discern the difference between a business with potential and a fad that will only be around for a year or two.

I never worried whether any of the mail order businesses I created were fads or not. In mail order, if you watch your ads and returns, the demise of a product never comes as a surprise. If an ad works, it will pull immediately. If it does not pull the first time out, it never will.

RETURN PERCENTAGES TO LOOK FOR

There are certain return percentages needed for mail order products. If your ad fails to meet the percentages, pull it and get out. For example, with *Entrepreneur* I always counted on a return of at least

150%. That is, if the ad cost $1,000, I expected to get $1,500 in orders. Realistically, that is not a great return, but it is meaningful because at *Entrepreneur* we had a significant backend, and could sell customers up to 10 times their initial order through future orders. With a strong backend you can afford to break even or even lose money on an initial mail order ad or direct-mail piece.

The longevity of ads vary. My "Who's Making A Bundle?" seemed to go on forever as did the first ad ("Science Has Finally Counterfeited a Perfect Diamond!") I wrote for Van Pler & Tissany. Actually, "Who's" and "Science" each lasted about the same length of time before they died (three and one-half years). For a space ad, that is a significant period of time.

Few, however, can match the late Joe Karbo's full-page ad that he created in order to sell "Lazy Man's Way To Riches." It is a prime example of the longevity of a good mail order ad.

Karbo was a car salesman who made a lot of money and then went broke. He kicked around for several years, barely making a living. Then he came up with an idea for a book, an instructional book that would tell people how to make money through mail order. His full-page ads are masterpieces of copywriting. They tell one long, fascinating story.

Karbo put it together a decade ago, and it made him millions. He passed away several years ago, but his family runs the same ad and it still pulls. That type of operation is only possible in the mail order field.

In 1983 I found a 20-year-old opportunity that showed as much (if not more) promise than Karbo's "Lazy Man's Way To Riches." On the front page of the classified section of a local newspaper I saw a full-page ad for simulated diamonds, more commonly known as cubic zirconias.

The ad sparked my interest. I am an opportunist, as all mail order enthusiasts should be. If you see something that appears to have potential, give it a second look. I did with the "CZs" and was amazed at what happened.

The stones had been on the market for nearly two decades, but no one had been able to sell them through mail order. They had, of course, been sold through department and novelty stores, but no mail order marketer had been able to create a successful business with them.

When I saw the product I was not looking for a revolutionary idea. At the time, I was searching for a mail order product that was drawing response, and I intended to revise the product, rework the ad,

and launch a new business. Borrowing someone else's idea? Perhaps, but the best mail order ideas are either out in the marketplace or are variations of existing ideas.

At *Entrepreneur* I traveled throughout the country giving seminars to mail order marketers. If you want to get into mail order, scan the magazines and mail order ads that are running. Find advertisements that are repeated; that is a sure sign the product is being sold. Rewrite the ad and see if you can say it better and sell the product more effectively.

Most mail order mavens already have a product in mind that they want to sell. Usually they came to the seminars with their ideas scribbled on matchbook covers or scrawled clumsily on scratch paper.

UNPROVEN PRODUCTS—ARE THEY WORTH IT?

One of the roads to mail order success is to find a new and unique way to sell a proven item. Try to avoid marketing unproven products.

I talked myself blue trying to convince the seminar attendees that inventing a new idea is putting the cart before the horse. There are many good products already in the marketplace that are filling needs. Start with a proven item. When you make enough, you can play with your own idea.

The desire to market an original idea has cost mail order marketers millions of dollars. Most successful enterprises sell a variation of what someone else is marketing. They may make a few changes in packaging, name, ad approach, and the appearance of the item, but the similarity is there.

Fortune 500 and other established companies do the same. Think of the number of jeans that are being sold and how much they all look alike. The same is true of toothpastes and automobiles. How different are the breakfasts that are being sold at fast-food franchises?

Smart marketers never reinvent the wheel.

The CZ ad I saw was poorly put together, but it was intriguing. I could envision millions of consumers being interested in purchasing an "affordable diamond"—artificial or not. It was also an item for the masses.

As I do with any item that intrigues me, I study it. A friend showed me one and I was amazed at the cubic zirconia's resemblance to a diamond. It was polished and brilliant. Jewelers had a difficult time telling the difference between a fine, polished CZ and a diamond.

Despite their appeal, no one had been able to use mail order to mass market them.

The ad I looked at was no exception. It ran once in one daily publication, a second time in a national weekly, and then it was pulled.

I knew it was not working, but why? My instinct told me that here was a product with a multimillion dollar future.

I began to research the history of CZs. I went to the library, called a trade association, and read several jewelry magazines. Long ago, I learned not to jump into something simply because it appeared to be an opportunity. Find out if it really is one. I replied to several of the CZ mail order ads and sent for the stones they were offering. In mail order, ordering from competitors is commonplace. Whenever I see a mail order item that appears to be of interest, I respond. At *Entrepreneur* I sold manuals to individuals and firms that not only purchased so they could inspect our approach, but also to determine the possibilities of becoming a competitor.

I was astonished at the stones that arrived. They bore no resemblance to the CZs my friend had. These were unpolished, poorly packaged, and they suffered in comparison to a diamond as well as a polished CZ. When set in a ring or necklace, the flaws were obvious to the naked eye.

One satisfied customer can create 10 additional mail order sales, while one unhappy buyer can kill 100 potential sales.

It was obvious that buyers were disappointed at what they saw when it arrived in the mail. Even worse, they probably bad-mouthed the stones to friends. Mail order marketers make this mistake often. They obtain a product at low cost, and insist on making more profit than necessary. They may cut the quality of the packaging or produce a substandard product.

Quality has a tremendous impact in mail order. Even low-priced goods depend heavily on the perception of quality when sold through the mail.

The CZ marketers looked upon the stones as a get-rich-quick scheme. There is no such animal when it comes to mail order. Sell quality and look for repeat business. Because mail order affords the marketer anonymity does not mean they can get away with selling inferior goods.

IMPORTANCE OF QUALITY

In mail order you must be quality-oriented. Too many believe they can get away by fulfilling orders with marginal goods. It may work

once, but never again. "Take the money and run" is the wrong approach. The mail order marketer who operates under that philosophy misses out on additional purchases by the buyer.

In the case of CZs, the additional purchases—or back end—could be 10 or 20 times greater than the initial buy. Most worthwhile mail-order products offer the same benefit—a strong back-end or repeat sale. The idea behind the CZ ads was to sell a consumer a stone at a low cost, and then have it sent back to be set. By designing the appropriate follow-up, a CZ marketer could sell bracelets, necklaces, rings, and pendants, and be setting the stones for buyers for years to come.

But a buyer who is disappointed with his or her goods is certainly not going to send the stone back to the marketer to be set. Yet, the CZ companies could not exist without the back end. They were not getting it.

I also believed that the mail order marketers were trying to sell the stones to the wrong market. Some companies were selling two-carat CZs in tabloids such as the *National Enquirer*. The *Enquirer* is great for certain types of mail order products, such as good luck charms, hernia medications, astrological charts, and so on, but not CZs.

If a buyer has no functional use for a product, he or she will not make the purchase regardless of how good the ad or appealing the offer.

CZs had a definite audience, but I did not believe they were reading the *Enquirer*. For example, someone who has been unemployed for six months is not going to buy a CZ for his wife simply because it is low-priced. The reason: None of their friends would believe it was a real stone. How could anyone buy a diamond if they are out of work? (Even if they did, it would be a ridiculous purchase and their friends would think them fools.)

CZ buyers were not in low income brackets. A two-carat stone in the hands of someone who was not making enough money to afford a real one lacks credibility. No one wants to be laughed at, and those consumers in lower income brackets would be laughed at if they purchased and wore the stones.

The market for CZ buyers were consumers in the middle and upper income bracket. I believed that but I did not just go by belief. I tested.

When test marketing a *new* mail order product, select isolated markets that are not havens for mail order marketers. Obviously, it is difficult to ascertain the havens for mail order entrepreneurs unless

you have been in the business for awhile. Typically, the major cities and the southeast are the home for most mail order marketers.

When testing the appeal of a *known* mail order item, you can use markets that are not isolated.

Testing in an isolated market gives the marketer some measure of protection against other mail order entrepreneurs who might be looking for ideas to copy. I am not interested in being ripped off before I get the product off the ground.

For example, I felt CZs would sell to an older market. Ft. Lauderdale, Florida is an ideal locale for this age bracket. If CZs had not been around for 20 years, I would not have used Ft. Lauderdale, because it is loaded with mail order entrepreneurs. The stones, however, had become commonplace and there was little chance that a mail order marketer would even notice another CZ ad.

THE BEST TEST MARKETS

There are certain markets that are excellent for testing. For instance, Dallas is a good predictor of the southwest. California, Oklahoma, and Kansas are also good.

Houston will also predict California—both are melting pots and growing cities. There is, however, an important distinction between melting pots and growing cities.

Melting pots (such as Houston and Los Angeles) draw population from all over the country. They are cities that show rapid growth. Growing cities (such as Dallas) are cities that draw most of their population from nearby areas.

In general, cities with rapid growth are melting pots. Houston drew because of NASA, which was the key. Contrast this with Chicago, a midwest market that has remained almost the same for the past 20 years. It gets an influx of people from the surrounding area, but immigration is low; most people are natives or from the immediate area.

As a test market, Washington, DC is an excellent east coast indicator; Ft. Lauderdale is good for the south and retirees; Shreveport, Louisiana is a typical southern market; Hutchison, Kansas a typical rural, farm-oriented area.

If a product test works well in a big market, it is no indication that it will sell in a small market. To determine if it will, use the *Editor & Publisher* guide and compare the profiles of the market.

For example, if you have sold a cosmetic product in a market, you

can assume that another, similar product will do well in the same city or area. If I sold *Entrepreneur* start-up manuals in one city, I knew I would be able to sell business tapes to the same market.

Although I have been in the mail order field for years, I still consult the guide to see if demographics in cities are changing. It has saved—and made—me millions of dollars.

I found the market for CZ buyers were consumers in the middle and upper income brackets. Obviously, someone with money would not be scoffed at if they suddenly showed up with a one or two carat diamond. Friends would believe the stone was real and would never question them.

Retirees were another market. If a person is living in a retirement community, few friends or acquaintances know their financial situation. They have no idea as to how much money they might have made when they were working. A retiree could wear one and not have anyone question whether they could afford it.

The initial marketers of CZs overlooked the "usability" factor in mail order. Few buy products so they can place them in a drawer.

WHY MAIL ORDER PRODUCTS FAIL

Mail order items can fail because of poor research. Before I market anything, I learn everything there is to know about it. Any good salesman does the same thing. It is impossible to sell a product through the mail, if you know nothing about it.

You must know how it works, what it does, what problems it solves, how it will benefit the user. Those are all questions that must be answered in a one-step mail order ad, or in the follow-up material that goes to prospects who were generated through a two-step ad.

In addition to my time at the library, talking to trade associations, and reading, I had heard about an ABC-TV *20/20* news show. A reporter had taken a CZ to the diamond mart in New York, and showed it to a jeweler along with a top quality real diamond. The jeweler was unable to tell the difference between the simulated stone and the real diamond, and said that "both were counterfeits." That was a powerful argument and gave top quality CZs, or simulated stones, enormous credibility.

But CZ marketers refused to take advantage of the edge the media had given them. Instead of selling quality, polished stones they took the easy way and fulfilled with unpolished, faulty gems.

The ads I saw were poor as well. They were full-pagers and ex-

pensive, but that does not mean an ad will draw. Every CZ ad I saw was cheaply put together. It had poor graphics, horrendous type styles, and huge white spaces with unbalanced headlines.

The marketers were trying to sell a simulated diamond, a stone that could replace a real diamond because it looked so good. Yet the ads looked cheap and poor. The ads reflected on the CZs they were trying to sell. The ad, although it was a full-page, looked cheap. Therefore the buyer construed the product as being cheap, too.

In addition, my research had shown that the market for the stones was the middle and upper class. This bracket would be instantly turned off by a poorly constructed ad.

Mail order has come a long way, but post office boxes are still suspect. You need as much credibility as possible when trying to get people to put money in an envelope. A P.O. Box does not enhance a consumer's opinion of your company. In many cases it makes them worry about where their money is going, and if they will ever see the product.

Credibility was important, especially in the case of the CZs. I needed a well-known address, an address that would lend stature to the product. Where else but Beverly Hills? There is not another name in the world that signifies riches, luxury, and class as much as Beverly Hills.

The selection of a name for a mail order company and/or product can be the difference between success and failure. I spent days jotting down ideas, forming combinations of words and sounds.

For the simulated jewelry company, I decided on Van Pler & Tissany. It had a sound, a ring to it. Later, a number of people told me they thought it was an established jewelry store they had heard of years before.

WHY PEOPLE BUY

Mail order sells for reasons such as practicality, romance, status, health improvement, and moneymaking.

A diamond is sold on the basis of romance, status, and its investment potential. A CZ does not have investment potential, but it does have romance, practicality, and status.

Status is a potent motivator for mail order. I sold millions of startup manuals through *Entrepreneur* on the promise of making money and gaining status. One went with the other. Start your own busi-

ness, make money, be admired, and have your friends look up to you when you are successful.

Starving Artists offered consumers status at a low price. Cadillac offers status, as does Mercedes. In today's marketplace, where attitudes about money, homes, and cars are paramount, status is a critical element in the sale of any product.

If you can offer status at a low price, as was the case with the CZs, you can have a phenomenally successful product. Status itself is never mentioned in the ad. However, it is implied, with phrases such as the "discerning few," which one well-known automobile manufacturer always uses.

I used "charged" words in the Van Pler ad. There was a sentence towards the beginning of the ad that read "the super rich were the first to buy Van Pler Diamonds as replacements for their expensive jewels."

If the super rich buy it, the stones are good enough for the rest of us.

It took me three hours to complete the full-page ad. I write rapidly when I know what I am talking about. I think the same is true for anyone. If you have the knowledge and can relay it, ads do not take long to put together. It is only when you lack knowledge that it becomes a struggle to write.

Whenever possible, mail order headlines should be newsworthy. My headline for the full-page CZ ad read "SCIENCE HAS FINALLY COUNTERFEITED THE PERFECT DIAMOND!"

It was called a scientific breakthrough, which is about as newsy as a headline can be.

There has always been controversy over the length of a headline. I believe a headline can be any length (within reason) as long as it piques the reader's curiosity. That means you do not have to condense a head into three or four words. It can be a sentence as long as the diamond headline.

The purpose of a head is to arouse curiosity. It can be two words, and if it does the job, fine. It must intrigue readers and get them to go on. It cannot be misleading. What is promised in the head must be given in the body copy of the ad.

With every headline, I use all capitals.

I followed it with numerous subheads. They told the entire story. If someone only read the headline and subheads, they would get the message. The first subhead read:

"Thousands of Jewelers and Pawnbrokers Fooled—It Cuts Glass!"

The second was courtesy of ABC's "20/20."

"ABC's 20/20 News Team Fools New York Diamond Mart Expert"

Each of the remaining subheads was designed to tell a story and pique the readers' curiosity in hopes they would go back and read the entire ad.

"Top Economist Says Consumers Would Be Foolish to Buy a Mined Diamond Now!"
"$15 a Carat for This Sales Only—Selling in Europe for $100!"
"Limit Per Customer—No Orders Accepted from Jewelers or Dept. Stores!"
"New York Magazine Says, More Beautiful than Mined Diamonds!"
"Expected to Be Hottest Gift of the Year!"
"More Indestructible than Mined Diamonds—Lifetime Warranty"
"Postdate Your Check for 30 Days—Free Inspection in Your Home!"

The subheads also addressed every possible objection and question a buyer might have. In a one-step, never leave doubts in the prospect's mind. ABC and *New York* magazine gave us credibility, the price relayed affordability, and the postdated check was my personal guarantee.

There is psychology in the well-written subhead. Limiting orders says to the buyer that the stones are going to be bought up quickly. They cannot delay, or they may miss out.

"No orders from jewelers or department stores" has an underlying meaning as well. It says that these stones are such a bargain that jewelers and department stores would be willing to buy them at the same price. The same ploy is utilized in other areas where the advertisement has a line that says "no sales to agents." It gives the buyer an impression of value.

TEASING THE BUYER

I try *not* to tell the entire story in the first few lines. I always tease and tantalize readers, and lead them from paragraph to paragraph.

Television does a marvelous job of teasing. Just before a commercial break in a television show, there is always something interesting going on, a reason why the viewer should stick around. "Dallas" did

an excellent job of teasing with its "who shot J.R.?" episode that ended one season and began another. Almost every television soap has adapted the same technique, and attempts to give the viewer a reason to tune in for the first episode the following season.

Whoever came up with the "Dallas" ploy would probably be a good mail order copywriter. Their sense of timing and what keeps people interested was on target.

I use the same technique in the direct-mail letters I write. At *Entrepreneur* I would send out four- and five-page letters, tease the reader, and get them to the last page where there was one logical conclusion—to order.

My CZ ad had those elements. I also use plain, easy to understand terms. I avoid multisyllabic words. It has nothing to do with talking down to an audience, but short, concise, recognizable words mean you will not lose readers.

The creation of a CZ may have been a scientific breakthrough, but you would never want to use technical terms to describe it.

I also take liberties in ads. They may be done in news style, but I use adjectives, which are seldom found in a news story. The ad should be filled with facts and information, but it should never be dry reading. Straight news stories are difficult for consumers to stick with. Good mail order ads have the news element, but they are embellished just enough to keep the reader's interest.

In the Van Pler ad there were statements such as "Now you can have jewelry that will truly impress everyone you meet" (adjectives and opinion). "Imagine a new wedding ring with a big, dazzling Van Pler Diamond" (adjectives and opinion).

In blending the two, the mail order marketer has to be careful not to go overboard and have the ad read like a full-page of hype. The objective news element must be present throughout.

Still, an ad needs excitement. I do not mean sensational, blaring headlines, but an ad has to move and motivate people. It has to announce something, make them aware of a product and the benefits it contains. And it has to make them want it *now*—that takes excitement.

WHAT IS AN OFFER?

Every ad still has to have an offer. I do not mean the product you are selling, but the offer that is being made to the prospect. Marketers sometimes confuse the two. The product in my ad was the diamond.

The offer was the bargain, $15 a carat, money-back guarantee, post-dated check, and free inspection. Those are offers. They are what ultimately sell the consumer.

One wrong word, a misleading line in a subhead, or the failure to sell an offer instead of a product, can kill an ad. There is no one line in an ad that works better than another. You must have them all. Mail order ads must flow and have a cohesiveness.

Graphically, an ad should be easy to read, and it should fit the image of the product. In all the CZ ads I examined, the typestyles were too diverse and the white space too obvious; the overall ad appeared as if it were thrown together at the last minute.

The Van Pler ad is an example of how graphics should be used. I prefer all capitals in the headline, but I use capitals and lowercase in the subheads.

There is white space so the prospect can easily follow the subheads, but there are no glaring holes.

One of the major departures between my ad and that of my competitors was in the term CZ. I wanted to get away from the mundane and traditional. Consumers had heard the word CZ. The term cubic zirconia is hard to pronounce, has no rhythm to it, and is unromantic and dull.

I changed it to the Van Pler Diamond.

Later, I ran into trouble as a result of complaints from jewelers who felt that consumers had the impression I was selling a real diamond. To alleviate the concern, I changed the name to the Van Pler Diamond X.

My first test ad was in the state of Washington. It was in a small town with a population of 40,000. The ad cost was $700 for a full-page in the local newspaper (circulation: 10,000).

The response was phenomenal. I generated 500%, or $3,500, in orders. I contained my enthusiasm, however, since one market does not mean you will be successful nationally. Before going on, I selected another market with similar characteristics, only with a higher percentage of retired people. The city was in Florida and the response was even better.

I tested two additional markets with a heavy percentage of white-collar workers. Both did extremely well. I found that the Sunbelt, because of retirees, was an exceptional area for the Van Pler Diamond, as was Florida and parts of the west coast.

In general, if a test goes well in the north, it will do well in the west. The west is the easiest market to penetrate. The northeast is the toughest because of its conservatism.

Once people respond to a mail order ad, the most important thing to overcome is buyer's remorse. We all have it. To overcome it, some marketers send thank yous or order acknowledgements before the product even arrives. I went one step farther—I made sure that every order was shipped within three days after we received it. That was an unheard of response time but I felt it was extremely important. Too many mail order companies take weeks to fulfill. Legally they may be within bounds, but they turn off the buyer.

WHEN TO DELIVER THE GOODS

When buyers order, they want it *now*. The longer you take, the more rapidly their interest fades. This can be especially critical with mail order operations that run a high percentage of CODs. If the order takes three weeks to reach a buyer, there is an excellent chance he or she will not accept it. That's why so many mail order COD operations run an astounding 50% return rate.

The best way to satisfy customers is to respond quickly and give them more than expected. Previous CZ marketers did exactly the opposite. I went overboard because I was counting on the back-end and repeat business.

Another element that contributed to the response was the fact that Van Pler could not be bought at the corner drugstore. There were thousands of outlets that marketed CZs, but none had the Van Pler Diamond.

That does not mean you cannot market items through the mail that are sold in stores. You can, but the price must be extremely competitive or the approach unique. If the Van Pler were a stone that could be bought at Sears, I would not have generated the response that I did. Prospects would have been spending their time comparing prices instead of clipping the coupon and mailing it.

Within a few months I was placing ads in most daily newspapers. When I tallied the results from my roll-out I was astounded. There was not a newspaper in the country that returned less than 200%. In many cases I had 800 to 1,000% returns. Even with my best-pulling ads for *Entrepreneur*, I never approached that kind of return.

I was inundated with business through the mail and at our store in Beverly Hills. We never did any consumer advertising for the Beverly Hills store, yet our business averaged more than $1,000 a day. Why? Because of our ads and catalogs that went to buyers. It contained our address, and many buyers preferred to stop in at the store

and see what was there. The mail helped the retail. It will do the same for most products.

I designed our Beverly Hills showroom so that it resembled those in the downtown jewelry mart. The showroom was dark, with black walls. The display case was dark as well. The blackness added to the lustre of the gems.

I installed closed-circuit cameras, the same equipment found in the mart. It all combined to give Van Pler & Tissany an authentic appearance. The stones were artificial but the store looked genuine and it paid dividends.

In mail order when you sell goods and use an address to help sell the product, you will get walk-in traffic. Some buyers want to be able to pick up the goods and feel them. They want more than what is pictured in a catalog.

I pioneered numerous advertising concepts with *Entrepreneur*, and I did the same with Van Pler. I was the first mail order marketer to take a full-page mail order ad in *USA Today*. No one had ever done it before and I understood why. It was a $15,000 investment. Selling stones from $10 to $60 requires a significant return to just break even.

Actually, the *USA* buy was not risky. In the months since I started selling the stones, I had a chance to examine the profile of our buyers. There were significant numbers of professionals and businesspeople.

USA Today has a heavy male readership. The majority of our buyers were male. This is in contrast to most merchandise offers, which attract primarily female buyers. The heavy male response was due to the headline, which stressed the "scientific breakthrough." It was loaded with logic and evidence. Women buyers are more motivated by emotional and romantic headlines and body copy.

USA Today also appeals to professionals and businesspeople. Equally as important, the majority of its circulation was newsstand. That meant the purchaser of the paper was serious about reading that particular day's edition, and there was an excellent chance that he or she would see my ad.

But nowhere in *USA Today* could I find any mail order ads. Why? Simply because no one had tried it. The publication was still relatively new. Other mail order marketers had examined it but they did not want to be the first to take the chance. To me, however, the publication was ideal to reach our market.

The vast majority who bought our stones were men who wanted to give their wives or girl friends a diamond without the insurance expenditure or worrying about theft. A number had even sent letters to us asking if we could duplicate a real diamond necklace or bracelet.

They wanted to keep the authentic goods in the safe and use the Van Pler. It was a practical decision by consumers who were facing increasingly high insurance rates.

I saved hundreds of thousands of dollars in advertising costs by placing all my Van Pler ads on a standby basis. Standby, which simply means your ad waits until there is a last-minute cancellation by another advertiser, can save mail order companies anywhere from 30% to 70% on the cost of the ad.

Most publications have standby rates. The only disadvantage with the system is that there is no way to predict the day it will run or its actual placement.

To give you an idea of the savings, one of the major metropolitan newspapers in Los Angeles can be purchased for $2,500 for a full-page on a standby basis. Contrast this with a page in the *Los Angeles Times* that runs around $16,000 without standby.

The original Van Pler & Tissany space ad pulled for more than three years. It ran seven and eight times a year in some daily newspapers, and the response seldom dipped below 200%. When it did fall, I cut the size of the ad (from a full-page to a half) in order to reduce the amount of response needed for a profit.

In 1987, I began testing another full-page space ad. This sold exactly the same products; however, it was geared to draw women. I had not purposely ignored females; however, the first headline I constructed was more appealing to men with its scientific thrust. The new ad I created had a headline that certainly piqued the interest of females. It read:

"What are Nancy, Liz, Jackie and Joan Wearing?"

I had another line right under the main headline that read:

—and Prince Phillip, too??

In addition, the ad was loaded with credibility. I had quotes from *New York*, the *Wall Street Journal*, ABC-TV, and several others.

Is it working? I do not know; however, I should have the answer by the time this book is published. If it goes the way I think it will, then Van Pler & Tissany could easily double its $6 million gross—the amount of sales we generated during our first six months of business, a figure that gives you an idea of the potential of an old mail order product that is repackaged and marketed to a new audience.

9

Getting Your Foot in the Door

The success of Van Pler & Tissany is an example of how rapidly a mail order company that develops the right merchandise concept can grow. It also illustrates—even more than *Entrepreneur*—the importance of back-end sales.

For more than three years, I sold loose stones successfully through the same one-step, full-page space ad that I outlined in Chapter 8. Selling half carat Van Pler Diamonds for $15, and one-carat stones for $25 was the first step, but the pricing was certainly not high enough to account for our phenomenal dollar volume.

What brought in most of the revenue was the back-end offer I made to every loose stone buyer. Earlier I discussed the importance of a mail order product's "usability."

What do you do with loose stones? Obviously, they have to be mounted in rings, pendants, bracelets, or some other jewelry. Not many buyers purchased loose Van Pler diamonds so they could stick them in a drawer. Most were interested in a setting.

A Van Pler & Tissany catalog accompanied every loose stone order. The catalogs, which started with fewer than 30 items, eventually grew to more than 200, and I was producing a revised edition every other month.

The catalog was filled with rings, necklaces, pendants, bracelets, watches, and every other type of jewelry imaginable. There was a special offer with the stone that buyers received along with their

catalog. If they purchased one of our settings, they could return their loose stones for full credit.

Nearly 80% of those who bought the stones returned them for credit and ordered a piece of jewelry. The $15 order was followed by a catalog order that averaged $177.

Obviously, one of the reasons for the ease of sale was the appearance of the initial stone I sold to our buyers. It answered the buyer's expectations.

MAGIC OF A POSTDATED CHECK

There were two other elements of our offer that convinced buyers that we were trustworthy. First, we let the buyers postdate their checks for 30 days. Second, we promised to ship goods within three days after receiving the order.

A company willing to accept a postdated check and ship within three days is a rarity in this business. Those promises cost but they were worth it. Occasionally, a buyer would send us a bad check, and I had to have an adequate, well-trained shipping department on hand at all times.

But nothing is as important as rapid fulfillment in mail order. When customers purchase products through the mail, they want them *now*.

Certainly, they know it will take time to fulfill, but the mail order marketer has stimulated their hot buttons, and they want the goods as soon as possible.

Unfortunately, the longer it takes for them to receive the product, the cooler they become toward it. They lose interest. They want to enjoy the product immediately. If they wait four to six weeks for delivery, there is a good chance they will return it.

With Van Pler & Tissany, my return rate is less than 1%. On the other hand, the average mail order company will run 10% returns because of their delivery delay. With CODs the return rates are much higher.

Doing everything to get that first order to the customer not only cuts returns, but it enhances back-end orders. Customers look at your second offer and they do not hesitate because they know they will receive it without delay.

The postdated offer does not result in hordes of returned merchandise, either. Less than 1% of those who purchased loose stones returned them for a refund. As for bad checks, less than 1% of those received bounced.

There is another factor that accounts for the low rate of bad checks—the audience. Van Pler & Tissany sells primarily to middle-aged and older consumers, many are retired, and few are "hustlers." Most are average law-abiding citizens who do not believe in passing bad paper. Before making a postdated check offer to customers, carefully analyze the potential market to ensure that returns or bad checks will not be too high. On the other hand, some mail order marketers run into hordes of bad checks because of the audience they are approaching. Selling get-rich-quick schemes usually attracts fast-buck artists who are prone to sending bad checks.

VALUE OF AN 800 LINE

In the catalog there was also a toll-free 800 number that customers could use to order additional merchandise. These 800 numbers can be a boon and a disaster. Initially, I retained an 800 service. They handled all our incoming toll-free calls from across the country. The 800 number enables prospects to act when they want; in other words, there is no delay or cooling off period.

On the downside, it is difficult to find a competent company with 800 lines. Operators are usually not highly paid. They must handle a variety of orders, they work different shifts, and they often get one product confused with another. This happens all the time despite the fact that most 800 operators work with a computer that has all the information they could possibly need about your product.

For three years I struggled and tolerated an 800 service. Early in 1987 I installed in-house 800 lines with trained salespeople. There was an astounding difference. Our average order jumped nearly 50% to more than $240.

The difference was not because of high pressure, however. Our buyers, when they used the 800 line, had catalogs and were seldom first-time customers. They were familiar with the company, its quality, and its rapid delivery. When they called they were ready to order. With that type of customer you do not want to twist arms or use high pressure. A simple suggestion ("had you thought about the matching bracelet to go with the necklace") was all it took.

I also give telephone salespeople leeway. They can create offers and discounts (as long as they follow company policy) of their own. It is, as I said, the offer that people buy.

The salespeople had one other thing that the customer could not find on our first 800 lines—product knowledge. That has become

critical in today's marketplace. How many times have you entered a store and found a clerk who could not answer a question about a product? How often have you decided to buy something and a clerk was unable to tell you the difference between two closely related items.

Frequently, of course. That's one of the problems with most retailers today, and a prime reason for mail order's growth. If you cannot get the answers when you take the time to go to the store, why bother? You might as well order through the mail.

Imagine the mail order company, however, that can provide the answers. At Van Pler & Tissany our telephone salespeople are trained. When customers call, they get every question answered and unlike many operations, by the time they hang up they feel comfortable about the order.

Although the full-page Van Pler & Tissany stone ad is a one-step, I equate it with a two-step. It is similar to the one-step subscription ads I placed with *Entrepreneur*. At *Entrepreneur* the idea was to get someone to buy the magazine initially; then we came back with our laundry list of manuals. This enabled us to up our average customer order. If customers bought manuals first, they might not purchase a subscription.

I used the same technique with Van Pler & Tissany. I did not send the jewelry catalog until the loose stones had been bought. The loose stones were the qualifier, the first step. If customers had initially seen the catalog, they might never have bought a loose stone, nor would their order have been as high. By delivering a quality, loose stone in a timely fashion, we enhanced our credibility with the buyer. They seldom hesitated to spend money after that.

The catalog was incredibly successful. Every mailing brought back seven to eight times our cost. It is similar to two-step marketing. If you get 100 inquiries off a small ad and you are selling a $40 product, you might sell 25 to 30 people with the right follow-up material. With a one-step, the ad might cost $2,000 and you would be lucky to get 50 people to respond.

With a two-step ad you can have less talent as a marketer and still succeed because of your follow-up material. With a one-step, full-page ad you have to hit the right media and customer the first time out—you do not get a second chance.

TELEVISION AND MAIL ORDER

Space and catalogs are not the only techniques for selling mail order products. The success of Van Pler & Tissany enabled me to explore

other ways to market the stones. Television intrigued me. It was never good for the business opportunity expos, but I felt it had possibilities for jewelry.

Although the typical 60- to 120-second direct-response commercials are still around, I was fascinated by "testimonial" type productions. They are all over the screen, especially on cable. Typically they are productions in which there are guests who talk about an opportunity, investment, product, or the like. There is usually a moderator who asks questions, and one or two guests are on hand to give testimony to the fact that they utilized the product (or whatever) and were successful with it.

At the conclusion of the show there is a toll-free 800 number that can be utilized to order the product or get involved in the opportunity. It is really a half-hour commercial made to look like an interview show. I loved the approach. It reminded me of the supplement we ran for *Entrepreneur*'s business shows.

The supplement and television show were both ads, but to the reading (or viewing) consumer they appeared to be editorial. They left viewers with the impression that the station had put the show together, not the owner of the product or investment opportunity.

Millions of dollars worth of books, tapes, real estate courses, and dozens of other opportunities are sold through this method. The producers, or owners of the show, usually work a barter arrangement to get the show aired. They may give the station up to 50% of the gross sales of the tapes or other products that are sold. In other cases, they may buy the time outright.

Cable television has become a competitive medium, and owners of stations are not all doing well. They are willing to barter and negotiate the sale of time. Fringe radio stations offer the same opportunity. The marketer can find stations in major markets that will sell half-hour blocks of time off the rate card.

Marketers using this approach have no commercial cost other than putting the show together. It is one of the newest and most creative ways of selling goods. It succeeds because it does not appear to be an ad, and whereas consumers are quick to switch off a 30-second radio or television commercial, they will watch a show that appears to be entertaining and informative.

I felt I could sell our stones the same way. I decided to put a new twist to the technique. Instead of making a half-hour, self-serving special on diamonds, I put together one that had more objectivity to it. It was entertaining, as well.

I hired an experienced crew, versatile producer and director, and

talented writers. They put the production together and included a segment where ordinary shoppers try to tell the difference between a Van Pler stone, a CZ, and a diamond. I wanted viewers to understand there was a difference between a CZ and a Van Pler.

I used celebrities as hosts. Politicians long ago discovered the value of a celebrity in a political commercial. They have credibility. They may no longer have it in political spots because they have been overused, but they do when it comes to variety and talk show programs.

To the average viewer our show is a legitimate, half-hour special. It is not a commercial. I retained one commercial spot at the end of the production for Van Pler & Tissany. The station could sell the remainder. The show cost $75,000, but it could double our business. Editing is being completed, and we will begin selling the show to independent television and cable stations shortly.

Our spot will have more impact when it is seen as one of three or four on the same show, instead of being the only commercial. Consumers recognize that there may be a relationship between commercials and endorsed products when they see the spot repeated continuously.

Once the television program airs, I expect to see even more competitors than we presently have. Knock-offs, however, have never bothered me. There are too many variables in an ad for someone to master, unless they copy it word for word. They may study one of my ads, substitute words, and change things around, but it will not impact our business.

If you are the first in the marketplace with a hot product, you will continue to dominate the market regardless of how many imitators come along.

CAN THEY RIP OFF YOUR IDEAS?

Imitators cannot hurt, but marketers who come along and put a new twist to an old approach certainly can. That is what I did when I started marketing the CZs. At least seven other people were selling the stones at the same time. None had the concept I did, nor did they think of upgrading the image of the stones and shooting for a higher income market. Eventually, I knocked every one of them out of the business.

Their approach was selling someone a stone that looked like a diamond but was cheaper. Not many consumers buy cheapness, especially when it comes to gifts. We do at the retail level when we see

the same brand of cereal advertised at one supermarket for 10% less. But brand name cereal can be compared, CZs cannot.

The success with Van Pler led me to explore the possibilities of marketing other imitation jewelry items. Once you have one winning product, it is easy and inexpensive to test additions to the line. In many cases it is imperative to add products. If I had failed to add manuals to *Entrepreneur's* catalog, the company would never have grown. Catalogs have to vary and differ. You cannot send the same material to the same buyers month after month. There have to be changes and additions—and new products.

If I had failed to add to *Entrepreneur's* catalog someone else might have come along, studied our approach, and entered the field with a rival publication that produced a greater variety of manuals that we did. I was never going to let that happen.

For Van Pler & Tissany, I found synthetic emeralds. They were even more realistic looking than the CZs. In Van Pler's case, I simply added a page to our catalog and continued mailing. Within a few weeks after the catalog was mailed, I had more than $400,000 on hand for emerald orders. In the next catalog I introduced pearls. I revamped the approach, and showed settings with emeralds, pearls, and diamonds together.

MAIL ORDER CATALOGS AND ADS—WHAT THEY SHARE

A mail order catalog is no different than a mail order ad. If the ad does not pull, you either change it or drop it. In a catalog, you must measure the income and response of each page and item. All items must pay for themselves and provide a good return. If an item stops pulling, we drop it from the catalog. If an item shows an excellent return, we give it more space. Only the winners survive. That's true with catalogs as well as businesses.

At Van Pler & Tissany our catalogs usually ran 36 pages, including the cover. To print, we might spend $40,000, plus another $20,000 for art and mailing costs. I took the total dollars expended for the catalog, and assigned a cost to each page. Within that page, each item incurred a cost. The more space it had, the more revenue it was responsible for generating.

If each page cost $2,000, I measured the return it generated to see if it (1) not only paid for itself, but (2) compared favorably with other

pages and items in the catalogs. Was there a page that drew twice as many sales as another? If so, it was clear evidence that buyers preferred the items on that page, and it was a sign that we should be giving those items more space in the next catalog.

I measured every page and item, regardless of whether they were new or old. We were able to introduce new products because customers had come to trust us, and believe that what Van Pler & Tissany sold was of value.

Most of the time, I tried to introduce products that had a certain amount of synergism with our established line. I introduced a line of "x," or slightly lower-priced jewelry. I created a full-page space ad for the "x" line and found that most of the ads, although profitable, seldom pulled more than 150%.

I was pleasantly surprised when I created a four-page mailer on the "x" and sent it to our existing list. Our 800 lines were flooded. Orders averaged close to $100, in contrast to the space ad orders which were around $50.

Once again, it was a matter of trust. Consumers who had bought from us previously knew us for our quality. They knew that although the "x" line was inexpensive, it was quality.

Interestingly, our "x" mailer aided our catalog sales. Recipients of the piece would call to place an order, and our salespeople would bring up our most recent catalog, ask if they had received it, and then ask if there was anything in the catalog they wanted. In about 20% of the cases, an "x" jewelry caller ended up buying both.

Not every product works in mail order and some produce such strange results that it is better to abandon them. I ran into one such product while searching for items that would go well with our jewelry.

I had been intrigued with collectibles. I saw firms make millions during high inflationary periods when gold and silver were the investment favorites. I also saw many of those firms survive and make an impact in good times.

I was looking for a collectible, something that would stand out from the rest, an item that could be marketed successfully.

In reading the financial pages, I had come upon a number of stories that were covering the sales decline of companies that were marketing collectible reproductions or specialized limited editions. Companies selling collectible coins were being hit the hardest.

One reason was that consumers had gone through a period of being besieged by coin (and other similar) offers. I find limited edition solicitations in my mailbox every day. After a while, consumers begin

to suspect the value of the edition, and they question just how limited the edition actually is.

THE NOSTALGIA CRAZE

By handling the marketplace in such a fashion, collectible marketers were burning it out. For the past decade, there has been a nostalgia craze sweeping the country. Music of the 1950s and shows depicting the era have become hits.

Consumers are hungry for original, antique items, items that reflect the good old days, simpler times. In lieu of those times they readily accept reproductions, but too many firms had cut corners.

In this environment I could see original collectibles selling but not reproductions. The product I sought would have to be an original with a true, limited supply.

I found it while reading. It was in an item in a newspaper that reported on the discovery of a cache of Roman coins that had been found by a British farmer while plowing. Some of them were more than 2,000 years old.

NOT ALL NAMES ARE THE SAME

If consumers are willing to buy coins and collectibles from the Franklin Mint, why not an authentic, 2,000-year-old coin from the "International Heritage Museum"—the name of my new company.

The success of *Entrepreneur* and Van Pler & Tissany is illustrative of the importance of a good name in mail order. What better name than International Heritage Museum? Most consumers regard museums as legitimate, nonprofit organizations that are out to preserve history. You do not have to be a museum to call your company one, nor do you have to be an association to call your mail order operation by that name.

I formed IHM. As was the case with the simulated diamonds, I spent days in the library researching Roman history and collectible coins. I called several coin associations, talked to dealers, sent for catalogs, and in a few weeks I became an authority on the subject. Once again, if I am going to sell something, I want to know everything about it.

I also decided to do some consumer research. Unlike the CZs,

coins required a substantial up-front investment. Before I bought a cartful, I wanted to show the product to people and get their reaction.

I obtained a small quantity of the coins and showed them to a number of people. I was only looking for one thing: their reaction. I did not care if they said they would buy or not. You can tell by someone's reaction if they are interested, and if they show interest they are a prospect. Interest comes into the picture long before price.

Everyone was fascinated by the coins. The historic value and charm of the item intrigued them. That told me something else—if they reacted to the coins in person, there was a good chance they would react to the coins in an ad, if the product was pictured. Describing Roman coins is one thing, but being able to see them is totally different.

Some might say basing an entire campaign on the reaction of a few friends is foolish, but I chose the respondents carefully. There was a cross section of people, and I knew them well. If you can find a cross section of consumers in a variety of economic brackets, you do not need 100 or 1,000. I can tell more from 10 people I know well than from 1,000 strangers who answer a survey.

It took me four weeks to negotiate for the sale of the rest of the coins. In the meantime, I started writing the ad. The similarities between the coins and my Van Pler & Tissany ad are apparent.

The headline:

"Hoard of Roman Coins Found in Potato Patch!"

Then came the subheads:

"Museum Offers Part of Incredible Discovery to Public!"

The credibility. I went on to tell the story of how a farmer in England had uncovered the coins, and how rare they were. My subheads took the reader through the ad, much as the subheads in the Van Pler & Tissany ad did.

You can own a 2,200 year-old ancient Roman coin!

Orders limited to 4 coins per person

400% increase in value in 10 years!

Magazines and investment advisors say coins best investment!

Tremendously undervalued—limited supply!

These coins are real—not reproductions

Museums's decree: available to individuals only—no dealer

30 day free examination—credit cards accepted

Limited quantity, first-come, first-served basis

Notice the similarities in the jewelry and coin ads. Limiting the amount of orders, endorsements from the media (magazines), the guarantee, and free examination. The ad stressed the rarity of the coins and their investment value.

I was selling practicality, romance (Old Roman coins), and status. The 400% increase appealed to one of our oldest motivations—greed. I backed the statement up with facts from investment houses.

Notice, too, that the museum will not sell to dealers, only individuals, an example of what an excellent bargain the coins were.

Before structuring the ad and deciding on prices, I thought carefully about the statements my friends had made when they saw them. Everyone had the feeling the coins were worth a great deal of money. It would be a mistake to sell them at a low price. Underselling is a mistake often made in mail order. Consumers are discerning and aware. Sometimes you can kill a product with too low a price. I always test when I am undecided about pricing. Major companies do the same thing.

It is, of course, impossible to predetermine what consumers will pay for your goods. A low price does not always mean a bargain. It may be an invitation (in the buyer's mind) to purchase something that is going to give them a great deal of trouble.

I had to decide price, and I was unsure of who the buyers might be. I selected four test areas, each isolated. A medium-sized midwestern town with a rural atmosphere was the first. The other three were major cities in the East, South, and Midwest. My prices ranged from $40 to $900, depending on the coin. I believed that those who were interested in coins and saw their potential, but did not have the money, would buy the $40 edition. Serious collectors would go for the high end.

In rural-oriented communities the ad pulled poorly; in cities it pulled 200% or more. The response was excellent, good enough to go for additional markets, but something happened that convinced me the coins were not for me.

In almost every case, anyone who bought the high-priced coins called me personally before they made a financial commitment. There was no telephone number in the ad, but to the buyers it did not matter. They were determined to run the "museum" manager down and talk to him personally before making the purchase.

Collector calls are far removed from an average consumer's questions. The collectors asked sophisticated questions, and I found myself spending anywhere from 15 minutes to a half hour on the telephone.

Coin collecting is a mammoth business. Next to stamps and dolls, it is the third largest collectible in the United States. But coin collectors are cautious. They have been burned before and they investigate before putting their money in an envelope.

The calls made me realize that the ad was good for collectors, but not the masses. I was more interested in selling thousands of $40 coins than a few hundred of the $900 variety. Specialized product sales to collectors can be time-consuming, as I found out.

I dropped the concept and canceled the ads, but I still had a load of coins I had purchased. I tried a different tact. In the next Van Pler & Tissany catalog, I put in two pages of ads for the coins. I also had several mounted on rings and pictured them in the catalog. In every case the price was as high (or higher) than consumers found in the coin ads. We sold the rings and the coins through Van Pler & Tissany's catalog, and never had to spend time explaining the background and so forth about the coins.

Why? Because the recipient of the Van Pler & Tissany catalog had already purchased goods from us. He or she believed in us and bought the item without question. (Interestingly, about 55% of Van Pler's list consists of men. This is in sharp contrast to most merchandise catalogs, which usually have women as a majority of buyers. Sharper Image is another catalog that has more than 50% of its buyers as men.)

The success of the coins within the Van Pler & Tissany catalog illustrates the potential that other similar goods might have. I began to think about merchandise that might be more closely aligned to the stones.

An item that we are in the process of testing is perfume—our versions of best-selling brands such as Opium and White Shoulders. In all, I selected more than 20 different, well-known fragrances that usually sell for $80 or more an ounce.

Our versions (names can be copywrited but not the fragrance) sell at a fraction of the cost of the originals. Initially, I ran a full-page space ads and tested them in four or five markets.

I stayed with the sophisticated markets such as Dallas (for the Southwest), a Florida market, one in the Sunbelt, and a Northern market.

Numerous companies had, of course, tried to market the same items; however, I believed they made several critical marketing errors. First, the perfume—because it will sell for a much lower price—is not necessarily going to appeal to a low-end market.

A low price does not mean that purchases will be made by those

in lower economic brackets. The success I have had with the Van Pler diamond proves that. I intended to take the same route with the perfume.

I also tested three different prices: $9.95, $14.95, and $24.95. When you are not sure, testing prices is a must. If possible, I try to get split runs in the same city so I can test two different prices in the same media. The higher price was designed to overcome a question I believed was in the consumer's mind—"How can it possibly be the same fragrance or any good for that low a price?"

So I created the $24.95 bracket. As was the case with Cadillac, the price had to be believable, and the incredibly low dollar figures may not have seemed so to buyers.

The buyers of perfume are, of course, primarily women. The space ad I designed reflected that. Instead of a lengthy, news headline, our ad had one large headline: "SALE."

The remainder of the ad did not have much copy, either. In my experience, I have found that most women are not interested in reading in-depth ads. Certainly, there are many who will read an in-depth piece, but the vast majority prefer little copy, and the one word that attracts their attention is SALE.

In addition, they were able to see the product, order blank, and price. As usual, the subheads told the entire story:

Blindfold test proves you cannot tell the difference

How can we do it?

No cruelty to animals

Be like the movie stars

Dazzle your man and your friends

Limited to customers—no orders accepted from stores

Postdate your check

Comparing the subheads on this ad to the Van Pler & Tissany or coin ad, it is obvious that the perfume ad appeals more to the emotions and romance. The references to cruelty animals, movie stars, and "dazzling your man and friends" are emotional pitches. There is rationale in the ad as well, with "How We Can Do It?" and "Blindfold Test Proves You Cannot Tell the Difference."

LOGIC SELLS MEN; EMOTION WOMEN

Good space and mail order ads vary, depending on the audience. When you are dealing primarily with males, you need more logic; with women more emotion.

Although it is still early, the initial results from our perfume ads are not encouraging. Returns are poor, and most of the ads did not break even.

Why? That is something I—or any other mail order marketer—will never know. I can surmise and second-guess. What I intend to do is rewrite the ad (especially the headline) and try again.

Previously, I have said that if an offer does not work, I do not beat it to death, and if the perfume were any ordinary product I certainly would drop it—now. However, there is a problem. I have 35,000 bottles on hand from my initial order.

So, I intend to try a new approach. One that hopefully will work. In the meantime, you can inspect my initial perfume ad effort in Chapter 10.

There is one place that I feel confident the perfume ad will work—our catalog. Once again, catalog readers are proven buyers, and trust the products we offer.

Regardless of how big or small the catalog gets, we will continue to utilize bulk mail. For catalogs, bulk mail is the only sensible mailing technique. And, in many cases, I believe it makes just as much sense as first-class—even when it comes to letters.

HOW TO PACKAGE THE ENVELOPE

The key to success, however, is not how a letter is mailed, but how it is packaged. There is probably more confusion in the direct-mail field about envelopes than any other element.

What causes a person to open an envelope? They open one because of what they "feel" about it. There are several schools of thought when it comes to handling envelopes. Some marketers believe in putting copy on the outside of an envelope, while others shy away from it.

The outside copy is designed to entice the recipient, get them to open the package. In many cases it works and the way you can tell is if you see the same technique repeated.

I have always preferred leaving copy off the outside of an enve-

lope. At *Entrepreneur* and Van Pler & Tissany, my direct-mail letters have always "pitched from the top." That is, I prefer to start the message with the letter inside and continue it until it is completed.

When copy is printed on the outside of an envelope, you "put" something in recipients' mind. The message may cause their minds to wander to other things, and if the outside line is particularly important they may even lose track of it by the time the envelope is opened.

They expect the rest of the letter or message to continue where the envelope left off. Too many copywriters put a misleading message on the outside in hopes of getting prospects to open the letter. Consequently, when the envelope is opened, prospects are disappointed because the copy inside bears no relationship to the outside. They have been deceived and resent it. As a result your offer and envelope go in the trash.

OUTSIDE ENVELOPE COPY—A MISTAKE

My philosophy has always been to catch the prospect's interest with what is inside. I regard copy on the outside of an envelope as a warning. If it is misleading or does not logically flow into the interior copy, you lose the prospect. I want to sell everyone I can. I know if there is any interruption anywhere within a direct-mail piece, the response will diminish.

In all my letters I try to be secretive and personal on the outside. I try not to give anything away. I use metered mail that appears to be first-class and does not print the bulk mail indicia. Many direct-mail pieces have "third-class bulk mail" printed on them. That is an immediate giveaway—this is junk mail, throw it away.

Time, of course, is a precious commodity for all of us. Regardless who you are trying to sell, they will look for a clue on the outside of the envelope. If they spot anything that indicates that this is a solicitation or junk mail, you have probably lost a chance at the sale.

Consumers will even look at the return address to determine if it is a familiar name. If so, and they can pinpoint it as a direct-mail firm, they may discard the piece as well.

Over the years I have found that you can use a company name on a return address, but do not hesitate to use a name they may not recognize. A DBA (Doing Business As) for instance. One that may spark interest and help get the letter opened.

Obviously, the best envelope is the one that has no label or win-

dow. It is typed or run off on a computer and has a personalized look to it. Personalization is a critical thing in mail order. Consumers have been "numeralized" to death with social security, license plates, and dozens of numbers that have been given to us by governmental and other agencies.

THE CONSUMER'S NEED FOR PERSONALIZATION

Consumers hunger to be treated as individuals, personalized. That's why personalized license plates have gone well. They give us an identity of our own, one that no one else has. The more personal the envelope in a mail order campaign, the better the chance it will be examined and opened by the prospect.

The next best thing is the window envelope that appears to have a check inside. Normally, it is an order card with a letter and brochure behind the card. The card is simply made to appear as if it were a check stub. It works.

The last option is the printed label on the envelope. The label, however, is a giveaway that there is junk mail inside and dramatically decreases your chances of getting the envelope opened.

One of the newest approaches has been the envelope with "urgent dispatch" or a similar message printed on the outside. Some marketers have used the envelope that says "$2,000 fine or five years in prison if this envelope is opened by anyone other than the addressee."

In both cases the object is to make the envelope appear official. It's like a letter from the IRS—we all open that one.

There is a question as to whether the post office will allow the "urgent" type packages to continue when they are merely disguises for a direct-mail message. If the post office does not pass regulations against their use, the technique will soon be copied by marketers throughout the country, and will eventually lose its unique feature.

THE "EUROPEAN CONNECTION"

If you watch direct-mail pieces you will soon discover a constant stream of new packages coming into the market on a regular basis. One of the latest—and hottest—is an envelope that has a return address from Hong Kong, West Germany, or some other location in Europe. The actual meter may read Medina, Ohio, or Peoria, Illinois.

But it is the return address that is the gimmick and appeal. Few notice the meter reading, and the charm and appeal of the package is "getting a letter from a foreign country." We are all fascinated by one.

Obtaining a European (or similar) address is not difficult. You do not have to live there. In the next year we will be running a similar promotion with a London address for Van Pler & Tissany. The postmark, of course, will probably read Beverly Hills.

There are no books or libraries that a marketer can visit in order to keep up on the latest packaging gimmicks. There are envelope companies that can be consulted, but the best way is to get on as many lists as possible. Respond to mail order advertisements. Once you are on one list, you will be amazed at the other literature that will begin coming your way.

I not only examine envelopes and read mail order pieces that come into the office, but I also file any that I think may be good or of interest later. One of the best mail order copywriters in the country is a young man who has four file drawers filled with mail order pieces, and another drawer containing best-pulling heads. He obtained the pieces by being on mailing lists. The heads he cut out from newspapers and magazines.

Present and potential mail order marketers have to realize they are not the masters of everything. Other people have good ideas, and you can learn from them, regardless of how long you have been in the business.

If you do not know what you want to sell, save everything; break them into categories such as insurance, books, health, and so on. I have an extensive jewelry file, and although Van Pler & Tissany is successful, I still examine every new piece that comes through the mail. I also study trade papers in the industry for new ideas.

Although many mail order marketers study the industry, most still slip when it comes to the basics or fundamentals. For example, did you ever notice how people open an envelope. In more than 90% of all cases, it is from the back. They do not open an envelope while looking at the front. Then they pull the entire package out.

With this in mind, what happens if marketers have not arranged their package so that there is an attention-getter facing the back of the envelope? Chances are they may lose the prospect before anything is even read.

Pay attention to the little things; they make or break a mail order piece. One word can turn someone off. A letter that is inserted the wrong way can wind up in the circular file.

The best mail order package is the one that is all together. That is,

is one continuous piece with the only exception being the order card. Everything else is in one letter. But even a piece that is together can be a problem. There is a tendency for the buyer to go straight for the order card to see what you are selling. If it is not right, you lose the customer. An order card that is hidden or not obvious is the best type.

Ideally, the best piece is a pitch (letter) that is joined together and attached to the order card. The prospect pulls it out and there is no way for a card or other literature to fall on the floor and enable the buyer to prejudge the package.

Mail order marketers deal with emotional people, which we all are. Typical buyers or consumers do not want to be bothered. They want to open and discard the mail as rapidly as possible; they try to figure ways not to open the mail; they try to come up with techniques by which they can automatically tell if a piece is junk mail and toss it.

Think about yourself when you sit down to open a letter or read the mail. What do you do? Why do you do it? What gets your curiosity?

I have always kept those questions in mind when composing a direct-mail piece. The package must be easy to open, and to read. If there are several pieces enclosed and you pull them apart, you might look at any one of them first. If each does not grab you, there is a good chance you will toss the entire package. The offer may be great, but the marketer may not have packaged it correctly.

I have found that mailers with a lot of pieces and a whole lot of writing on the envelope are disasters. They are usually produced by large companies that are just getting into the field and do not care. They have money to burn, and no conception of how the business works.

Time magazine can afford to give away two million calculators at $1.20 each. They rely on giving away the store and they hope they will make it up in ad revenue. The typical mail order entrepreneur cannot.

Mail order is an exciting and rewarding business, a challenge that no corporate position could possibly match. It is also a much-maligned occupation, one that offers incredible opportunities to anyone, regardless of education, background, or beliefs.

I have owned and operated many businesses, but my best ideas were those that related to mail order. It does not require a high school diploma or college degree. Anyone and everyone has a shot to make it. To do so, you have to keep a number of things in mind.

Do not expect everyone to be a potential customer. If you do, you are in for a disappointment. With 250 million people, you only need a fraction of a percent to be a success. With *Entrepreneur* my total market was only five million—less than 2% of the population in the entire country. Yet I was able to create a mail order firm and sell it for close to $4 million in less than 10 years.

NARROW MARKET, HIGHER COSTS

Remember, too, the narrower the market you appeal to, the higher the price your product has to be in order to cover costs. There is a world of difference between *Entrepreneur* and Van Pler & Tissany. With Van Pler my audience is in excess of 100 million. That was one of the reasons why I could sell a stone for $15.

The key to mail order success is, once again, sensitivity; understanding consumer attitudes, and realizing that they change.

Recognizing these changes will enable mail order marketers to develop products and services that will be the giant businesses of the 1990s and beyond.

Luck? Certainly you need it in business as you do in life. But it is not the determining factor. In mail order, more than any other business, the critical link to success is you; your ability to read people and relate to them.

If you have those abilities, you are on the way.

10

Letters, Mailing Pieces, Ads

One of the first direct-mail letters written by Chase Revel was the following three-page letter by John C. Revel to those who answered his first inquiry ad ("How Much Money Does Joe's Business Make?").

At the time, Revel was an unknown business consultant, and the letter was designed to convince those who answered his $44 *Wall Street Journal* ad that *Insider's Report* was worth the subscription price ($16.75).

In looking back at the letter, Revel says "there is nothing I would change in it. Although it is more than a decade old, the principles in it still work."

Revel is referring to a number of techniques that are illustrated by the letter. Note the letterhead and the lines "member: Santa Monica Chamber of Commerce" and "member: American Management Association." Associations and chamber of commerce affiliations connote stability and enhance credibility. Notice, too, the professional appearance of the letterhead.

The letter is long, but easy to read. It is broken up by underlined words and phrases, as well as short paragraphs. The language is easy to understand. There are no complex words or phrases that would lose the reader.

The 21 points that every *Insider's Report* features are designed to answer all the possible needs a buyer (present or potential small business owner) could have. Little is left out.

The letter is written on a "one-to-one" basis. That is, it is as if Revel is talking to you personally, and not to an entire group of

people. Successful mail order letters follow the same one-to-one format.

The P.S. is not an afterthought. As is the case with other direct-mail pieces that use postscripts, the message is put there so that the reader will notice it. Revel's P.S. has a special message: buy now and get a special bonus. In other words, it has the offer in it. Studies show that the P.S. portion of a letter is one of the most read parts of any correspondence. Thus an important part of the message is inserted in the P.S.

Aside from describing his offer in depth, Revel also gives the reader insight into the author's background and why he is capable of writing the advice he is selling. Every conceivable question the prospect may have is answered in the letter.

John C. Revel

. BUSINESS INVESTIGATION • MANAGEMENT CONSULTANTS
1445 FIFTH STREET
SANTA MONICA, CALIF. 90401

MEMBER:
SANTA MONICA
CHAMBER OF COMMERCE

MEMBER:
AMERICAN MANAGEMENT ASSN.

Re: INSIDER'S REPORT & Who's Making A Bundle

We've all wondered just who is making it "hand-over-fist."
The guy who is sure isn't telling everyone—I'll guarantee that.

Probably everyone has wondered how much profit a particular
business makes—in actual dollars and cents. No doubt you can
think of a business that you thought about recently.

Also, you probably asked yourself: How much cash (minimum)
is needed to start that business? What kind of knowledge or
experience is needed? How do they get their customers? Who do
they buy from? How about locations, financing, etc.?

Knowing who is making "a bundle" and exactly how their
businesses operate is part of my profession.

I've made my living during the past 18 years researching
and investigating various businesses for investors, banking and
lending institutions. I've investigated practically every business from popcorn stands to multi-level consumer and industrial
manufacturing organizatons.

During this time, I have started and made successful 14
different small businesses of my own. Obviously, with my inside
knowledge, I picked only the most profitable businesses around.

Like most of my friends and acquaintances who are constantly
asking me for information, I'm sure you would like to have the
knowledge that I have acquired in the past years. Many of my
friends have become wealthy from my knowledge.

With some common sense, a little money and the ability to
follow instructions, you can cash in on my experience. If you
are a real go-getter, you'll probably make more than I have (in
the 7-figure area).

I will reveal the inside details of every small and very

(Continued on next page)

189

profitable business known. This experience is available in my bi-monthly INSIDER'S REPORT. I don't bother with the business that has low profits. And I concentrate on small businesses (you're not interested in General Motors), small enough for the average buy to get into with a small investment. I even include tricks for getting the money if you don't have it all.

If you are interested in vague, get-rich-quick schemes or petty, unproven, unheard-of gimmicks for making money, INSIDER'S REPORT isn't for you. I report on nothing but solid, established and proven businesses.

EVERY INSIDER'S REPORT FEATURE CONTAINS EVERYTHING* YOU NEED TO KNOW TO START AND RUN THAT BUSINESS:
(*All Exact Figures from Case Histories)

1. The pitfalls — how to avoid them.
2. Profit — how much to expect.
3. Exact costs — of everything to set up, open and operate.
4. Equipment — what to buy and where to find it.
5. Ways to save money on equipment, fixtures and etc.
6. Rent — how much to pay.
7. Location — how to choose the best.
8. Leases — how to negotiate important points.
9. Licenses, Permits — what to expect and how to get them.
10. Merchandise — what to buy, how to buy, where to buy
11. If Retail — how to lay out your store and display your wares.
12. Decorating Ideas — quick, cheap and impressive.
13. Signs — how much, how big, where, and what to say.
14. Employees — who to hire, what to pay, and how to get the best performance.
15. Advertising — how, where, when and how much.
16. Promotion — best gimmicks completely detailed.
17. Insurance — what you need and how much.
18. Knowledge — where to find it, buy, or rent it.
19. Financing — how to finance your opening costs.
    — how to finance your sales to customers.
20. Customers — how to bring them in and how to keep them.
21. Pricing — what price to sell your products or service.
AND HUNDREDS OF OTHER MINOR DETAILS......

In other words, practically every question you can imagine is answered in detail. I gained my reputation by being thorough—so be prepared for it. INSIDER'S REPORT is not a two-page newsletter, but a magazine-size manual averaging over 50 pages per issue.

I make it easy for you. When I decide to feature a business that's proven to be very profitable, my staff searches out businesses of that type for the best formula.

We investigate the most successful in the field to find out why. We find out what locations are best and why, what merchandise sells best, who has the best sales techniques, who has the most effective advertising gimmicks, who has the best internal controls, and on and on.

Therefore, the businesses featured in each manual may often be composites of successful techniques taken from several proven and profitable operations in that field.

In each issue I will feature four businesses along with various newsworthy items which may be used in any enterprise. Of the four featured, two will be budget businesses directed toward those who don't have a lot of cash. The investment range is from $100 to $2,000. The net profit range shown in articles to date has been from $15,000 up.

The other two reports have an investment range of $2,500 to $25,000, and have shown annual net profits ranging from $20,000 to $235,000 in those manuals printed to date.

This is the smart way to get into business. Just sit back and read the features on various profitable businesses. Or, order back issue collections featuring enterprises that evoke your interest. When one hits your liking, everything is right there in front of you —everything that you need to know to start that business. Your cost for the INSIDER'S REPORT is only $1.16 per business (based on a two-year subscription).

Why give you such valuable information at such a low price? First, it is physically impossible for me to take advantage of every exceptional opportunity. Presently I'm involved in five enterprises. In fact, occasionally I wish I didn't have so many businesses. Sometimes I can't golf, fish, hunt or sail when I want to because of pressing business demands.

Check me out. In fact, if you are in or visiting Los Angeles stop at my offices in Santa Monica and have a cup of coffee with us. Otherwise, have your local consumer protective organization such as the Better Business Bureau request a report on me from Los Angeles. I'm listed under "Insider's Report."

After you receive your first issue and Bonus Reports, if you are not pleased just mail them back to me within 30 days, and I will refund all of your money immediately by return mail.

There's a subscription card enclosed. Fill it out and send it to me with your payment in the enclosed prepaid envelope. Or you can charge your order to your BankAmericard or Master Charge.* You will get the current issue immediately, and on the first of every other month the new reports will be mailed to you. Good luck!

Sincerely,

John C. Revel

JCR/er

P.S. Earlier this year I did a Special Report on what I feel is the HOTTEST, NEWEST, MOST PROFITABLE BUSINESS around (in the low-investment range). It's really a winner, and people are standing in line at each location for this new, unusual service. This Report, No. 400, is FREE to you when you subscribe for one year.

If you subscribe for 2 years, you will receive 3 bonus reports. In addition to Report No. 400, you will get Report No. 210, THE BUSINESS WITH A MILLION-DOLLAR ANNUAL PROFIT POTENTIAL, and Report No. 500, BUSINESS START-UP TRICKS & ANGLES. See last page for more details on these Special Bonus Reports.

*For fast service on BankAmericard and
Master Charge orders only, call us collect.

◀─────────── Please Turn Page Here

Revel completely changed the format and direction of *Insider's Report* when he renamed it *Entrepreneur*. Instead of having a publication that was geared primarily toward mail order sales, he went to a slick, glossy look and introduced it to consumers via newsstand sales.

The following excerpt from *Editor & Publisher's Market Survey & Guide* shows the importance of this information to the mail order marketer.

The Houston, Texas listing gives the mail order entrepreneur an excellent feel for the market. For example, out of more than one million job holders, less than 10% are in manufacturing. The remainder are in service-oriented businesses, which are primarily white-collar jobs.

Notice the other categories, which range from a listing of department stores to newspapers and shopping centers.

Contrast this listing with the one next to it (Huntsville) and its principal industries. Obviously, Huntsville, with its heavy chemical, repair, lumber, and rock quarries, is a blue-collar market, and despite sharing the same state as Houston, the audience response for mail order products would be totally different.

HOUSTON, TEX.

1—LOCATION: Harris County, E&P Map E-4. (SMSA) On Houston Ship Channel; 23 mi. from Galveston Bay; 50 mi. from Gulf of Mexico; 252 mi. SE of Dallas; 219 mi. E of San Antonio; 50 mi. NW of Galveston; 95 mi. W of Beaumont. On U.S. Hwys. 59, 90, 75, 290; Interstate 10, 45; State Hwys. 35, 73, 225, 288.

2—TRANSPORTATION: Railroads—Santa Fe; Southern Pacific; Missouri Pacific; Missouri-Kansas; Texas; Rock Island; Ft. Worth & Denver (Burlington Lines).
Motor Freight Carriers—37. (120 Regulated Special Carriers).
Intercity Bus Lines—Continental Trailways; Greyhound; Kerrville; Texas.
Freight Steamship Lines—50.
Airlines—American; Air France; Eastern; National; KLM; Braniff; Pan American; Texas International; Continental; Delta; Southwest; Aeromexico; Air Canada; British Caledonian Airlines.

3—POPULATION:
Corp. City 70 Cen. 1,232,802;
Loc. Est. 1,623,000
City Zone ABC: (70) 1,741,912; (78) 2,191,600
RTZ-ABC: (70) 618,930; (78) 805,900
City & RTZ-ABC: (70) 2,360,842 (78) 2,997,500
County 70 Cen. 1,741,912; Loc. Est. 2,191,600
SMSA 70 Cen. 1,999,316; Loc. Est. 2,577,400
Demographic Information available from Newspaper. See paragraph 14.

4—HOUSEHOLDS:
City 70 Cen. 393,555; Loc. Est. 523,762
County 70 Cen. 540,929; Loc. Est. 758,300
SMSA 70 Cen. 614,287; Loc. Est. 881,200
City Zone ABC: (70) 540,855; (78) 758,300
RTZ-ABC: (70) 184,012; (78) 265,400
City & RTZ-ABC: (70) 724,867; (78) 1,023,700

5—BANKS:	Number	Deposits
Commercial Banks	158	$16,053,874,753
Sav. & Loan Assn.	39	$ 3,857,986,241

6—PASSENGER AUTOS: County 1,258,373

7—ELECTRIC METERS: Res. Co. 630,679

8—GAS METERS: Res. Co. 472,029

9—PRINCIPAL INDUSTRIES (SMSA): Industry, Number of Wage & Salary Earners—Wage and Salary Total 1,136,700; Manufacturing 187,100; Durable Goods 106,700; Lumber & Wood Prods. 2,600; Furniture & Fixtures 1,300; Stone, Clay & Glass 8,000; Primary Metals 8,300; Fabricated Metal Prods. 28,900; Machinery (exc. Elec.) 41,200; Electrical Machinery & Equip. 8,000; Transportation Equip. 3,600; Other Durable Goods 4,800; Nondurable Goods 80,400; Food & Kindred Products 13,600; Textile Mill Products 300; Apparel & Fin. Products 1,300; Paper & Allied Products 4,300; Printing & Publishing 11,200; Chemicals & Allied Prods. 29,300; Petroleum Refining 15,900; Other Nondurable Goods 4,500; Nonmanufacturing 949,600; Mining 46,600; Contract Construction 119,600; Transp., Comm., & Utils. 80,900; Transp. & Allied Services 49,500; Communications 15,400; Utilities 16,000; Trade 283,400; Wholesale Trade 95,000; Retail Trade 188,400; Fin. Ins. & Real Estate 64,100; Service Esc. Priv. Hsld. 222,700; Bus. & Personal Services 104,100; Med. & Prof. Services 114,900; Agri. Serv., For. & Fish. 3,700; Government 132,300; Federal 17,300; State 24,900; Local 90,100.

10—CLIMATE: Min. & Max. Temp.—Spring 59-80; Summer 73-92; Fall 59-80; Winter 45-65.

11—TAP WATER: Alkaline, hard.

12—RETAILING: Principal Shopping Center—9 blocks on Main St.; 9 on Fannin St.; 9 on Travis St.
Neighborhood Shopping Centers—There are about 180 shopping centers in the area.

SHOPPING CENTERS

50 or More Stores: Almeda Mall; Gulfgate; Highland Village; Laura Koppe; Memorial City; Northwest Mall; Palm Center; River Oaks; Sharpstown; Town & Country; Meyerland; Northline; Westwood Mall; Galleria; Greens Point 5; Woodlake; Baybrook Mall; Town & Country; Carillon West.

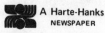

31 to 50 Stores: Briargrove; Campbell; King Center; Oak Forest; Pasadena Oaks; Spring Village; Woodland Acres; Northtown Plaza.
21 to 30 Stores: Braeswood; Galena Park; Garden Oaks; Greenbriar; Lakewood; Lantern Lane; McGregor Place; Maplewood; Merchant's Park; Pasadena Plaza; Spring Branch; Westbury Square; Sears-Harrisburg; Greenway Plaza Underground; Spring Shadows Plaza; Sugar Creek Village.
11 to 20 Stores: Alabama Shopping Center; Allendale; Avalon; Ayrshire; Bellaire Theatre; Belway; Braesheights; Bunker Hill; Campbell; Crawford-McGowen; Edgewood; Fashion Square; Fulton Village; Lamar-River Oaks; Lamar Terrace; Mangum Square; Market Center; Montclair; Northwood; Oak Meadows; Parkview Manor; Port City; Post Oak; Red Bluff; Richmond Plaza; Ridgecrest; Southland; South Main; Speedway; Stella Link; Tower; Willow Bend; Windsor Plaza; Winfield Center; 6600 So. Main District; No. Main at Quitman; Kempwood Plaza; Northbrook; North Oaks; Southgate; Westchase; Bellaire Triangle; Stafford Plaza; Camino South; Alabama S.C.; Ashford Sq.; Deauville Sq.; Hammerly Plaza; Ponderosa Forest.
10 or less Stores: Beekman; Berry Road; Fontaine; Greens Bayou; Jester Village; Kety Road; Melcher; Mosher; North Shepherd; Oak Village; Pinewood Village; Plum Creek; Richmond Village; Robindell; South Hill; Southway.
Principal Shopping Days: Department Stores—Thurs., Sat. Food—Thurs., Mon.
Stores Open Evenings: Department Stores—Many open till 9 every weekday. Food—Most open till 9 weekdays.

13—RETAIL OUTLETS: Department Stores—Battlestein's 7; Craigs 8; Foley's 8; Leonard's 9; Lord & Taylor 2; Meyer Bros. 1; Montgomery Ward's 7; Neiman-Marcus 1; Palais Royal 15; Penney's 10; Joske's 7; Sakowitz 6; Saks Fifth Avenue 1; Sears Roebuck & Co. 9; Weiner's 32.
Discount Stores: Fed Mart 4; Gemco 4; K-Mart 14; Sage 3; Target 6; Woolco 7.
Variety Stores: Ben Franklin 2; Kresge 2; Kress 2; TG&Y 20; Variety Values 4; Wacker G. F. Stores 6; Woolworth 9.
Chain Drug Stores: Cunningham's 4; Doyle's 3; Eckerd's 60; Jones Apothecary 10; Medic Pharmacy 4; Ralston 18; Sage Pharmacy 4; Save-On-Drugs 5; Sommers 3; SupeRx 14; Walgreen's 32.
Chain Food Supermarkets: Baby Giant 12; Cheri's Superette 3; Clayton's 3; Continental Finer Foods 2; Corner Food Stores 4; Doyle's Drive Inn 6; Eagle 15; Food City 7; Food Giant 4; Food Land 3; Gerland's 19; Handy Andy 7; JMH 2; Korner Pantry 6; Kroger 30; Kwik Stop 2; Lucky-Seven 28; Midget Market 3; Minimax 12; Mr. M. Food Stores 27; Mr. Mercury 4; P. M. Superette 3; Randall's 8; Rice 43; Richie 3; Safeway 37; Samperi's 2; Save Mart Discount Foods 3; Seller's Bros. Super Drive Inn 6; Seven-Eleven 183; Sultana 3; Sunny's 25; Super Quik 8; Super Duper 55; Tick Tock Foods 3; U-Tot-Em 150; Weingarten's 58; Stop & Go 139.
Other Chain Stores—Men's Clothing: Leopold, Price & Rolle; Men's Warehouse, Zindler, Graham's; Shoes: Baker's Shoe Stores 9, Brucal's Shoes 4, Chandler Shoe Stores 5, Fayva Family Shoes 10, Flagg 4; Florsheim Shoe Stores 12, Hanover Shoe 3, Kinney's Shoe Stores 14, Naturalizer Shoe Shops 3, Pay-Less Shoe 10, Pix Shoe 3, Red Cross Shoe 10, Shoe Box 10, The Shoe Gallery 3, Standard Make Shoes 9, Thom McAn Shoe 10, Vogue Shoes 6, The Wild Pair 4, Others: Singer Co. 12, Firestone 19, Goodyear 24, General Tire & Rubber 3, Edison Bros., Western Auto 26, Finger's Furniture 4, White 17, Levitz Furniture 2, Dinnettes & Barstools Unlimited 3, Furniture in the Raw 3, Haverty's 5, Levitz 3, Rattan Furniture Shop 4, Star Furniture 9, Ladies Clothing: Graves Fashion Shops 7, JM's 4, Judy's 4, Kinda Dray 4, Lane Bryant, Lerner Shops 7, The Limited 5, Margo's La Mode 8, Mr. Leonard's 3, Pic-a-Dilly 6, 5-7-9 Shop 5, Susie's Casuals 5, Suzette's Dress Shop 4, Shelly's Tall Girl Shops 4, Total Look Fashions 5, The Woman's Shop 5.

14—NEWSPAPERS: CHRONICLE (e-Mon. to Fri.) 322,762; (Sat. m) 337,552; (S) 416,934; Mar. 31, 1978 ABC.
POST (m-Mon. to Fri.) 303,447; (Sat. m) 335,464; (S) 360,603; Mar. 31, 1978 ABC.
Local Contact for Advertising and Merchandising Data: A. C. Bright, Natl. Adv. Mgr., CHRONICLE; Keith Butler, Natl. Adv. Mgr., POST.
National Representatives: CHRONICLE, Sawyer-Ferguson Walker Co.; POST, Branham/Newspaper Sales.

HUNTSVILLE, TEX.

1—LOCATION: Walker County, E&P Map E-4; County Seat. Diversified farming, cotton seed milling, lumber, rock quarries. Sam Houston State University. 70 mi. N of Houston; on U.S. Hwy. 190; State Hwy. 30, 94; Interstate 45.

2—TRANSPORTATION: Railroads—Missouri-Pacific.
Motor Freight Carriers—3.
Intercity Bus Lines—Continental Trailways.
Airlines—Most National, some International lines at Houston.

3—POPULATION:
Corp. City 70 Cen. 17,610; Loc. Est. 26,671
County 70 Cen. 27,680; Loc. Est. 44,346

4—HOUSEHOLDS:
City 70 Cen. 4,141; Loc. Est. 9,052
County 70 Cen. 6,851; Loc. Est. 15,796

5—BANKS:	Number	Deposits
Commercial Banks	3	$98,100,000.00

6—PASSENGER AUTOS: County 11,561

7—ELECTRIC METERS: 7,340

8—GAS METERS: 5,379

9—PRINCIPAL INDUSTRIES (CZ): Tank Trailer Repair; Coors Beer Dist.; Chemicals; Rock Quarries; Lumber & Timber; Cottonseed Oil Mills; Farming.

10—CLIMATE: Min. & Max. Temp.—Spring 42-73; Summer 70-100; Fall 42-72; Winter 24-65. First killing frost, Oct. 10. Last killing frost, Mar. 28.

11—TAP WATER: Alkaline, hard.

12—RETAILING: Northwest Shopping Ctr.-11th St. (9 stores).
Neighborhood Shopping Centers—Downtown (Ave. L & 13th St.); University Hts. S/C (5 stores); South Plaza S/C (4 stores); Brookhaven S/C (12 stores).
Principal Shopping Days: Fri. & Sat.
Stores Open Evenings: Some in Northwest S/C to 9 p.m.

13—RETAIL OUTLETS: Department Stores—J.C. Penney; Sears Catalog; Ward's Catalog; K-Mart; TG&Y; Duke & Ayres.
Discount Stores (CZ): Howard's.
Variety Stores—K-Mart; TG&Y; Duke & Ayres.
Chain Drug Stores (CZ): Eckerd.
Chain Food Stores: Piggly Wiggly; Safeway; Rice's.
Other Chain Stores—Zale's Jewelry; Firestone; Goodyear; Western Auto; Baskin-Robbins; TSO; Radio Shack.

14—NEWSPAPER: ITEM (e-tues. to fri.) 4,127; (S) 5,350; sworn Mar. 31, 1978.
Local Contact for Advertising and Merchandising Data: David F. Kramer, Pub., ITEM.
National Representatives: Branham/Newspaper Sales; Harte-Hanks Newspapers, Inc.

HURST, TEX.

1—LOCATION: Tarrant County (In Dallas-Fort Worth SMSA). E&P Map E-3. 12 mi. NE of Fort Worth; 17 mi. NW of Dallas. North Central Texas. Near Hwys. 121, 183, 377.

2—TRANSPORTATION: Railroads—Rock Island; T&P; MK&T, St. Louis & Southwestern.
Intercity Bus Lines—Continental Trailways; Greyhound; Texan Motor Coach.
Airlines—American; Braniff; Frontier; Continental; Delta; Eastern; Trans-Texas (Adjoins new Dallas-Fort Worth International Airport).

3—POPULATION:
Corp. City 70 Cen. 27,215; Loc. Est. 31,603
CZ ABC: (70) 81,959; Cities of Hurst & Bedford, Villages of Euless and towns of North Richland Hills and Richland Hills (78) 91,400
SMSA 70 Cen. 2,377,979; Loc. Est. 2,594,612
County 70 Cen. 716,317; Loc. Est. 735,397

4—HOUSEHOLDS:
City 70 Cen. 7,651; Loc. Est. 10,183
County 70 Cen. 225,873; Loc. Est. 259,744
SMSA 70 Cen. 752,381; Loc. Est. 920,082
CZ ABC: (70) 31,643 (78) 28,300

5—BANKS:	Number	Est. Deposits
Commercial	6	$233,533,634

6—PASSENGER AUTOS: County 454,593

7—ELECTRIC METERS: Residence 31,514

8—GAS METERS: Residence 23,444

9—PRINCIPAL INDUSTRIES (CZ): Metals; Helicopters; Welding Supplies; Galvanizing; Sand & Gravel; Refining; Forges; Builders Supplies; Mattresses; Refrigerators; Plastics; Paper Prod.; Auto Air Conditioners; Paint Mfg.; Furniture; Bag & Box Mfg.; Tile; Tower Const.; Fiberglass Engrg.; Neon Signs; Felt; Pet foods; Hermetics; Aircraft Component.

10—CLIMATE: Mild; Av. Annual Temp. 66; AV. Annual Rainfall 33 in.

11—TAP WATER: Artesian Wells; fluoridated.

12—RETAILING:
Nearby Shopping Centers—Hurstview; Pipeline; Val Oaks; Hurstgate; Shady Oaks; Belaire; Richland Plaza; Richland Center; Wilshire; Norrich; North East Mall; Village Square; The Willows.

Nearby Shopping Centers

Name of Shopping Center	No. of Stores	Principal Store and/or Supermarket
Bellvue	11	N.A.
Hill's	8	Buddies
Hurst Belaire	34	Sears, Moses Variety
Hurstgate	15	N.A.
Hurst Plaza	8	
Hurstview	9	
Myers	7	Myers
Northeast Mall	100	Mitchett's, Zales, Penney, Sears, Montgomery Wards, Lerner, Striplings, Dillards
Pipeline Road	6	N.A.
Plaza Grande	7	Tom Thumb
Shady Oaks	29	Ace Hardware
Stonegate	8	Winn Dixie
Uptown Medical Plz	—	N.A.
Village Square	22	Safeway, Skillerns
White's Plaza	7	Whites
Val Oaks	26	Cloth World
Willows	12	Safeway

Principal Shopping Days: Thu., Fri., Sat.; Most stores open evenings.

13—RETAIL OUTLETS: Department Stores—Myers; Montgomery Ward; J. C. Penney; Lerner; Anthony's; Mitchell's; Watson Bros.; Dillard's; Striplings; Sears.
Variety Stores—M. E. Moses; Mott's.
Discount Stores: Gibson's; K-Mart; Treasure City; Best; H. S. Wilson.
Chain Drug Stores—Revco; Treasury Drug; Eckerd; Skillern's; Town & Country; Skagg's.
Chain Food Supermarkets (CZ): Buddie's 6; Safeway; Kroger; Save-U; Thom Thumb; Winn Dixie.
Other Chain Stores—White's; Goodyear; Firestone; Sears.

14—NEWSPAPER: MID-CITIES NEWS (e-Mon. to Fri.) 8,923; (S) 9,027; Mar. 31, 1978 ABC.
Local Contact for Advertising and Merchandising Data: John Huckabee, Pub., Stan Wilson, Adv. Mgr., MID-CITIES NEWS.
National Representatives: Texas Suburban Dailies.

IRVING, TEX.

1—LOCATION: Dallas County (In Dallas-Ft. Worth SMSA). E&P Map E-3. Light Manufacturing, North Central Texas. 10 min. from Dallas and 20 min. from Fort Worth.

2—TRANSPORTATION: Railroads—Frisco; Rock Island.
Motor Freight Carriers—40.
Intercity Bus Lines—Continental.
Airlines—American; Braniff; Continental; Delta; Ozark; Eastern; Frontier; Mexicana; Texas Int'l.

3—POPULATION:
Corp. City 70 Cen. 97,260; Loc. Est. 110,923
CZ ABC: (70) 97,260; (78) 107,600
SMSA 70 Cen. 2,377,979; Loc. Est. 2,594,612
County 70 Cen. 1,327,321; Loc. Est. 1,404,874

4—HOUSEHOLDS:
City 70 Cen. 28,831; Loc. Est. 36,867
County 70 Cen. 421,919; Loc. Est. 497,857
SMSA 70 Cen. 752,381; Loc. Est. 920,082
CZ ABC: (70) 28,831; (78) 35,500

5—BANKS:	Number	Est. Deposi
Commercial	5	$110,000,00
Sav. & Loan Assn.	5	$ 60,000,00

6—PASSENGER AUTOS: County 840,825

7—ELECTRIC METERS: Residence 23,275

8—GAS METERS: Residence 22,844

9—PRINCIPAL INDUSTRIES (CZ): Petroleum Distributio Chemicals; Aluminum Prods; Heavy Equipmer Precision Tools; Food Distribution; Chemical Asphalt; Tool & Dies; Sash & Doors; Trailers; C Refining; Truck Transport; Food Processing.

10—CLIMATE: Min. & Max. Temp.—Spring 62-8 Summer 72-93; Fall 48-68; Winter 41-61.

11—TAP WATER: From Wells and Lakes.

12—RETAILING:
Neighborhood Shopping Centers—Williamsburg; Irvin gate; Downtown; Plymouth Park; Village Irvin North; Ridgecrest; Irving Plaza; K-Mart; Northga Plaza; Cortez Plaza.

Nearby Shopping Centers

Name of Shopping Center	Number of Stores	Principal Sto and/ Supermark
Carvel Square	10	Safewa
Central Pk. Plz.	33	Ward Dru
Citizens Center	20	Pulido
Cortez Plaza	20	Page Drug, Tom Thum
Freeway	—	N.A
Irvingate	10	Sea
Irving Mall	78	Sears, Penney, Lerner
Irving North	—	Rexa
Irving Plaza	—	N.A
Irving Shpg. Villa.	17	A&P, TG&Y, Skillern
MacArthur	—	N.A
Martinique	—	N.A
Plymouth Pk. No.	15	Buddies, Mkt., Ward Dru
Plymouth Park	100	Penney, Kroger, Safeway Woolco, Tom Thum
2nd & Jefferson	—	N.A
Story	—	N.A
Williamsburg	6	A&P, Moses Varie

Principal Shopping Days: Fri. & Sat.
Stores Open Evenings: Mon. & Thurs.

13—RETAIL OUTLETS: Department Stores—J. C. Penney Sears; White Stores; Neal's Dry Goods; Sange Harris; Western Auto; Int'l. Super; K-Mart; Gibson Woolco; Leonard's, Titches.
Variety Stores—Duke & Ayres 2; M. E. Moses S.S. Kresge; T.G.Y.; Motts; Ben Franklin.
Chain Drug Stores—Big State 3; Ward Cut Rate Dekoven 1; SupeRx 1; Skagg's 1; Skillern's 2.
Discount Stores: Gibson's; K-Mart; Treasure City Woolco (planned).
Chain Food Supermarkets: Safeway 3; Worth; Buddie 2; Reese's; Minyard's 3; Morris; Korger 3; L & 2, Tom Thumb, Skaggs Albertsons.

14—NEWSPAPERS: NEWS (e-Mon. to Fri.) 11,81 (S) 12,820; Mar. 31, 1978 ABC.
Local Contact for Advertising and Merchandisin Data: Larry T. Beasley, Pub.
National Representatives: U.S. Suburban Press, Inc.

JACKSONVILLE, TEX.

1—LOCATION: Cherokee County, E&P Map E-3 Shipping & distribution Ctr. for E. Texas agri mfg. & lbr. area. College ctr. in E. Central Texas 110 mi. SE of Dallas; 110 mi. SW of Shrevepor La.; 180 mi. N of Houston & 145 mi. SE of Texar kana.

2—TRANSPORTATION: Railroads—Missouri Pacific Southern Pacific (frght.); Cotton Belt (frght.).
Motor Freight Carriers—9.
Intercity Bus Lines—Continental; Central Texas Texas Lines.

3—POPULATION:
Corp. City 70 Cen. 9,734; Loc. Est. 9,860
CZ Local Est. 16,500
Retail Trading Zone, Local Est. 21,000
County 70 Cen. 32,008; Loc. Est. 34,957
City & Retail Trading Area; Loc. Est. 37,500

4—HOUSEHOLDS:
City 70 Cen. 3,420; Loc. Est. 4,024
County 70 Cen. 10,478; Loc. Est. 13,278

Revel took a major gamble in 1977, when he put on the first of more than 40 business shows. The expos, which were sponsored by *Entrepreneur*, were held in major cities throughout the country.

The prime promotion tool was a four- to six-page supplement he put together in an editorial/advertising format. The format, which was the first of its kind to be used by a promoter, is an advertisement but is written as editorial matter.

Notice the "news" appearance of the stories.

Start Your Own Business Expo opens next Friday

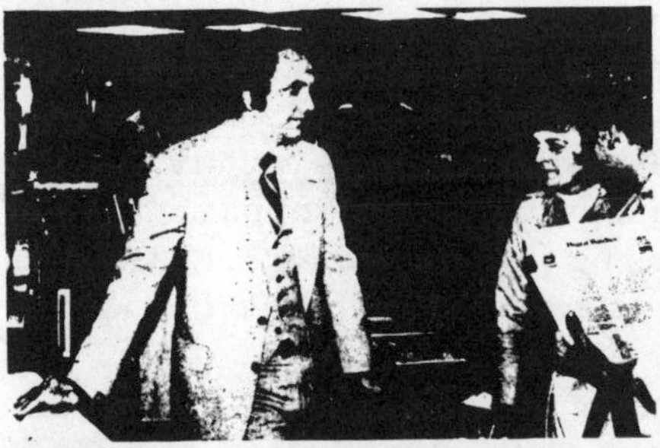

101 EXHIBIT BOOTHS—Some of the newest and most unique small business investment opportunities will be on display at the Start Your Own Business Expo. More than 80 different types of small businesses will be displayed in 101 booths at the expo. A series of seminars is also slated.

Three-day show at Convention Center to feature seminars by experts, displays

The Start Your Own Business Expo '77, the largest show of its kind to be held in Los Angeles in more than a decade, is set for the Convention Center next Friday through Sunday, Aug. 5-7.

The highlight of the expo will be seminars conducted by experts on a wide range of subjects relating to small businesses and exhibits manned by 101 franchisers and distributors displaying unique small businesses that can be started for from less than $1,000 to more than $100,000.

The 50 hours of seminars, which are all "how to" sessions, include such topics as "how to finance your business" and the "hottest new businesses and trends in the country."

The seminars will be cosponsored by the U.S. Small Business Administration, Mayor Bradley's Office of Small Business Assistance and the International Entrepreneurs' Assn.

Eleven experts from across the country have been gathered to conduct the seminars.

On display will be several investment opportunties that have never before been displayed in Los Angeles, including such innovative concepts as computer stores and computer photographs. A number of the investments represent opportunities for both absentee, part-time or full-time management involvement.

Owners of about 81 franchises and distributorships will be on hand to answer questions.

Another unique display will be a "voice stress analyzer," which has taken the place of the polygraph in many police departments. The analyzer, which is being increasingly utilized in business and industry, will be demonstrated throughout the run of the show.

Admission is $2.50 for adults. Children under 12 are free.

Seminars are $10 each, $35 for four or $65 for all nine sessions.

Reservations for seminars are not required but may be made by calling (213) 394-3787 or (213) 451-5743. Those attending a seminar will be admitted to the expo free.

Show hours are noon until 9 p.m. Friday; 10 a.m. until 9 p.m. Saturday; and 10 a.m. until 6 p.m. Sunday.

Chicken's unbeatable in new tic tac toe game

A chicken that plays tic tac toe?

Better than that. A Northern California firm, Money Making Opportunities, has made a practical application of the Pavlov experiments on animal conditioning to develop a unique game.

The firm has conditioned chickens to respond to a series of lights to play tic tac toe. And they have never been beaten.

One of the talented chickens will be on display at the Start Your Own Business Expo '77 and will take on all challengers.

When you insert a coin in the game machine, a light goes on telling the chicken to make the first move. Then you make a move, and another light goes on telling the chicken of your move. The game progresses from there.

When the chicken has won or played to a tie, he gets a reward, a kernel of corn.

Money Making Opportunities has a flock of birds available for the coin-operated games. A number of the games have been sold in Europe at fairs and shopping centers, and the firm guarantees the chickens will be unbeatable.

They are so sure of the birds that the firm will pay $5 to anyone at the business expo who beats the chicken.

Los Angeles Times

START YOUR OWN BUSINESS EXPO '77

SUNDAY, JULY 31, 1977 PART VIII

Special Advertising Supplement

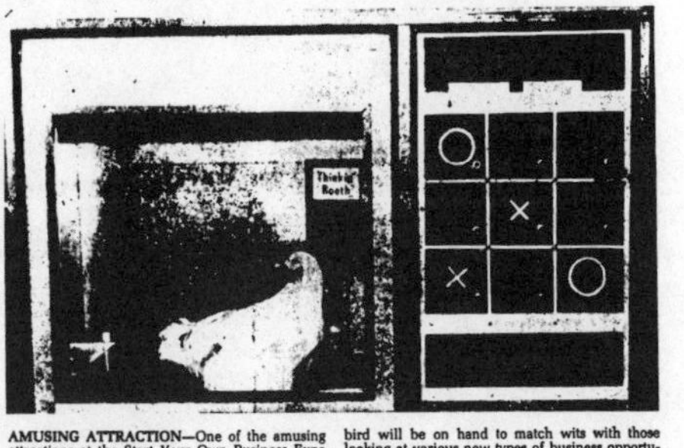

AMUSING ATTRACTION—One of the amusing attractions at the Start Your Own Business Expo is this tic tac toe-playing chicken. The trained bird will be on hand to match wits with those looking at various new types of business opportunities. Anyone who can beat the chicken wins $5.

A BABY'S BATH AID

Widow parlayed dream into success

If you're an eighth grade dropout, a $3-an-hour assembly line worker and a widow with a family to raise, what do you do?

Pansy Essman was in that predicament, spent her last dollar on a dream and turned it into a $1 million-a-year manufacturing business.

Her idea was a new bath aid for babies. Ms. Essman, who will conduct a two-hour seminar for women on "how to start their own business" as part of the Start Your Own Business Expo next Saturday, dreamed about a pillow-like piece of sponge that conformed to the baby's body and supported the child when it was in the tub. The pillow enabled mothers to free both hands when working with the baby.

"Manufacturing is not the typical women's business," she said, "but there's great opportunity in it for them if they can surmount the obstacles."

Among her obstacles were suppliers who refused to believe she was serious even though she had the money to pay for the materials.

"I couldn't get anyone to service my company with the raw materials we needed," she said. "Finally, there was one salesman who took me seriously. If it wasn't for him, we would never have made it."

At first, Ms. Essman tested her products in local stores in Northern California. As she suspected, they sold quickly. Still, she needed national distribution. Local sales alone were not enough to keep her doors open and meet her payroll.

So she took her last dollar and a sample of her products and went to a trade show in New York. Within a matter of hours, she had five national distributors for her products.

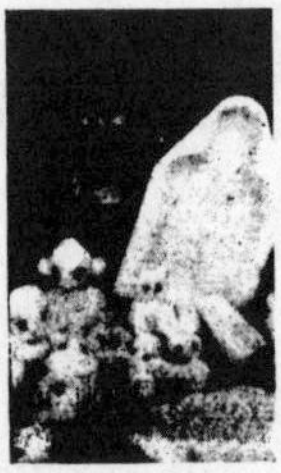

DREAM REALIZED—Pansy Essman, who turned a dream into a $1 million-a-year business, will conduct a seminar for women on business opportunities in the manufacturing field.

"I learned a great deal about the business world and how it views women," she said. "I learned about the subtle resistance women find when venturing into it.

"I think the manufacturing area is an ideal place for women. Most of the time, when women enter business, it's usually in the service area because they don't think any other doors are open to them. They're wrong. Today, things have changed a great deal. The climate is different and women have a special knowledge and understanding that makes them ideal for manufacturing."

Her perseverance was such that the National Business Council named her "Businesswoman of the Year" in 1976, and organizations throughout the country have asked her to give seminars on starting a manufacturing enterprise.

"Too many potential entrepreneurs, whether they are men or women, say they don't have the experience or the knowledge or the education," she said. "Believe me, those things are all secondary to the key ingredient—desire. That's one of the things I try to point out and explain at my seminars.

"Certainly, there's a fear in starting your own business—all gamblers get afraid occasionally. But the bottom line is always keep a positive mental attitude and use what you know."

Nine seminars on business scheduled

Eleven experts to discuss all phases of starting a small business

An intensive series of nine seminars conducted by 11 experts at the Start Your Own Business Expo '77 will cover practically every aspect of small business development.

A top priority for new businesses is financing. Many potential entrepreneurs are blocked due to lack of funds, lack of knowledge in preparing business plans to facilitate borrowing and ignorance of the vast pool of investment capital available for solid business proposals.

Promoting and advertising is another important area. When some basic principles of advertising are understood, the entrepreneur can draw on professional talent at practically no cost relative to return.

Chase Revel, director of the International Entrepreneurs' Assn., said that the reason for the mass of mediocrity in small business is the hangup of cutting corners financially.

"Potential businessmen are usually concerned with having the newest of ideas and the direction of business trends. Most fail to recognize trend indicators until the trend is fully developed," Revel said. "The reason is clear. Few have access to sufficient information from a wide range of sources to see the pieces going together."

The research department of the entrepreneurs' association assimilates masses of information from all over the world each month, covering practically every area of small business interest. The IEA is the only organization in the nation that specializes in small business research.

Please Turn to Page 3, Col. 4

International Entrepreneurs' Assn. passes on unpublicized ideas for neophyte businessmen

People are constantly looking for new ways to make money. Most of the ideas are unpublicized, and when the average person does hear about them, it is usually too late to make any money.

Suppose you had a friend in every city of the world constantly watching for new, profitable ideas. If all these friends reported back to you, you would have a formidible choice of exploitable ideas.

Chase Revel, a management consultant and now director of International Entrepreneurs' Assn. (IEA), the creator and key sponsor of the Start Your Own Business Expo, made this theory a reality. The association has more than 30,000 members throughout the world constantly feeding new ideas into the central headquarters in Santa Monica where they are compiled and disseminated to members.

Several years ago, Revel realized that the Tuneupmasters low-priced, quick tune-up concept was very profitable and could work in any city. The firm had only eight shops at the time—they now have 53. He told IEA members that he felt this was one of the hottest new business ideas of that year.

Some European members reported several years ago that discos were beginning to catch on over there. Revel passed on this information to members in the United States and now, as everyone knows, discos are everywhere.

Not only are new ideas and concepts passed between members, but news of new dynamic products are included.

Association officials will be on hand at the business expo to show you the latest new ideas gleaned from around the world and answer questions about membership in IEA.

Opportunities abound for the absentee owner

Is it possible to work for someone else and still own your own business?

According to industrial psychologist Phill Beane it is not only possible, but "absentee ownership is becoming one of the most popular forms of small business investment in the United States."

Beane, who has studied behavior patterns of middle-management executives for the past two decades, says that of the men and women he has studied, there is a growing uneasiness with the firm in which they work.

"They can't afford to quit because they're making too much money. Yet, they can't really get ahead," he said. "They're looking for some alternative."

In the 1960s that alternative was the stock market. Recently, however, with the stock market showing erratic growth, investors are turning to

Please Turn to Page 3, Col. 6

Voice analyzer proves better than polygraph

The Mark II Voice Analyzer will not only be one of the most unique small business investment opportunities at the Start Your Own Business Expo '77, but will also be one of the most promising.

The Mark II, which measures the changes in stress in a person's voice when he is answering questions, has proven to be more accurate than the traditional polygraph machine, and its utilization is much broader.

Aside from police departments, a growing number of companies and industries are adopting the compact machine, which fits into a briefcase, for everything from interviews with potential employees to breaking internal theft rings.

The device, which was developed after nearly 10 years of research, is simple to operate, and anyone can easily be trained in its use.

Marcon Ltd. of Long Beach will display and demonstrate the Mark II at the expo and conducts intensive training classes as part of its sales and distribution program.

"The use of the machine in the past few years has been nothing short of phenomenal," said Sam Lowery, president of the firm, "but even though industry is anxious to utilize the equipment most companies don't have the time to send their people through an indoctrination course.

"That's where the real opportunity comes in. Many of our distributors act as consultants."

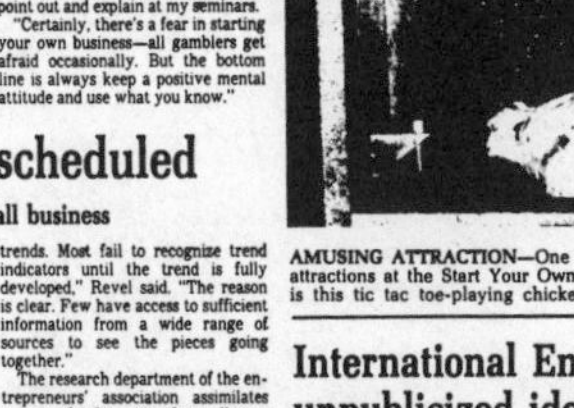

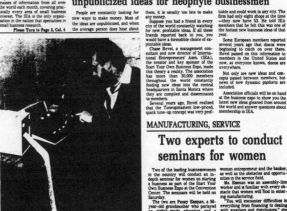

OUTPERFORMS POLYGRAPH—The voice stress analyzer, a machine with the ability to overhear a telephone conversation and predict whether the person on either end of the line is telling the truth, is just one of the many small business opportunities on display at the Start Your Own Business Expo, which opens at the Los Angeles Convention Center next Friday for a three-day run.

Mayor's office offers help

Unknown to many small businessmen is an office on the 20th floor of the Los Angeles City Hall that could mean thousands of dollars in additional business to firms throughout the city.

The office is the Mayor's Office of Small Business Assistance, which was established in April, 1975, by Mayor Bradley to foster increased commercial dealings between the City and small businesses in the area.

MANUFACTURING, SERVICE

Two experts to conduct seminars for women

Two of the leading businesswomen in the country will conduct an in-depth seminar for women on starting a business as part of the Start Your Own Business Expo at the Convention Center. The seminars will be held on Saturday.

The two are Pansy Essman, a 56-year-old grandmother who parlayed an eighth-grade education and a dream into a $1 million-a-year business, and Virginia Mullen, vice president and treasurer of Scope Industries and a director of the First Women's Bank in Los Angeles.

Ms. Essman will describe the opportunities and obstacles in the manufacturing field. Ms. Mullen will discuss the relationship between the woman entrepreneur and the banker, as well as the obstacles and opportunities in the service field.

Ms. Essman was an assembly-line worker and is familiar with every obstacle that women will find in entering manufacturing.

"You will encounter difficulties in everything from financing to dealing with suppliers and distributors," she said, "but all of these problems can be overcome. Women are missing enormous opportunities in the manufacturing area."

Ms. Mullen, who has been in industry for her entire business career, has viewed women in business from a different perspective.

Please Turn to Page 3, Col. 5

Who's Who, Report #26

If your biography were in *Who's Who*, wouldn't you want a copy? That's the reason they sell so well. The price ranges from $35 to $50 per copy. Publish a *Who's Who* of your area and net upwards of $125,000. Easy to compile and sell because all business is transacted by mail. Minimum cash needed—$20,000.

Free Style University, Report #89

Heliotrope college grossed over $500,000 last year with a 30% net simply offering classes on unusual subjects with no classrooms of their own. The teachers teach in their home and split the tuition with the college. Most cities are wide open for this but you'll need about $15,000 in capital.

Tune-Up Shop, Report #9

New specialty. Originator has 31 shops in only three years of operation. Most net $40,000 before taxes. Only $4,000 investment and entire country is wide open. Mechanic/managers readily available everywhere for absentee-owners. Easy to control.

No Smoking Clinic, Report #17

A $280,000 average annual profit on an investment as low as $15,000. Thirty-six million Americans want to quit smoking. Clinics using "aversion therapy," an extension of Pavlov's conditioned-reflex theory, make it easy. Our editor quit a two-pack-a-day habit with one hour of treatment, and had no desire for a cigarette at all, nor any withdrawal symptoms. You don't need to be a doctor or have any medical background to open this clinic. We include all details, plus an actual narrative of the therapy.

Dive For A Pearl, Report #1

Customers pay $3.75 to pick an unopened oyster guaranteed to have a pearl in it. Strange as it may seem, the company we report on has fourteen stores with a b/t profit exceeding $30,000 per store. $4,000 in cash will start you out, and no experience in jewelry is necessary. Market is virgin.

Psychic Training, Report #46

Teach people how to use their mindpower to perform unusual phenomena, including becoming a psychic. This fantastic concept is sweeping the country. One instructor nets $10,000 for a five-day lecture. Anybody can do it—complete dialogue and source of training, $2,000 start-up cost.

Day-Care Centers, Report #58

Tremendous growth business but only very profitable when certain criteria are met. Some net $150,000 before taxes on as little as $20,000 investment. Most centers are running at capacity. Ideal absentee owner business. We show you the only way to start one for high profits.

Instant Print Shop, Report #13

Even though you see lots of instant printing shops around, few realize half of their potential. Where they are missing the boat is clearly outlined here, with a case history of a retired Army Sergeant grossing $122,000 his first year in business, and netting $45,000 b/t. He had no printing experience, but realized how ignorant his competitors were. His total investment was less than $5,000.

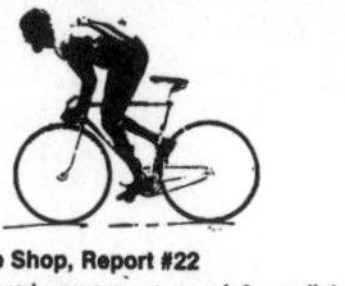

Bicycle Shop, Report #22

Bike rental operators get started for as little as $1,800 and get their investment back in the first month. To start a bike shop you'll need about $5,000 in cash. The profit margin is not the highest, but we found one store that grossed nearly $900,000 in 1973. Today the big demand is for repair shops.

Pinball Arcade, Report #100

A local neighborhood arcade can become a teen hang-out and show over $25,000 annual profit on an investment of less than $1,000. Locations in shopping malls are the big money-makers, with many netting over $70,000 per year on a cash investment of $10,000.

Car Wash, Report #76

The owners are "doing it at the car wash." The top ones we found were netting over $125,000 a year. The investment is substantial with the lowest in the $15,000 range and the average between $35,000 and $50,000. However, scientific methods exist for choosing a location and estimating the gross.

Dry Cleaners, Report #37

There are numerous dry cleaning shops in every city. Some make average profits and some make phenomenal take-home earnings. We have investigated and discovered the reason—and how you can make over $50,000 per year in this common business venture. The instructions are simple and you will receive assistance all along the way. $15,000 to $20,000 is the minimum cash investment.

Coffee Shop Restaurants, Report #59

$250,000 pre-tax profit for some who found the key to a successful shop. We tell their experiences and angles. Investment could be as low as $5,000.

Trade Schools, Report #47

We profile a *Bartender's Training School*, but report covers starting any type of trade school. Easy to start and operate, and has become a booming field. $1,000 per week is not unusual. Start-up costs, $6,000 minimum.

Employment Agency, Report #51

Minimum investment needed for this one is $5,000. A high-profit business under the right conditions—and we tell you what they are.

Miniwarehouse, Report #42

A 62% return on investment—plus equity gain. Amazing, but under the right conditions these consumer storage facilities are top money-makers, with as little as a $15,000 investment. We cover construction of a new warehouse, as well as conversion of an existing building.

Self-Service Gas Station, Report #68

A new concept is sweeping the oil industry. Full-service gas stations will soon be a thing of the past. New government controls protect operators from unproportionate deliveries in any energy crisis. Some are netting over $75,000 on investments as low as $5,000.

Contest Promotions, Report #30

Believe it or not, many people will pay to enter a contest to try to win money. One company has been running these contests for over 8 years and had over a million contestants from ads in pulp magazines. Strictly legitimate—and like having your own private state lottery. The company we report on nets close to one-half million dollars annually. Takes a minimum of $7,500 cash to start.

Auto Paint Shop, Report #50

We researched the most successful chain, Earl Scheib, who has over 200 locations—and found plenty of room for competition. Average gross of $337,640 can show profits of over $57,000 with as little as $4,000 invested. Painting cars is simple, as we show you.

Figure Developers, Report #64

Exercise-type bust developers actually work and the majority of women want larger bust line. These units have been sold exclusively through mailorder for years.

However, we discovered a brand new exciting way to capitalize on this untouched market. $3,000 cash needed as minimum investment.

Fried Chicken Restaurant, Report #55

Take-out chicken restaurant owners have found you don't need the Kentucky Fried Chicken name to be a success. Independents gross almost as much with higher net profit percentages. Some net near a whopping $150,000 a year. Included in this report are the ingredients to Col. Sander's "secret recipe." Start as low as $5,000.

Tool & Equipment Rental, Report #28

This is one of the fastest-growing businesses around. Some stores are experiencing a 20% increase in sales each year. We found one wholesaler of tools and equipment who will take you by the hand, teach you everything about the business, finance 75% of your inventory and fixtures, and give you advice any time you need it—all for buying your inventory from him. And we couldn't beat his prices anywhere. $15,000 to $30,000 cash is required. Profit before taxes ranges from $20,000 to $70,000 for new operations. Step-by-step instructions are included for those who want to start independently.

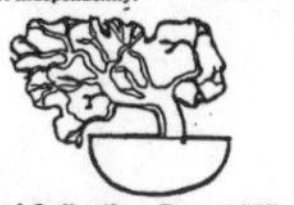

Bonsai Collecting, Report #57

A 28-inch-high bonsai tree recently sold for $8,500. Most small trees sell in the $100 to $500 range. Experienced collector shows how you can dig these trees from the forest, naturally bonsaied, and find an immediate market—collectors abound. $100 starts and there's a $25,000 potential in the first year just working weekends.

Plant Shop, Report #2

Take advantage of the booming interest in green plants with this business. We picked the most successful merchandiser around and describe his unique process of selling plants. Very low start-up costs—$1,500 to $7,000. Net $40,000 to $50,000.

Furniture Store, Report #11

A unique method of running this store makes it highly profitable—an annual pretax net of $84,000 plus, from an investment as low as $7,000. Many furniture stores throughout the U.S. but plenty of room for more. Experienced personnel are plentiful and ready to show an absentee-owner the way to go.

Liquor Store, Report #24

The seemingly depression-proof liquor business is perfect for the person who wants large profits with minimum risks. Liquor stores show one of the lowest mortality rates of any retail business. Distillers directed us to the most profitable stores in the country, and from them we have created a composite of the perfect store. Investment can be as low as $5,000 in some states—though $30,000 is a more realistic average figure. Profits range from a low of $20,000 to highs of $150,000—the average is around $40,000 annually.

Art Show Promoter, Report #21

You don't need to know anything about art to start this one. There are thousands of artists in every city who can't get an art gallery to show their work. They will jump at the chance to participate in an art show. With $100 to $500 you can put on a show each weekend for these artists and net over $35,000 per year. One of the easiest businesses to start that we've seen. Two case histories included.

Burlwood Tables, Report #93

Tables made from tree stumps sell for $300 to $600. The stumps are free for the taking. Two entrepreneurs we found sold between $50,000 and $60,000 in two months. Minimum investment $500; Average investment $15,000.

Green Plant Leasing & Service, Report #49

Green plant rental and maintenance is a new industry riding on the tails of the fantastic boom in indoor nursery products. Many people are finding that caring for plants is a problem and a nuisance especially the managers of restaurants and office buildings. Thus, the emergence of the plant serviceman. Can be started part-time with $1,000 or less. Nets of $3,000 to $4,000 per month are not unusual. And you don't need to know the first thing about plants.

Old-Fashioned Ice Cream Bar, Report #36

Hand dip ice cream bars in chocolate like they did in the 1800's, and make a bundle. Started three years ago at a ccounty fair, over 40,000 bars were sold at 35 cents each in two weeks. The re-creator of this method now has 10 shops that will gross close to a million dollars this year. A few had start-up costs of less than $300.

Stuffed Toy Animals, Report #39

We've all seen plush toy animals being sold roadside at some time or another. With the help of an interpreter, we interviewed a Mexican immigrant who was grossing over $40,000 per year, and netting more than $17,000 profit before taxes. His starting capital was a borrowed $200. The amazing fact was that he spoke only a few words of English. Several other case histories are included that are equally amazing.

Computer Handwriting Analysis, Report #8

No matter how corny or carney it sounds, we couldn't resist reporting on this unusual money-maker. No experience of any kind is needed; as little as $800 in cash starts you, with case histories showing $22,000 to $60,000 profit per year.

Janitorial Service, Report #34

Some office building management companies pay a million dollars per year just to keep the floors spotless, the ashtrays clean, wastebaskets emptied and windows shining. You can enter this billion-dollar business with just a few hundred dollars and little talent. Case histories show men netting $30,000 their first year on a $300 investment, and $50,000 the second year. Easy to get into, and the competition is generally uneducated.

Earring Shop, Report #60

Shop specializing in ear-piercing and earrings is the new hit on the retail scene. Mark-ups range from 300% to 1,000%. Market untapped as only a few are operating. You can even start at flea markets and swap meets for as little as $600. Shops net around $25,000, absentee-owned.

Pet Shop, Report #7

If you or your wife like animals, this is the business for you. The net profit percentage is one of the highest in retail sales, and some started with as little as $5,000 cash.

Digital Watch Repair, Report #95

Digital watches are creating a headache for consumers and jewelry stores because many of the manufacturers have gone out of business due to competition from the big five and no repair services exist yet. Repair is simply replacing simple parts or a chip. Any electronic technician can handle. A wide open market with unknown potential over 12-million watches are out there with no place to be repaired. Minimum investment $1,500; average investment $4,000.

Custom Rug Making, Report #66

Companies, businesses and individuals will pay high prices for individualized handmade rugs as wall and floor decor showing their trademark, logo or crest. Start from your home with $75. Profit potential $15,000 to $30,000.

T-Shirt Shop, Report #43

Decaling T-shirts with a small heat-transfer machine is a small business which some started for under $500. Profits are high—we found one store netting $6,000 per month. A simple, easy absentee-owner business.

Popcorn Man, Report #25

Popcorn, caramel corn, cotton candy and snow cones have the highest margin of profit of any snack food—with a cost as little as 10% of the retail price. You can get into this business with as little as $250, and we show several case histories of profits of $20,000 to $40,000 for small operators working only part-time.

Window Cleaning, Report #12

An investment of less than $50 can put you into this unusual business. There's practically no competition and the business requires no skill and little business knowledge. Two case histories reveal profits from $3,000 to $4,000 per month.

Furniture Stripping, Report #52

The antique craze has created an unyielding demand for this simple service. Most strippers are booked solid for weeks in advance. New simple system makes it possible to get into this business for less than $900—and you can even begin at home.

Ghost Dog Manufacturing, Report #29

Here's a hot item anyone with a minimum of intelligence can make in his home. You'll find a lucrative market. All you need is a few simple hand tools and less than $100 for materials. Case history shows one producer netting $28,000 his first year. The market is practically virgin for this humorous and unusual product.

Mattress Shop, Report #72

Specialty mattress shops net from $20,000 to $45,000 on an investment of around $8,000. Easy to start and operate. Great for an absentee owner.

Consignment Car Sales, Report #18

Get into big-time auto sales with as little as $900 in cash. An amazing concept! Not only do you sell cars for people, the big profit area is in buying cars for customers at wholesale prices. All the ins and outs explained. A great new gimmick shows one dealer netting $8,000 per month, and two others over $5,000.

Photocopy Shop, Report #38

Lease a photocopier and a small shop—and net over $3,000 per month. Many shops do over 150,000 copies monthly, and we found one hitting the half-million mark. Demand is astounding! Cash needed: $2,000.

Parking Lot Striping, Report #31

Hundreds of thousands of parking lots in this country need daily, weekly, monthly or annual maintenance. If you can draw a straight line with a ruler and have approximately $200 in cash, you can earn in excess of $25,000. A detailed case history shows how one man started with the parking lot where he worked and built his business from there.

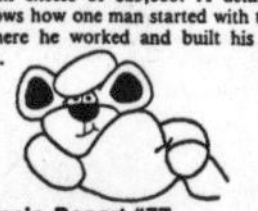

Vinyl Repair, Report #77

On first assumption we thought this was a low income business. But on investigation we found several operators netting over $50,000. In surveying the country we found many cities without this service but the need was there. Prime market is car dealers. A shoe-string investment would be $450. Realistically expect to invest more.

Sunglass Specialists, Report #65

We found a shop in a mall specializing in just sunglasses, netting over $27,000 annually for the last three years. Mark-up is high—300% to 500%. We found another lady at a flea market with a $400 inventory netting $125 per day.

Carpet Cleaning, Report #53

You can't roll up wall-to-wall carpet and sent it out for cleaning. This means it must be cleaned "on location." You can enter this profitable business with little cash, and we have outlined all the steps and how to select the right equipment.

Muffler Shop, Report #44

A $6,000 cash investment return $118,000 b/t profit the first year. Believe it or not, there's a virgin market for mufflers because of a new concept that has Midas scared. Large complicated inventories are no longer needed. Several case histories.

Hamburger Is King, Report #16

The inside way to start a unique hamburger stand for as little as $800, and net $20,000 annually. You could be next door to McDonald's and still do it—probably with more profit. No cooking skills are needed. This report will show you how to have the best-known hamburger stand in town.

Pizzeria, Report #6

You don't need to be Italian or know how to cook. Proven recipes and complete instructions are included in this report. Easy to start—you can "shoestring" it for as little as $600 and net better than $20,000 annually. The food business is an easy place for those with short capital to make a bundle.

Hot Dog Stand, Report #73

Years ago hot dogs outsold hamburgers as a fast food. Market trends indicate their cycle is coming back. We show an angle several people have used where you can open a shop for as little as $950. A few case histories show profits exceeding $40,000.

Mobile Restaurant or Sandwich Truck, Report #56

Many areas still don't have this service that provides hot and cold sandwiches for factory and office workers. $500 starts. Sandwiches can be made at home. Profits reported as high as $48,000 for a one-truck operation. Expansion potential unrestricted.

Auto Jockey, Report #48

Valet parking service for restaurants. A few hours of work per day pays one operator servicing only six restaurants a $54,000 b/t net annually. He started with $400 in cash. Another company grosses over a million dollars every year.

Order manuals by number and title

1. Dive-For-A-Pearl Shop—$10
2. Plant Shops—$15
3. Balloon Vendor—$10
4. Tennis Club—$15
5. Athletic Shoe Store—$15
6. Pizzaria—$15
7. Pets Shop—$15
8. Handwriting Analysis—$10
9. Tune Up Shop—$15
10. A Rose For The Lady—$10
11. Furniture Store—$15
12. Window Washing Service—$10
13. Print Shop—$15
14. Adult Book Store—$15
15. Mailorder Business—$15
16. Hamburger Shop—$10
17. Quit Smoking Clinic—$15
18. Consignment Used Car Lot—$10
19. Cheese Shop—$45
20. Flea Market Promoters—$15
21. Art Show Promoters—$10
22. Bicycle Shops—$15
23. Rental Agency Publisher—$15
24. Liquor Store—$15
25. Popcorn Vendor—$10
26. Who's Who Publishing—$15
27. Antique Photo Shop—$10
28. Tool & Equipment Rental—$15
29. Ghost Dog, Hot Product—$10
30. Contest Promoters—$15
31. Parking Lot Maintenance—$10
32. Antiques Stores—$15
33. Pet Hotel and Grooming—$15
34. Janitorial Services—$10
35. Do-It-Yourself Auto Repair Shop—$10
36. Old Fashioned Ice Cream Bars—$15
37. Dry Cleaning—$15
38. Photocopy Shop—$15
39. Stuffed Toy Animals—$10
40. Adults Only Motel—$15
41. Robot Lawn Mower—$10
42. Mini Warehouses—$15
43. T Shirt Shop—$10
44. Muffler Shops—$15
45. Worm Farming—$10
46. Psychic Training Seminars—$15
47. Trade Schools—$10
48. Auto Jockey—$10
49. Rent A Plant—$15
50. Auto Painters—$15
51. Employment Agency—$15
52. Furniture Stripping—$10
53. Carpet Cleaning—$10
54. Ten Minute Oil Change Shop—$15
55. Southern Fried Chicken Store—$15
56. Mobile Restaurant—$10
57. Bonzai Collecting—$10
58. Day Care Center—$15
59. Coffee Shop—$15
60. Earring Shop—$10
61. Stained Glass Window Manufacturer—$10
62. Sugar-Free Low-Calorie Bakery—$15
63. Lie Detection By Voice Analysis—$10
64. Bust Developers Product—$10
65. Sunglass Shop—$10
66. Customized Rug Making—$10
67. Newsletter Publishing—$15
68. Self-Service Gasoline Station—$15
69. Flea Market - Items How To Find—$10
70. Candy Stand, Roadside—$10
71. Promoting A Seminar—$15
72. Mattress Shop—$15
73. Hot Dog Stand—$10
74. Electronic Mosquito Repeller—(Not Avail.)
75. Hot Tubs—$15
76. Car Wash—$15
77. Vinyl Repair—$10
78. Franchise Pros & Cons—$5
79. Frozen Yogurt Shop—$25
80. Weight Control Clinic—$15
81. How To Chose A Franchise—$5
82. Skateboard Parks—$25
83. Cookie Shop—$25
84. Computer Store—$25
85. SBA Financing-New Business—$25
86. SBA Financing-Existing Business—$25
87. Hidden Franchise Laws—$10
88. Roller Skate Rental—$15
89. Free Style University—$15
90. Roller Skating Rinks—$15
91. Burglar Alarms—$15
92. Import/Export—$15
93. Burlwood Tables—$15
94. Homemade Cake Shop—$15
95. Digital Watch Repair—$15
100. Pinball Arcade—$15

MAIL TO:

RC___AM___SH___ SLP____CL ___EN NM AD CK

International Entreprgneurs Association
631 Wilshire Blvd., Santa Monica, CA 90401

Payment Enclosed: $__________

Charge It To My: ☐ BankAmericard or Chargex ☐ Master Charge

NO. __________

EXP. DATE ______ M.C. Interbank No. ______

Send the following manuals immediately:

Report # ______ Title __________________ Price ______
Report# ______ Title __________________ Price ______
Report# ______ Title __________________ Price ______
Report# ______ Title __________________ Price ______
Report# ______ Title __________________ Price ______

Total ______

Plus 6% Sales Tax Calif. Res. ______

Net Total ______

NAME __________________

ADDRESS __________________

CITY __________ STATE __________ ZIP __________ 480

Revel's first catalog was in the early days of *Entrepreneur*. In it he sold manuals to prospects. A present day catalog, which features more than 200 start-up manuals follows. Throughout the catalog there are success stories detailing the lives of people who entered a business they read about in *Entrepreneur* and became successful because of the advice they garnered from the manual.

Would you mind if we filled your mailbox with money?

Dear Friend,

No, we're not sending you cash. But what you have in your hands is even better, in the long run. Inside this catalog you'll find over 250 PROVEN moneymaking opportunities. . . one (or more) of which can be your ticket to successful business ownership.

Turn this page and discover how millions of people (most with no great talent or experience) have reaped the multiple rewards of entrepreneurship. Each description highlights the attractive benefits of owning a particular moneymaker and tells you how to get the detailed, inside story on starting that particular business.

The full story on each business can be found in the appropriate _Entrepreneur_ manual--YOUR START-UP GUIDE-- covering every important aspect of successfully running the business.

Our experienced and resourceful research specialists have tapped into their personal information networks to pry out the secrets and tried-and-true techniques of the experts in each business. We pass this expertise on to you in the manuals so that you can start the business(es) of your choice way ahead of the rest of the pack.

If you have any questions after reading this catalog, please give us a call on our toll-free lines (1-800-421-2300, in CA 1-800-352-7449). Our friendly business counselors will help you obtain the materials you need. If you can't decide which of these profitable businesses is best for you, or if you just have some questions about entrepreneurship, give us a call. We're here to help you make the right entrepreneurial moves.

Now go ahead and start reading. There's a lot of money and opportunity here waiting for you.

Sincerely,

Wellington Ewen
President/Publisher

.S. Make sure you read about _Entrepreneur_ Magazine's ¬edictions for 1987's "hottest businesses" elsewhere in this talog. These are 10 businesses I know you'll want to explore.

Promotional Gimmicks

Why pay expensive advertising fees to promote your business when our manual tells you how you can promote your business FREE!

Besides being low-cost or FREE, each and every one of these methods is readily adaptable to your product or business. Here are just a few:

- An outrageous window display used by Tiffany's that cost about $1 per window and got incredible comments, attention, and media publicity
- An ingenious way retailers can capitalize on the dieting craze and draw customers who otherwise probably would never have entered their store
- How a $35 junked auto quadrupled receipts for a New Hampshire grocery store owner
- How a car stereo dealer in Sacramento drew such overflow crowds he could barely handle business. His gimmick—a vat of Jell-O
- How a 6-foot-by-4-foot block of ice and a simple handwritten sign drew 2,000 customers in a 48-hour period for Janney's Ace Hardware
- What would happen if you used homing pigeons to announce your grand opening to the local newspaper, radio, and TV stations? (We'll tell you!)
- How a local business sent out 10,000 postcards carrying a discount coupon that brought in over 4,600 families within two weeks!
- An ingenious promo gimmick involving hermit crabs that boosted patronage in a Southwest nightspot by over 1,000 people

Request **Manual No. X1111, "Promotional Gimmicks."** The price for members is $24.50; nonmembers, $29.50.

Mobile Restaurant/ Sandwich Truck

Factories and offices are a hidden gold mine for anyone wanting to bring sandwiches, drinks, and snacks by three times a day. All you need is a van—you can buy the food from local caterers.

Earnings can run upwards of $50,000 a year for owner-operated vans. However, for as little as $250, you can tie in with a local caterer who'll provide the van and give you the food on consignment. Your profit won't be quite as high, but this is a dynamic business and some areas are still wide open. Our manual will tell you everything you need to get started in this lucrative business.

Request **Manual No. X1056, "Mobile Restaurant/Sandwich Truck."** Members, $39.50; nonmembers, $45.00.

Teacher's Agency (Free-Style University)

One college we found grossed over $500,000 one year with a 30 percent net simply by offering classes on unusual subjects often, with no official classrooms of their own. The teachers conduct classes in various locations and split the tuition collected with the college. There are still opportunities galore in this field.

Request **Manual No. X1089, "Teacher's Agency."** The special member price is just $44.50; nonmembers, $49.50.

Private Mailbox Service

The demand for post office boxes is so great, waiting lists at local post offices are quite often several months long. Obviously, businesspeople—particularly those that are home-based—and other consumers can't afford to wait that long just to obtain a mailing address.

And that's where the country's rapidly expanding cadre of private mailbox services are cashing in. Not only can almost any private mailbox service offer a business or individual *immediate* mailbox space, many of them can provide an important added benefit that the U.S. Postal Service cannot match—a prestigious address of the customer's choice.

All the results of *Entrepreneur*'s extensive research are available in this completely updated manual, which contains actual figures from currently operating businesses, including:
- Complete start-up projections;
- How to price your boxes;
- High-profit extras you can offer;
- How to advertise your new business;
- What equipment you will need, and its cost;
- How to choose your site and set up your location;
- A chapter devoted to daily operations.

The start-up capital required for this business can be as low as $10,000, and our research shows some owners grossing as much as $55,000. This is a growing field, and many opportunities still exist to establish private mailbox services throughout much of the nation. Request **Manual No. X1147, "Private Mailbox Service."** The special members' price is just $54.50; nonmembers, $59.50.

Furniture-Stripping Service

Furniture stripping is not new; people have been doing it for years whenever they wanted to prepare an old piece of furniture for refinishing. There have always been commercial furniture-refinishing shops. But specialty houses doing furniture stripping as a consumer service are relatively new. There's a good chance to make big bucks in this field.

To get your copy, request **Manual No. X1052, "Furniture-Stripping Service."** The special member price is just $34.50; nonmembers, $39.50.

201

Package inserts are sales pieces. They are ways to test a mailing list, and are relatively inexpensive compared to space advertising.

The piece may share a package with several other inserts. They are put into packages along with the merchandise that has been ordered by the customer. When the customer receives his merchandise, he or she also gets the inserts.

A mail order marketer can test a list in this manner. If the response is good, the marketer can purchase the remainder of the list and do a special mailing to it. If the response is poor, they can forget the list.

Naturally, by sharing a package with other mail order companies, response is diluted; however, the package insert still remains an effective way to test.

Notice, too, the necessity to put as much information as possible in a small space. This insert was for Revel's Van Pler & Tissany. He tested 10 lists with it and found 4 that warranted further mailings.

Please Read Privately!

Dear friend,

You'll understand the reason for the secrecy shortly. It all began in Russia many years ago.

I'm an executive with one of the largest jewelry companies in the country. Van Pler and Tissany in Beverly Hills. One day a Russian diplomat came to see me. He handed me a beautiful three carat diamond ring and asked how much it's worth. I looked at it carefully under the microscope. The diamond was perfect — not a flaw, and it had much more brilliance than the average diamond.

I rubbed it against a piece of test glass. It cut the glass easily. I told the Russian that the retail value was about $20,000. He laughed and said, "Are you sure?"

I called in Lloyd, my head jeweler, to look at it. Lloyd is 59 years old and had grown up in the jewelry business. After a minute or so of examining the diamond, he came to the same conclusion — "It's perfect and has exceptional brilliance."

The Russian diplomat laughed again and said, "It's a counterfeit!"

We were astonished and couldn't believe it. But the Russian went on to explain. "Our scientists have counterfeited a perfect diamond! And I'm here to see if you are interested in obtaining the formula from us on a royalty basis."

I did and everyone that sees it is fooled. ABC's "20/20" TV show took the counterfeit to New York's famous Diamond Mart for appraisal. Without any suspicion several diamond experts gave the counterfeit appraisals in the thousands of dollars.

New York Magazine stated in a recent article, "...it looks even better than a mined diamond."

THAT'S THE REASON FOR THE SECRECY!

It is called "The Van Pler Simulated Diamond." (We'll refer to it as just the "Van Pler Diamond" from here on.) A short time ago it was introduced in Europe with tremendous acceptance. It's retailing there now for over $100.00 a carat.

$25.00 A CARAT FOR THIS SALE ONLY!

As a giant promotional campaign to introduce the incredible, new Van Pler Diamond, only the first 5,000 people in each state will be allowed to buy these beautiful

FOOTNOTE: The only people in Russia who can have a diamond, ruby, emerald, sapphire or pearl are a handful of political leaders, even though they mine millions of carats of these gems every year. (The second largest diamond mines in the world are in Russia.) Outside of industrial use, they sell all their real gems to the free world market. Their Communist laws forbid the people to waste money on such extravagances, however, the common people demanded and were allowed to have jewelry, but with simulated gems. As a result, over many years, the Russians have become the world experts in making high quality counterfeit jewels.

jewels at a sensational low price of $25.00 a carat on a first-come, first-served basis.

There is a limit of two Van Pler Diamonds per order unless the order is postmarked before January 1, 1987. Orders postmarked before then may request a maximum of 7 diamonds.

Since this is a promotional campaign to introduce the Van Pler Diamond to the nation at a cost way below our regular wholesale price, no orders from jewelers or department stores will be accepted.

Due to the tremendous acceptance of the Van Pler Diamonds in Europe, Americans are expected to respond even more enthusiastically. I believe everyone has felt how wonderful it would be to give someone you love a diamond.

The Van Pler Diamond is not as brittle as a mined diamond and is resistant to shattering because it was created at the incredible temperature of over 5000° Fahrenheit. The hardest steel melts at only 2,786°F.

The Van Pler Diamond will last many, many lifetimes without any worries. In fact, you will receive a Lifetime Warranty against any defects.

We are so certain you will be very pleased with a Van Pler Diamond that we will let you examine them in your home without risking a dollar. If for any reason you do not like the Van Pler Diamond, just mail it back to us within 30 days and we will return your postdated check uncashed.

Use any Major Credit Card. All unmounted diamond orders shipped in four working days, First Class Insured Mail. Jewelry is shipped in 10 working days.

Imagine how exciting it will be to show off your new diamond to your friends. And remember, it's warranted for a lifetime in writing.

Sincerely,

Gene Rowland

Gene Rowland
Executive Director

P.S. Mail your order before January 31, 1987, and receive FREE
— a one carat real amethyst, topaz or citrine gemstone.

INSIDE
VERY UNIQUE JEWELRY AT
INCREDIBLY LOW SALE PRICES

Van Pler & Tissany Fine Jewelers

465 S. Beverly Drive, Beverly Hills, CA 90212

☐ Mr.
☐ Ms.
☐ Mrs. _____

Address:_____ Apt. #_____

City: _____

State:_____ Zip:_____

IMPORTANT: Ladies Rings over size 9, add $10.00 per size above 9. For example, size 11 is $20.00 additional.

Men's Rings over size 11, add $10.00 per size above 11. For example, size 13 will be $20.00 additional.

No refunds on ladies rings over size 10 or under size 4, or men's rings over size 12 or under size 8.

Order Number	Item Name	How Many	Ring Size	Color: White/Yellow Gold or Sterling Silver	Price

	Sub Total	
☐ Payment Enclosed	Calif. Res. Add 6½% Sales Tax	
(No C.O.D.s) (All personal checks will be verified with your bank).	Shipping & Insurance	$3.00
Postdated Checks Accepted ONLY for Unmounted Diamonds not jewelry.	Total U.S. Dollars	

Bill my credit card: ☐ VISA ☐ Mastercard ☐ Am Express
Card No.:

Exp. Date: _____
(No orders shipped without expiration date)

Sign if Charging:_____
X534

How to Determine Your Ring Size

Cut out and wrap around finger. Make sure it will slip over knuckle. The point where A meets the number is your size. Half way between is a half-size.

0 1 2 3 4 5 6 7 8 9 10 11 12 13 14

A

"Confessions of a Hard-Nosed Millionaire" was one of Revel's first mailing pieces that detailed his life story. It was *Entrepreneur*'s most effective subscription piece.

Notice the hardened appearance Revel has in the cover picture. The cover follows.

Confessions
Of A Hard-Nosed
Millionaire

The following is a page taken from *Standard Rate & Data Service,* another must for mail order entrepreneurs.

Note the rundown on this page of "consumer lists." For example, *The Sharper Image* (a catalog) goes to consumers. The "description" of its buyers and "list source" are extremely important. Males account for 82% of its list, with an average purchase of $150, which is one of the highest figures of any catalog.

Compare their list to some of the other publications listed on the page. SRDS is a resource that also contains list brokers and managers.

553 General Merchandise Mail Order Buyers

SAMSUNG ELECTRONIC EQUIPMENT BUYERS—cont

1. PERSONNEL
List Manager
Ed Burnett Consultants, Inc., 99 W. Sheffield Ave., Englewood, NJ 07631. Phone 201-871-1100. Toll free 800-223-7777 outside NJ.
All recognized brokers.

2. DESCRIPTION
Buyers of TVs, VCRs, modular display screens, microwave ovens and other electronic equipment.

3. LIST SOURCE
Warrantee cards.

4. QUANTITY AND RENTAL RATES
Rec'd March, 1986.

	Total Number	Price per/M
Total list	253,000	50.00
Hotline (monthly)	25,000	55.00
Microwave ovens (1984-85)	120,000	50.00

Selections: product, 5.00/M extra; state, SCF, sex, 2.50/M extra.
Minimum order 5,000.

(D-C)

S.A.V.E.
(This is a paid duplicate of the listing under classification No. 612.)
Media Code 3 553 6547 9.00   Mid 021348-000
Member: D.M.A.
Participant D.M.A. Mail Preference Service.
G.R.I. Corporation.
65 E. Southwater, Chicago, IL 60601. Phone 312-977-3670.

1. PERSONNEL
President—Frank Wittosch.
General Sales Manager—Michael T. Colucci.
Sales Administrator—Ametra Carrol.
Branch Office
New York 10036—1212 Avenue of the Americas. Phone 212-869-6155.
Broker and/or Authorized Agent
All recognized brokers.

2. DESCRIPTION
Purchasers of package goods collections on a continuity club basis about every two months. Multi-buyers purchased two or more collections. Former buyers have purchased multiple kits and paid for all collections before discontinuing membership. Trial buyers have purchased only the introductory offer.
Average unit of sale 10.00.

3. LIST SOURCE
Direct mail, package inserts, direct response space ads.

4. QUANTITY AND RENTAL RATES
Rec'd February, 1986.

	Total Number	Price per/M
Buyers	900,000	52.50
Multi-buyers	516,000	57.50
Former multi-buyers (12 months)	575,000	50.00
Former trial buyers (12 months)	170,000	47.50
New names added	142,000	55.00
New multi-buyers	121,000	60.00
Hotline multi-buyers	281,000	*

Selections: age groups (A: 18-24, B: 25-34, C: 35-49, D: 50+), marital status, children (1, 2, 3 or more), ages of children (0-2, 2-5, 6-11, 12-17), apartment/homeowner, 3.00/M; telephone (yes or no), 5.00/M; income (25,000.00+, 17,000.00 - 25,000.00, 14,000.00-17,000.00, less than 14,000.00), income index of social position, Catholic surname, 6.00/M; state, SCF, 3.00/M; census block group, running charge, 5.00/M extra; ZIP Code, credit card, 5.00/M; keying (4-digit), no extra charge; keying (5 or more digits), .75/M; telephone numbers 30.00/M; prism clusters, 10.00/M extra.

5. COMMISSION, CREDIT POLICY
20% commission to all recognized brokers.

6. METHOD OF ADDRESSING
4/5-up Cheshire labels. Pressure sensitive labels, 4.00/M extra. Magnetic tape (9T 1600 BPI), 15.00 nonrefundable fee.

7. DELIVERY SCHEDULE
Two weeks from receipt of order.

8. RESTRICTIONS
No cosmetic offers. Sample mailing piece required with order. Mailing dates must be cleared in advance.

9. TEST ARRANGEMENT
Minimum 10,000.

11. MAINTENANCE
Updated quarterly.

(D-C8)

SCINTILLA SATIN SHOP, INC.
Media Code 3 553 6636 0.00   Mid 019553-000
Scintilla Satin Shop Inc.

1. PERSONNEL
List Manager
Names & Addresses, Inc., 3605 Woodhead Drive, Suite 101, Northbrook, IL 60062. Phone 312-272-7933.

2. DESCRIPTION
Mail order buyers of satin sheets, bedspreads, loungewear, intimate apparel, negligees, nightwear and accessories, 60% female.
Average unit of sale 60.00.

3. LIST SOURCE
Catalog mailings and space ads in Wall Street Journal, Playboy, Playgirl, Ebony, Cosmopolitan, Redbook, House Beautiful, Oui, Harpers Bazaar, etc.

4. QUANTITY AND RENTAL RATES
Rec'd January, 1984.

	Total Number	Price per/M
Buyers (1978-83)	19,000	60.00
Inquiries (1978-83)	17,500	50.00

Selections: state, SCF, 2.50/M extra; ZIP Code, sex, 5.00/M extra; keying (up to 5-digits) 1.00/M extra.
Minimum order 5,000.

6. METHOD OF ADDRESSING
4/5-up Cheshire. Pressure sensitive labels 6.00/M extra. Magnetic tape (9T 1600 BPI).

8. RESTRICTIONS
2 sample mailing pieces required for approval.

SCOTTISH & IRISH IMPORTS, LTD.
Media Code 3 553 6662 6.00   Mid 038441-000
Scottish & Irish Imports, Ltd.

1. PERSONNEL
List Manager
The Listworks Corp. List Management Division, 40 Radio Circle, P.O. Box 459, Mount Kisco, NY 10549. Phone 914-241-1900.

2. DESCRIPTION
Mail order catalog buyers of tartans, tam o'shanters, coats-of-arms, crests, coins, bonnets, brogues, brooches, shortbreads and puddings, musical instruments and recordings, travel, history and legend books, etc.
Average unit of sale 50.00.

3. LIST SOURCE
Direct mail.

4. QUANTITY AND RENTAL RATES
Rec'd March, 1986.

	Total Number	Price per/M
Total list (1985)	37,628	70.00

Selections: state, SCF, 3.50/M extra; keying, 1.50/M extra; ZIP Code, 4.00/M extra.
Minimum order 5,000.

6. METHOD OF ADDRESSING
4-up Cheshire labels. Pressure sensitive labels, 7.50/M extra. Magnetic tape (9T 1600 BPI), 25.00 nonreturnable fee.

8. RESTRICTIONS
Sample mailing piece required for approval.

SELECTIVE SHOPPER
Media Code 3 553 6688 1.00   Mid 018494-000
A.A.S., Inc.

1. PERSONNEL
List Manager
Names & Addresses, Inc., 3605 Woodhead Dr., Suite 101, Northbrook, IL 60062. Phone 312-272-7933.

2. DESCRIPTION
Doctors, dentists, presidents, lawyers and C.P.A.'s who have purchased personal and gift merchandise. 95% men; median age 43.1.
Average unit of sale 99.00.

3. LIST SOURCE
25% direct mail; 75% space ads.

4. QUANTITY AND RENTAL RATES
Rec'd March, 1986.

	Total Number	Price per/M
Total list (1985)	6,257	75.00
1984-85	12,194	
1983-85	26,783	70.00
1982	11,809	60.00

Selections: recency, 5.00/M extra; state, SCF, ZIP Code, 3.00/M extra; keying, 1.00/M extra.
Minimum order 5,000.

5. COMMISSION, CREDIT POLICY
20% commission to recognized brokers.

6. METHOD OF ADDRESSING
4/5-up Cheshire labels. Pressure sensitive labels, 6.00/M extra. Magnetic tape (9T 1600 BPI).

8. RESTRICTIONS
Two sample mailing pieces required with order.

10. LETTER SHOP SERVICES
Return mag tape to: John Clure, A-1 Computer Serv., 112 Main St., New Canaan, CT 06840.

(C-C2)

SERVICE MERCHANDISE MAIL ORDER BUYERS
Media Code 3 553 6741 8.00   Mid 023363-000
Service Merchandise Catalog Showrooms.

1. PERSONNEL
List Manager
Woodruff-Stevens & Associates, Inc., 345 Park Ave. So., New York, NY 10010. Phone 212-685-4600.
All recognized brokers.

2. DESCRIPTION
Mail order buyers of jewelry, garden, automotive, household accessories, kitchen appliances, toys, sports equipment, etc.; 40% male (families).
Average unit of sale 70.00.

3. LIST SOURCE
Direct mail.

4. QUANTITY AND RENTAL RATES
Rec'd March, 1986.

	Total Number	Price per/M
Total list (1985)	29,088	50.00
Hotline (90 days)	11,784	55.00

Selections: ZIP Code, over/under 50.00, 5.00/M extra; state, SCF, sex, 3.00/M extra; keying, 1.00/M extra.
Minimum order 5,000.

6. **METHOD OF ADDRESSING**
4-up Cheshire labels. Pressure sensitive labels, 5.00/M extra. Magnetic tape (9T 1600 BPI).
8. **RESTRICTIONS**
Sample mailing piece required with every order.

SHAPE MAGAZINE SUBSCRIBERS
(This is a paid duplicate of the listing under classification No. 556.)

Media Code 3 553 6748 3.00   Mid 031183-000
Weider Health & Fitness.
1. **PERSONNEL**
List Manager
American List Counsel, Inc., 88 Orchard Rd., CN-5219, Princeton, NJ 08543. Phone 201-874-4300. Toll free 800-526-3973. QWIP 201-874-4433.
All recognized brokers.
2. **DESCRIPTION**
Subscribers and expires to Shape, a magazine on health and fitness for women. Median age 28.4; 98% female. Average unit of sale 20.00.
3. **LIST SOURCE**
95% direct response sold; 5% space ads.
4. **QUANTITY AND RENTAL RATES**
Rec'd February, 1986.

	Total Number	Price per/M
Subscribers	169,092	55.00
Direct response sold	152,182	+5.00
Students	19,155	*
Expires (last 8 months)	63,000	45.00

Selections: state, ZIP Code, SCF, recency, 5.00/M extra; key coding, 1.00/M extra.
5. **COMMISSION, CREDIT POLICY**
20% commission to all recognized brokers.
6. **METHOD OF ADDRESSING**
4-up Cheshire labels. Pressure sensitive labels, 7.50/M extra. Magnetic tape (9T 1600 BPI), 20.00 fee.
7. **DELIVERY SCHEDULE**
Ten working days.
8. **RESTRICTIONS**
Two sample mailing pieces required for approval.
9. **TEST ARRANGEMENT**
Minimum 5,000.
11. **MAINTENANCE**
Updated monthly.

(D-C3)

THE SHARPER IMAGE®

Media Code 3 553 6756 6.00   Mid 019931-000
The Sharper Image.
1. **PERSONNEL**
List Manager
The Listworks Corp., List Management Division, 40 Radio Circle, P.O. Box 459, Mt. Kisco, NY 10549. Phone 914-241-1900.
All recognized brokers.
2. **DESCRIPTION**
Mail order catalog buyers of electronic products and personal accessories; 82% men.
Average unit of sale 150.00.
List is computerized.
3. **LIST SOURCE**
90% direct mail; 10% space ads in Smithsonian, Science '84, Time, Signature, Esquire, The Wall Street Journal, and Popular Science.
4. **QUANTITY AND RENTAL RATES**
Rec'd March, 1986.

	Total Number	Price per/M
Last 6 months	230,000	*90.00
Last 12 months	400,769	*
1983-84	663,000	75.00

(*) Fundraisers, 65.00/M.
Selections: year, state, SCF, ZIP Code, recency (12 mos.), 5.00/M extra; keying, 1.50/M extra; sex, hotline (3-6 mos.), credit card, 50.00 plus buyers, 10.00/M extra; 100.00 plus buyers, 20.00/M extra.
Minimum order 5,000.
5. **COMMISSION, CREDIT POLICY**
20% commission to all recognized brokers.
6. **METHOD OF ADDRESSING**
4/5-up Cheshire labels. Pressure sensitive labels, 8.00/M extra. Magnetic tape (9T 800/1600 BPI), 20.00 nonreturnable fee.
8. **RESTRICTIONS**
Sample mailing piece required with every order.

(D-C2)

THE SHELBURNE COMPANY
Media Code 3 553 6779 8.00   Mid 024914-000
The Shelburne Company.
110 Painters Mill Rd, Owings Mills, MD 21117. Phone 301-363-4304, /1347.
1. **PERSONNEL**
List Manager—John Popowski.
Broker and/or Authorized Agent
All recognized brokers.
2. **DESCRIPTION**
Mail order catalog buyers of products for the home and office.
Average unit of sale 125.00.
ZIP Coded in numerical sequence 100%.
List is computerized.
3. **LIST SOURCE**
Ads in Wall Street Journal, Popular Science, New Shelter, Washington Report, etc., 10% catalog and package inserts 90%.
4. **QUANTITY AND RENTAL RATES**
Rec'd February, 1984.

	Total Number	Price per/M
Total list (last 12 months)	200,000	80.00

Selections: keying (1-5 digits), 1.00/M extra; state, SCF, sex (80% male), 3.00/M extra; ZIP Code, 5.00/M extra; 6 months recency, 10.00/M extra; 3 months recency, 25.00 plus buyers, 15.00/M extra; 50.00 plus buyers, 20.00/M extra.
5. **COMMISSION, CREDIT POLICY**
20% to recognized brokers.
6. **METHOD OF ADDRESSING**
4-up Cheshire. Pressure sensitive labels, 6.00/M extra. Magnetic tape (9T 800/1600); 15.00 non-returnable charge.
8. **RESTRICTIONS**
Sample required for prior approval.
11. **MAINTENANCE**
Updated monthly.

SHEPLERS
Media Code 3 553 6790 5.00   Mid 019052-000
Sheplers, Inc.
1. **PERSONNEL**
List Manager
Rubin Response Management Services, Inc., 3315 W. Algonquin Rd., Rolling Meadows, IL 60008. Phone 312-394-3400.
All recognized brokers.
2. **DESCRIPTION**
Mail order catalog buyers of western gear and apparel; 55% men.
Average unit of sale 58.00.
3. **LIST SOURCE**
Direct mail.
4. **QUANTITY AND RENTAL RATES**
Rec'd November, 1985.

	Total Number	Price per/M
Buyers (90 days)	70,000	*65.00
Last 12 months	270,600	60.00
Multi-buyers (last 12 months)	182,400	70.00
Credit card (last 12 months)	125,500	*
Catalog requestors (last 12 months)	310,400	55.00

(*) Fundraisers, 55.00/M.
Selections: state, SCF, 3.00/M extra; ZIP Code, year, sex, monetary, 5.00/M extra; keying, 1.00/M extra; ZIP select minimum 25.00.
Minimum order 5,000.
6. **METHOD OF ADDRESSING**
4/5-up Cheshire labels. Pressure sensitive labels, 5.00/M extra. Magnetic tape (9T 1600 BPI), 15.00 nonrefundable tape fee.
8. **RESTRICTIONS**
Sample mailing piece required for approval.

S&H GREEN STAMP REDEEMERS
Media Code 3 553 6796 2.00   Mid 037377-000
Sperry & Hutchinson Co.
1. **PERSONNEL**
List Manager
Media Marketplace, P.O. Box 2245, Princeton, NJ 08540. Phone 609-896-1900.
2. **DESCRIPTION**
Green stamp redeemers.
4. **QUANTITY AND RENTAL RATES**
Rec'd March, 1986.

	Total Number	Price per/M		Total Number	Price per/M
Mail	86,000	45.00	In-store	194,000	*

Selections: sex, SCF, ZIP Code, state, 2.50/M extra; hotline, 5.00/M extra; key coding, 1.00/M extra.
Minimum order 5,000.
5. **COMMISSION, CREDIT POLICY**
Net 30 days from mail date.
6. **METHOD OF ADDRESSING**
4-up Cheshire. Pressure sensitive labels, 7.00/M extra. Magnetic tape, 20.00 flat fee.
8. **RESTRICTIONS**
Sample mailing piece required for approval.
11. **MAINTENANCE**
Updated monthly.

SHOPPING INTERNATIONAL
Media Code 3 553 6802 8.00   Mid 019414-000
Participant D.M.A. Mail Preference Service.
Arizona Mail Order.
1. **PERSONNEL**
List Manager
Qualified Lists Corp., 135 Bedford Rd., Armonk, NY 10504. Phones: 914-273-6700; 212-409-6200.
2. **DESCRIPTION**
Mail order buyers of fashions, handicrafts and jewelry; includes catalog requests; mostly women.
Average unit of sale 55.00.
3. **LIST SOURCE**
Direct mail.
4. **QUANTITY AND RENTAL RATES**
Rec'd February, 1986.

	Total Number	Price per/M
Mail order buyers (1983-85)	383,023	65.00
Last 6 months	96,858	+10.00
Last 12 months	173,223	+5.00
Catalog requests (1983-85)	170,569	40.00
Credit card buyers (1983-85)	152,937	70.00
Fundraisers		50.00/M

Selections: keying, 1.00/M extra; ZIP Code, state, SCF, handicrafts, 20.00 + buyers, 2.00/M extra; multi-buyers, garment, 50.00 + buyers, 10.00/M extra; jewelry, 15.00/M extra.
Minimum order 5,000.
6. **METHOD OF ADDRESSING**
4-up Cheshire labels. Pressure sensitive labels, 5.00/M extra. Magnetic tape (9T 800/1600 BPI), 15.00 nonreturnable fee.
8. **RESTRICTIONS**
Sample mailing piece required for approval.

A CBS Magazines Publication

Media Code 8 676 2112 0.00   Mid 001117-000
Published monthly by CBS Magazines, a division of CBS, Inc., One Park Avenue, New York, NY 10016. Phone 212-503-4256.
For shipping info., see Print Media Production Data.

PUBLISHER'S EDITORIAL PROFILE
THE RUNNER is a magazine edited for runners interested in health, fitness and an active lifestyle. Articles concern developments in physiology, sportsmedicine and nutrition, as well as major events worldwide and the personalities that infulence the sport. Race highlights, results and events are covered in each issue. Rec'd 11/8/85.

1. PERSONNEL
Publisher—George A. Hirsch.
Advertising Director—Belle Jauchen.
Production Manager—John Ansaldi.

2. REPRESENTATIVES and/or BRANCH OFFICES
Boulder, CO 80301—John Cabell, 3393 Iris Ave., Suite 104. Phone 303-444-7055.
Bloomfield Hills, MI—Premier Publications Representatives.

3. COMMISSION AND CASH DISCOUNT
15% of gross to recognized agencies. No cash discount.

ADVERTISING RATES
Rates effective January, 1986 issue.
Rates received September 4, 1985.

5. BLACK/WHITE RATES

	1 ti	6 ti	12 ti	18 ti	24 ti
1 page	8,320.	8,020.	7,855.	7,705.	7,545.
2/3 page	6,275.	6,060.	5,940.	5,810.	5,685.
1/2 page	5,015.	4,830.	4,740.	4,630.	4,555.
1/3 page	3,225.	3,100.	3,035.	2,960.	2,920.
1/6 page	1,700.	1,670.	1,620.	1,570.	1,530.
Agate line	24.93	24.11	23.61	23.11	22.62

FREQUENCY DISCOUNTS
Earned by using 6 or more insertions. Orders for 1/3 page or larger earn frequency discounts for larger units when used. An advertiser using 4 or more insertions totalling a minimum of 3 pages in a single issue will earn an additional 5% discount. 4 to 7 pages earn a 10% discount, 8 pages earn 20% discount. Ads must be inserted within one year of the first insertion to earn a frequency discount rate.

6. COLOR RATES
2 color:

	1 ti	6 ti	12 ti	18 ti	24 ti
1 page	10,415.	10,045.	9,845.	9,655.	9,430.
2/3 page	7,970.	7,665.	7,505.	7,355.	7,210.
1/2 page	6,410.	6,170.	6,035.	5,905.	5,795.
1/3 page	4,860.	4,665.	4,585.	4,480.	4,390.
1/6 page	2,630.	2,565.	2,500.	2,450.	2,400.

4 color:

	1 ti	6 ti	12 ti	18 ti	24 ti
1 page	12,480.	12,030.	11,780.	11,555.	11,320.
2/3 page	10,015.	9,635.	9,450.	9,245.	9,040.
1/2 page	8,180.	7,880.	7,720.	7,555.	7,415.
1/3 page	6,300.	6,060.	5,950.	5,800.	5,690.

7. COVERS

	1 ti	6 ti	12 ti	18 ti	24 ti
4th cover (4 color)	18,905.	18,225.	17,925.	17,575.	17,145.

9. BLEED
Extra 15%

11. CLASSIFIED/MAIL ORDER
Commercial Classified:
3.85 per word; minimum 15 words 57.75.
Personal Classified:
Running events only, 2.30 per word.
Expand-Ad Classified:
5.80 per word; minimum 15 words 86.25.
Regular Bold Face 4.60, Regular Grey 4.80, Regular Bold and Grey 5.55.
Expand Bold 6.55, Expand Grey 6.75, Expand Bold and Grey 7.50.
Illustrated Classified:
90.00 per column inch (maximum 3″). Must be used in conjunction with either regular or Expand-Ad Classified.
Display Classified:

	1 ti	6 ti	12 ti		1 ti	6 ti	12 ti
1 inch	175.	170.	165.	3 inches	525.	510.	495.
2 inches	350.	340.	330.				

DISPLAY CLASSIFICATIONS:
MAIL ORDER/RACE
BLACK AND WHITE RATES:

	1 ti	6 ti	12 ti	18 ti	24 ti
1 page	5,275.	5,100.	4,980.	4,885.	4,755.
2/3 page	3,970.	3,850.	3,755.	3,690.	3,600.
1/2 page	3,165.	3,090.	2,990.	2,930.	2,875.
1/3 page	2,055.	1,965.	1,935.	1,890.	1,845.
1/6 page	1,090.	1,070.	1,050.	1,020.	970.
Agate line	15.86	15.31	14.91	14.68	14.28

COLOR RATES:
2 color:

	1 ti	6 ti	12 ti	18 ti	24 ti
1 page	6,590.	6,370.	6,250.	6,110.	5,945.
1/2 page	5,045.	4,875.	4,755.	4,675.	4,555.
1/3 page	4,050.	3,925.	3,845.	3,745.	3,665.
1/3 page	3,085.	2,970.	2,905.	2,840.	2,775.
1/6 page	1,670.	1,635.	1,595.	1,550.	1,520.

4 color:

	1 ti	6 ti	12 ti	18 ti	24 ti
1 page	7,915.	7,650.	7,475.	7,330.	7,135.
2/3 page	6,340.	6,130.	5,980.	5,875.	5,735.
1/3 page	5,170.	5,015.	4,880.	4,790.	4,690.
1/3 page	4,000.	3,855.	3,760.	3,690.	3,600.

15. MECH. REQUIREMENTS
For complete, detailed production information, see CBS Print Media Production Data.
Printing Process: Web Offset.
Trim size: 8 x 10-3/4; No./Cols. 3.
Binding method: Saddle stitched.
Colors available: AAAA/ABP, Matched, 4-Color Process (AAAA/MPA).

DIMENSIONS—AD PAGE

1	7 x	10	1/3	2-1/4 x	10
2/3	4-5/8 x	10	1/3	4-5/8 x	5
1/2	7 x	5	1/6	2-1/4 x	5
1/2	4-5/8 x 7-1/2		1/6	4-5/8 x 2-1/2	

16. ISSUE AND CLOSING DATES
Published monthly; issued approximately the 20th of month preceding cover date.
Insertion orders and material due the 1st of 2nd month preceding cover date.

SPECIAL FEATURE ISSUES
April—Total Fitness.
July—Nutrition Issue.
October—Fashion Issue.
November—Shoe Issue.

17. SPECIAL SERVICES
A.B.C. Supplemental Data Report September 1985 Issue.

18. CIRCULATION
Established 1978.
Summary data—for detail see Publisher's Statement.
A.B.C. 12-31-85 (6 mos. aver.—Magazine Form)

Tot.Pd	(Subs.)	(Single)	[Assoc]
279,492	219,274	60,218	...

Average Total Non-Paid Distribution (not incl. above):
Total 29,722
TERRITORIAL DISTRIBUTION 9/85—283,044

N.Eng.	Mid.Atl.	E.N.Cen.	W.N.Cen.	S.Atl.	E.S.Cen.
16,949	39,361	44,840	22,074	38,483	11,180
W.S.Cen.	Mtn.St.	Pac.St.	Canada	Foreign	Other
23,549	18,056	46,053	7,311	9,557	3,631

Publisher states: "Effective with January, 1985 issue rate base of 275,000."

Runner's World

A Rodale Press, Inc. Publication

Media Code 8 676 2125 2.00   Mid 001118-000
Published 12 times a year by Rodale Press, Inc., 33 East Minor St., Emmaus, PA 18049. Phone 215-967-5171, TELEX; 847338.

PUBLISHER'S EDITORIAL PROFILE
RUNNER'S WORLD is edited for the mature runner, from those just beginning to discover the joys and benefits of running to veteran runners and marathoners. Features deal with training, medical research, nutrition, personalities, races, adventure runs, and other subjects directly or indirectly related to the runner's enjoyment of the sport. Columns cover feet and shoes, medical advice, training and racing, late-breaking news in the sport, running for beginners, women and over-40 runners. Rec'd 4/2779.

1. PERSONNEL
Publisher—Michael S. Perlis.
Advertising Director—Marcia Godelesky.
Production Coordinator—Deborah Dorn.

2. REPRESENTATIVES and/or BRANCH OFFICES
New York 10017—Stan Singer, Debbie Walsh, 708 Third Ave. Phone 212-697-2040.
Emmaus, PA 18049—Marie Whitaker, 33 E. Minor St. Phone 215-967-5171.
Chicago 60601—Laurie McGlade, 75 East Wacker Dr. Phone 312-726-0365.
Los Angeles 90010—Colleen Sopp, 3660 Wilshire Blvd. Phone 213-383-2237.
San Francisco 94108—Alan Levy, Caryl Richmond, 601 California St., Suite 2004. Phone 415-398-8183.
Birmingham (Detroit)—Peter C. Kelly Incorporated.

3. COMMISSION AND CASH DISCOUNT
15% to recognized agencies. Late payment service charge of 1-1/2% per month on any balance outstanding more than 30 days from billing date. Invoices rendered on 10th of month preceding date of issue. Cash with order except to those that have established credit. No commission on production charges.

4. GENERAL RATE POLICY
Publisher reserves right to revise rates upon 60 days notice in advance of the closing date of the first issue affected.

ADVERTISING RATES
Rates effective October, 1985.
Rates received August 30, 1985.

5. BLACK/WHITE RATES

	1 ti	3 ti	6 ti	9 ti	12 ti
1 page	8,310.	8,120.	7,810.	7,645.	7,310.
2/3 page	6,440.	6,290.	6,055.	5,925.	5,670.
1/2 page	5,405.	5,280.	5,080.	4,970.	4,755.
1/3 page	3,745.	3,660.	3,520.	3,445.	3,295.
1/4 page	2,660.	2,600.	2,500.	2,450.	2,340.
1/6 page	1,995.	1,950.	1,875.	1,835.	1,755.
2 pages	15,790.	15,425.	14,840.	14,525.	13,895.

Frequency discounts apply to the number of issues in which units are used during the contract year. Short rate will apply if advertiser has not earned billed rate at end of contract period. Rebate will be made at end of contract period if advertiser has used sufficient insertions to earn lower rates.

6. COLOR RATES
2 color:

	1 ti	3 ti	6 ti	9 ti	12 ti
1 page	10,355.	10,115.	9,735.	9,525.	9,110.
2/3 page	8,030.	7,845.	7,550.	7,390.	7,065.
1/2 page	6,730.	6,575.	6,325.	6,190.	5,920.
1/3 page	4,660.	4,550.	4,380.	4,290.	4,100.
2 pages	19,675.	19,220.	18,495.	18,100.	17,315.

4 color:

	1 ti	3 ti	6 ti	9 ti	12 ti
1 page	12,455.	12,170.	11,710.	11,460.	10,960.
2/3 page	9,650.	9,430.	9,070.	8,880.	8,490.
1/2 page	8,095.	7,910.	7,610.	7,450.	7,125.
1/3 page	5,605.	5,475.	5,270.	5,155.	4,930.
2 pages	23,665.	23,120.	22,245.	21,770.	20,825.

7. COVERS
Non-cancellable.

	1 ti	3 ti	6 ti	9 ti	12 ti
2nd or 3rd cover (4 color)	13,700.	13,385.	12,880.	12,605.	12,055.
4th cover (4 color)	15,960.	15,590.	15,000.	14,680.	14,045.

8. INSERTS
Bind-in cards available.

9. BLEED
No charge.

10. SPECIAL POSITION
Centerspread .... 31,140.

11. CLASSIFIED/MAIL ORDER
70.00 for 20 words or less, 3.50 for each additional word. Phone numbers, addresses, abbreviations and each dictionary-word counted as one word. Zip code, no charge. First 3 or 4 words set in Bold Capital letters. Business name and address set in bold type. Bold type and italics not available in body type. Prepayment required.
Mail Order Discount, less 15% on regular display advertising.

MARKETPLACE NATIONAL EDITION

Box size:	1 ti	3 ti	6 ti	Box size:	1 ti	3 ti	6 ti
1 inch	230.	205.	185.	3 inch	750.	675.	600.
2 inch	475.	425.	375.				

Typesetting charge 50.00 (for material not camera-ready). Other artwork, drawing, layout and camera ready will be billed accordingly. All ads are 2-1/4" wide. All ads must be prepaid. No agency discounts. Frequency discounts apply when total amount prepaid.

RACE ADVERTISERS—SPECIAL RATES

A 30% discount will be allowed for national race advertising. Non-profit advertising earns 20% discount. Clinics, product promotion and tours do not qualify.

13a. GEOGRAPHIC and/or DEMOGRAPHIC EDITIONS
Regional rates offered to racing and retail advertisers with a regional message. There is a 10% race discount. Guaranteed placement and color do not apply to regional editions. Advertisers can select a maximum of 3 of the 4 regionals.
Runner's World race co-sponsorship participants earn a 20% discount off of regional rates. National advertisers desiring a regional rate will pay a pro-rated portion of the national rate plus a 20% premium.

WESTERN EDITION

Covering the states of California, Hawaii, Oregon, Idaho, Washington, Nevada, Arizona, Utah, Montana, Wyoming, Colorado, New Mexico, Alaska, Saskatchewan, Alberta, British Columbia.
BLACK AND WHITE RATES:

	1 ti	3 ti	6 ti	9 ti	12 ti
1 page	1,800.	1,760.	1,690.	1,655.	1,585.
2/3 page	1,300.	1,270.	1,220.	1,200.	1,145.
1/2 page	1,010.	985.	950.	930.	890.
1/3 page	720.	705.	675.	660.	635.
1/4 page	575.	560.	540.	530.	505.
1/6 page	415.	405.	390.	380.	365.

CIRCULATION:
Publisher states: "Rates based on a circulation average of 90,000."

CENTRAL EDITION

Covering the states of Michigan, Ohio, Indiana, Illinois, Wisconsin, Minnesota, Iowa, Missouri, North Dakota, South Dakota, Nebraska, Kansas, Oklahoma, Manitoba, Texas.
BLACK AND WHITE RATES:

	1 ti	3 ti	6 ti	9 ti	12 ti
1 page	1,700.	1,660.	1,600.	1,565.	1,495.
2/3 page	1,225.	1,195.	1,150.	1,125.	1,075.
1/2 page	950.	930.	895.	875.	840.
1/3 page	680.	665.	640.	625.	600.
1/4 page	545.	530.	510.	500.	480.
1/6 page	390.	380.	370.	360.	345.

CIRCULATION:
Publisher states: "Rates based on a circulation average of 85,000."

SOUTHEAST/MID-ATLANTIC EDITION

Covering the states of Arkansas, Louisiana, Mississippi, Alabama, Georgia, Florida, Tennessee, Kentucky, North Carolina, South Carolina, Virginia, West Virginia, Maryland, Delaware, District of Columbia.
BLACK AND WHITE RATES:

	1 ti	3 ti	6 ti	9 ti	12 ti
1 page	1,000.	975.	940.	920.	880.
2/3 page	720.	705.	675.	660.	635.
1/2 page	560.	545.	525.	515.	495.
1/3 page	400.	390.	375.	370.	350.
1/4 page	320.	315.	300.	295.	280.
1/6 page	230.	225.	215.	210.	200.

CIRCULATION:
Publisher states: "Rates based on a circulation average of 50,000."

NORTHEAST EDITION

Covering the states of New York, Pennsylvania, New Jersey, Connecticut, Rhode Island, Massachusetts, New Hampshire, Vermont, Maine, Quebec, Nova Scotia, New Brunswick, Newfoundland, Prince Edward Island, Ontario.
BLACK AND WHITE RATES:

	1 ti	3 ti	6 ti	9 ti	12 ti
1 page	1,300.	1,270.	1,220.	1,195.	1,145.
2/3 page	935.	910.	880.	860.	820.
1/2 page	730.	710.	685.	670.	640.
1/3 page	520.	510.	490.	480.	460.
1/4 page	415.	405.	390.	380.	365.
1/6 page	300.	290.	280.	275.	265.

CIRCULATION:
Publisher states: "Rates based on a circulation average of 65,000."

14. CONTRACT AND COPY REGULATIONS
See Contents page for location—items 1, 2, 7, 8, 10, 12, 14, 24, 25, 27, 30, 32, 35, 36, 37, 42.

15. MECH. REQUIREMENTS
For complete, detailed production information, see SRDS Print Media Production Data.
Printing Process: Web Offset.
Trim size: 8 x 10-3/4; No./Cols. 2&3.
Binding method: Saddle-stitched.
Colors available: Publisher's Choice; 4-Color Process (AAAA/MPA).

DIMENSIONS-AD PAGE

1	7-1/8 x 9-7/8	1/4	3-1/2 x 4-7/8
2/3	4-5/8 x 9-7/8	1/6	4-3/4 x 2-1/4
1/2	7-1/8 x 4-3/4	1/6	2-1/4 x 4-3/4
1/2	4-5/8 x 7-1/4	1/4	3-1/2 x 4-7/8
1/3	4-3/4 x 4-3/4	Sprd	15-1/2 x 9-3/4
1/3	2-1/4 x 9-7/8		

16. ISSUE AND CLOSING DATES
Published 12 times a year.
Space reservation and material closing 20th of 3rd month preceding issue date.
All copy changes must be in writing.
No cancellations after closing.

SPECIAL FEATURE ISSUES

April & October—Reader Information Service.

17. SPECIAL SERVICES
A.B.C. Supplemental Data Report released October, 1985 issue.

18. CIRCULATION
Established 1966. Single copy 2.50; per year 19.95.
Summary data—for detail see Publisher's Statement.

A.B.C. 12-31-85 (6 mos. aver.—Magazine Form)

Tot.Pd.	(Subs.)	(Single)	(Assoc.)
286,355	211,556	74,799	...

Average Total Non-Pd Distribution (not incl. above):
Total 9,899

TERRITORIAL DISTRIBUTION 10/85—289,596

N.Eng.	Mid.Atl.	E.N.Cen.	W.N.Cen.	S.Atl.	E.S.Cen.
17,836	36,829	42,924	19,127	37,049	9,3502
W.S.Cen.	Mtn.St.	Pac.St.	Canada	Foreign	Other
22,981	18,114	55,571	13,882	9,849	6,184

Publisher states: "Effective with October, 1985 issue, guaranteed net paid circulation average of 300,000."

(C-C)

Running Through Texas

Media Code 8 676 2162 5.00 **Mid 038787-000**
Published bimonthly by Tel-Aire Publications, P.O. Box 470467, Dallas, TX 75247. Phone 214-438-4111.
For shipping info., see Print Media Production Data.

PUBLISHER'S EDITORIAL PROFILE

RUNNING THROUGH TEXAS is a magazine directed to the serious runner. The articles cover training, nutrition, general fitness, runner profiles, race previews and results on a statewide basis. There is a two-month event calendar. Rec'd 3/7/86.

1. PERSONNEL
Advertising Director—Jan Walton.
Editor/General Manager—John Bayne.

3. COMMISSION AND CASH DISCOUNT
15% to recognized agencies. 2% 10 days. Net 30 days.
1-1/2% charge on accounts over 30 days.

ADVERTISING RATES
Card received March 7, 1986.

5. BLACK/WHITE RATES

	1 ti	2 ti	3 ti	4 ti	5 ti	6 ti
1 page	736.	713.	684.	644.	624.	605.
2/3 page	661.	632.	598.	558.	542.	525.
1/2 page	430.	418.	400.	379.	368.	355.
1/3 page	258.	250.	240.	228.	221.	215.
1/6 page	170.	166.	160.	152.	148.	144.

6. COLOR RATES
Per color, extra .... 150.
Matched color, extra .... 75.

7. COVERS

	1 ti	2 ti	3 ti	4 ti	5 ti	6 ti
2nd cover	975.	937.	898.	850.	825.	800.
3rd cover	825.	800.	776.	752.	730.	708.
4th cover	1242.	1205.	1154.	1100.	1066.	1034.

8. INSERTS
Available.

9. BLEED
Extra 10%

10. SPECIAL POSITION
Extra .... 50.

14. CONTRACT AND COPY REGULATIONS
See Contents page for location—items 1, 3, 6, 8, 10, 12, 13, 14, 16, 17, 18, 22, 23, 24, 25, 28, 32, 33, 34, 36, 38, 39, 42, 43.

15. MECH. REQUIREMENTS
For complete, detailed production information, see SRDS Print Media Production Data.
Printing Process: Sheetfed Offset.
Trim size: 8-1/2 x 11.
Binding method: Saddle-stitched.
Colors available: 4-Color Process (AAAA/MPA).

DIMENSIONS-AD PAGE

1	7-1/2 x 10	1/3	4-3/4 x 4-7/8
2/3	4-3/4 x 10	1/3	2-1/4 x 10
1/2	7-1/2 x 4-7/8	1/6	2-1/4 x 4-7/8

16. ISSUE AND CLOSING DATES
Published bimonthly.

Issue:	Closing	Issue:	Closing
Jan	11/30	July 1	5/31
Mar	1/31	Sept	7/31
May 1	3/31	Nov	9/30

SPECIAL FEATURE ISSUES

July-Aug/86—Running Vacations, Track Highlights.
Sept-Oct/86—Texas Marathon Preview.
Nov-Dec/86—Sports Medicine Clinics & Athlete's Gift Guide.

17. SPECIAL SERVICES
Advertising Preparation Services.

18. CIRCULATION
Established 1982. Single copy 2.50; per year 12.50.

SWORN 12-31-85 (6 mos. aver.)

Total	Non-Pd	Paid	(Subs.)	(Single)	[Assoc.]
7,500	2,500	5,000	2,000	3,000	...

Unpaid Distribution (not incl. above):
Total 7,500
Publisher states: "Effective with February, 1986 issue, guaranteed net paid and non-paid circulation average of 7,500."

A Meredith Publication

Mid 000138-000
Charlestown Navy Yard, 100 First Ave., Charlestown, MA 02129. Phone 617-241-9500.
See listing under classification No. 6.

One way to generate interest is through a "public service" booklet or pamphlet. The "fraud" book that follows was utilized by *Entrepreneur* to generate names. It was given free (50 cents for postage and handling), and the names proved to be excellent prospects.

BUSINESS OPPORTUNITY FRAUDS

BY CHASE REVEL

Provided as a Public Service
By International Entrepreneurs' Assn., Inc.

ENVELOPE STUFFING

I suppose everyone would like a business they could operate from their homes with no overhead, no employees to worry about, and make a nice living with only a few hours of work.

Well, a business like that is **so rare** it is practically unknown and definitely on the endangered species list.

There are, however, tens of thousands of con men out there selling "home work schemes." Our research department monitors all areas of small business including mail order, and each week we must receive a dozen or more "co-op mailers"—little catalogs containing hundreds of mail-order ads.

Practically every ad in these things are some form of rip-off; 99% operate from post office boxes. We traced a few through the post office and interviewed the men behind the schemes. Most felt they were perfectly legitimate, ethical and even openly proud of their con-game mail-order gimmicks. A few appeared nervous and afraid, and couldn't understand how we'd obtained their home addresses.

Envelope Stuffing

We found eleven variations on this deceitful scheme that still preys on poor trusting people across the nation. A couple of companies doing this promotion wrote some of the cleverest advertising copy that we have read in years. It's a shame their talent is being wasted or misused.

Here's how the envelope stuffers work: Some provide the literature that you mail free, while others sell the literature and mailing lists. After extracting two to five dollars for instructions, some offer a start-up package for $10 to $150. One, through some ingenious phrasing, implied that the $25 price would be refunded, but it was actually a credit toward a larger package costing $85 to $125.

A few just sold lists of companies, some categorically, others individually, who use outside addressing/mailing services. Ironically, one listed a dozen companies which, upon investigation, turned out to be mail-order firms selling—*envelope stuffing schemes!*

One of the operators we investigated pulled out all the stops for a quick response, claiming buyers had a good chance to win $1,000,000. Actually, this con man supposedly held a drawing each month, and the winner would get a free $1 ticket in the monthly Illinois State Million-dollar Lottery.

In addition to the million-dollar prize, he also showed a lucky number which buyers were supposed to match to their order coupon number. If the numbers matched, the buyer would receive a $37.50 value surprise package, along with his order. Just imagine, all of this for only $12.50.

Postal inspectors regularly issue mail-stop orders against these con men, but they just surface again somewhere else. In the latest issue of the Post Office "Memo to Mailers," two were listed as receiving stop orders: NASCO, in Columbus, Ohio, and Ross, in District Heights, Maryland.

The Results

We purchased one of these packages for $25.00, and received 200 brochures promoting envelope stuffing. We had to buy the envelopes, and because of the weight of the brochure, the first-class postage would come to 26 cents per piece. A gummed label mailing list of 200 names was also enclosed.

Just to test the results, we had our mailroom stuff and mail these winners. To my amazement, we actually received **two** orders for **$3.00 each.** We were required to send half to the guy from whom we'd bought the original package so he could fill the order—a drop-ship arrangement.

His original literature promised $500 profit on every 1,000 pieces of mail we stuffed. Here's how we actually made out:

Instruction	$ 3.00
Package	25.00
200 brochures & names	
200 Envelopes	4.00
Retail	
Postage for 200 at 26 cents	52.00
For Return Address on Envelope & Order Form	
Labor	No Charge
Five Hours	
Total Expenses	$84.00
Earnings	3.00
2 orders at $3, less $3 commission to con-man	
NET LOSS	$81.00

Need we say more about envelope stuffing?

Maybe some day soon the legislatures will enact laws and controls to outlaw rip-offs like these in the mail-order field—the kind of thing that hurts legitimate firms.

The State of California recently made a move in the right direction. All mail-order firms operating in California must now show their street address if they have a post office box in any ads or literature. Maybe this will scare away a few of the really shady operators.

This is just a small move in the right direction—we hope other states will adopt similar measures.

In closing, we suggest the following criterion for you to employ in spotting potential frauds. It won't work in all cases, but will be helpful in most. "If the offer is to make money and someone only requires a few dollars to show you how it's done, the offer is probably worthless."

LETTERS, MAILING PIECES, ADS

In 1978, Revel began writing a syndicated column on small businesses for the *Los Angeles Times*. The column served a dual purpose: It not only made him better known throughout the country, but it also earned him (and *Entrepreneur*) additional credibility in the eyes of consumers.

inside small business
by Chase Revel

CONCEPT: Factual, meticulously researched reports on small businesses: how they are started, how they are run, what start-up costs are and what profits can be expected. Chase Revel, the foremost authority on small business in the nation, constantly seeks out, investigates and reports on new small business ideas. The columns also deal with basic rules for starting a small business, small business financing and pitfalls to avoid. They are written in straight-forward prose void of financial cant or business jargon. It is aimed at the millions of newspaper readers who dream of being their own boss as well as business owners who want to keep up with latest business developments.

AUTHOR: Chase Revel made a million dollars in the construction business by the time he was 21. The business failed in the 1957 housing recession and Revel was selling vacuum cleaners door-to-door at 22. Launching new business enterprises then became Revel's profession. By 1973, after having started and operated 18 businesses, his wife suggested the business Revel is in today—giving information and advice on small business.

A $45 ad in the Wall Street Journal brought in the first subscriptions for his newsletter, which is today International Entrepreneurs magazine, with a circulation of 30,000 (at $35 a year). Revel and his staff regularly conduct small business seminars in convention centers throughout the United States. Attendance often sets local records. Interest in small business and the independence it promises is intense and INSIDE SMALL BUSINESS is the only feature in syndication designed to satisfy this reader need and demand for information.

SECTION: Business, lifestyle, living, classified.

FREQUENCY: One column a week.

FORMAT: 700 words. Scanner manuscript copy in Courier 12 or Perry 199.

Los Angeles Times
SYNDICATE

TIMES MIRROR SQUARE

LOS ANGELES, CALIFORNIA 90053 ● **TOLL FREE (800) 421-8603** **OR CALL COLLECT (213) 972-7987**

Not everything works. That was especially true with this ad for "501 Best Pick-Up Lines," which failed to even pay for itself.

220   LETTERS, MAILING PIECES

"The Best Source of Expansion Capital" worked well, and part of the credit goes to the photograph of Boston's Mayor Kevin White, a supporter of small business, who joined Revel.

"Science has finally counterfeited . . ." was the full-page space ad that launched Revel's successful high-line simulated jewelry company, Van Pler & Tissany.

This was another intriguing space ad that Revel created in order to sell Roman coins. Note the similarities between this and the preceding ad on the "counterfeit diamonds."

101

One of Revel's most recent ads is the one that follows. It was designed to attract more female buyers to Van Pler & Tissany. Previously, a majority of the company's jewelry buyers were male, primarily drawn by the "scientific" approach of Revel's initial ad ("Science counterfeits perfect diamond . . .")

This ad certainly has more of a romantic and emotional impact.

Index